Being THERE

100 Sports Pros

Talk About the

Best Sporting Events

They Ever Witnessed

Firsthand

Edited by Eric Mirlis

The Lyons Press
Guilford, Connecticut
An imprint of The Globe Pequot Press

The Lyons Press is an imprint of The Globe Pequot Press.

10 9 8 7 6 5 4 3 2 1

Printed in the United States of America

Designed by Maggie Peterson

ISBN: 978-1-59921-027-8

Library of Congress Cataloging-in-Publication Data is available on file.

To Keri
I couldn't have done this without you.

CONTENTS

FOREWORD

By Kenny Albert, Fox Sports/MSG Network

Whether you purchased this book or received it as a gift, you are part of a sub-culture whose lives are defined by sporting events. Years aren't measured by hours, days, weeks, and months; in our world, a year is comprised of the pre-season, regular season, postseason, and off-season.

Why else do we remember intricate details of games our favorite teams played decades ago, but have no idea where the car is parked at the mall? Or what we had for lunch yesterday?

If you are flipping through these pages, I guarantee that if you are old enough, you know exactly where you were when Mike Eruzione scored in Lake Placid; when the ball went through Bill Buckner's legs; and when Scott Norwood's kick sailed wide right.

I am just like you. In fact, in my world, major family moments are marked by sporting events. I met my wife Barbara for the first time on June 9, 1994—after I called the Vancouver Canucks' victory over the New York Rangers in Game 5 of the Stanley Cup Finals. Three days later, I took her to Game 3 of the NBA Finals between the New York Knicks and Houston Rockets.

Our older daughter Amanda was born on October 5, 1999 . . . hours after Al Leiter pitched the New York Mets to a 5–0 victory over the Cincinnati Reds in a one-game playoff. Our younger daughter Sydney entered the world on January 27, 2003 . . . less than twenty-four hours after the Tampa Bay Buccaneers won Super Bowl XXXVII. These games are embedded in my mind, and I often associate them with the births of my children.

When Eric Mirlis asked me to compile a list of the Top Five Sporting Moments I've seen in person, my mind wandered back to so many of the great games I've had the fortune of attending. How would I narrow my list down to five?

It is mind-boggling to think that fellow contributors were at the Polo Grounds when Bobby Thomson and the Giants won the pennant in 1951; at

Yankee Stadium when Don Larsen pitched his perfect game; and at Lambeau Field for the "Ice Bowl." Villanova-Georgetown. The Doug Flutie Game. Ali-Liston.

Can you believe that an eighteen-year-old named Maury Povich was Bob Wolff's statistician at the "Greatest Game Ever Played" in 1958 between the Baltimore Colts and New York Giants?

These events—and hundreds more—magically come to life on the following pages.

Since Eric has trusted me to write this foreword, I will take the opportunity to list some of the events I've attended that did not make my Top Five. My "honorable mention" list includes Roy Jones getting robbed of a medal at the 1988 Seoul Olympics, the "Jeffrey Maier" game at Yankee Stadium in 1996, and Terrell Owens stomping on the star at Texas Stadium in 2000.

I attended the first game at Giants Stadium (1976), the last game at Baltimore's Memorial Stadium (1991), the first game at Camden Yards (1992), the first game at Montreal's Molson Centre (1996), and the last game at Busch Stadium (2005).

By the way, I first met Eric during our collegiate years at New York University, after we both signed a petition to have the dormitory wired for cable television. Why? So we could watch sporting events 24/7.

I hope you enjoy reading these one hundred lists as much as we all enjoyed reliving the special moments that will be cherished forever.

ACKNOWLEDGMENTS

You can't do a book like this without calling in dozens of favors. I must thank the following people for helping me get this project done: David Abrutyn, Marty Aronoff, Marty Blake, Ryan Blake, Ben Bouma, Adam Caparell, Jerry Caraccioli, Jason Chaimovitch, John Cirillo, Dave Cohen, Dennis D'Agostino, Michael Frank, David Fried, Jessica Garrison, Bryan Graham, Jen Gunderson, Pat Hanlon, Steve Hirdt, John Huet, Tom Huet, John Kollmansperger, Doug Kroll, John Labombarda, Matt Litke, Mark Mandel, Keith Marder, Arash Markazi, Pete Macheska, Billy Matthews, Elliot Olshansky, Billy Proctor, Jillian St. Charles, Alan Sanders, Jon Scher, Steve Serby, Paul Sheppard, Eric Spitz, Gene Sweeney, Ben Tuliebitz, Lynn Vandenberg, Larry Webman, Barry Werner and Jason Wormser. I need to thank Josh Rosenberg from The Lyons Press, who led the charge in their editorial department.

A special thank you to my editor Ken Samelson, who has been my guide throughout the entire process, from pitch to publication. Extra thanks to Rich Ackerman for planting the idea in my head that this was a better idea than I originally thought. Enormous thanks to Stefanie and Dan Kaufman — Stefanie for inviting basically everyone at *Sports Illustrated* to participate, and Dan for all of the ideas, contacts, and hours of discussions, even though we both should have been working. And a very special thank you to Kenny Albert, for not killing me despite my asking him to introduce me to everyone in the sports world, and for patiently fulfilling my every pain in the neck wish along the way.

Most importantly, I have to thank the one hundred generous individuals who took the time out of their busy schedules to put a list together for this book. Without these contributions, this book would never exist. You all wrote it—I just put it in order.

Personally, I want to thank my family, both immediate and extended, but especially my parents, Michael and Carole, and my sister, Hope, for always being there throughout my career. Most importantly, though, I must thank my wife, Keri, who was with me every step of the way and offered nothing but rock-solid support throughout the long process of putting this book together, all eighteen months. Now that it is done, we can finally go on vacation.

INTRODUCTION

What are the most memorable sporting events you've ever seen in person?

That question might be one of the more enjoyable you will ever answer. Every sports fan, regardless of team or sport allegiance, has a favorite. Or multiple favorites. But no matter what the event is, the moment someone asks that question, the flood of memories comes rushing back and the events are relived. Isn't that what being a sports fan is all about?

What exactly makes a sporting event memorable, though? There are many reasons. In no particular order, here are some common themes you will find throughout this book:

—A singular memorable moment: These are the plays that made you say, "Wow!" They are unforgettable and in many cases legendary. Two home runs from vastly different eras come to mind as perfect examples—Bobby Thomson in 1951 and Kirk Gibson in 1988.

—An individual performance for the ages: In the zone. Sports fans have heard that phrase so many times, it has become a part of American culture. A player has one of those games that is unprecedented and unforgettable. Don Larsen's perfect game in the 1956 World Series is the only postseason no-hitter for a reason.

—A history-changing event: Super Bowl III signaled the beginning of a new era in football and led to the merger of two rival leagues. But it doesn't have to be a single game or moment to be historically important. No one will ever be able to deny the impact the Dream Team had on the sports world when they took the court in the 1992 Summer Olympics. These are the teams and nights that forever changed the sports map.

—An emotional crowd reaction: When the New York Rangers won the Stanley Cup in 1994, it was more than a team winning a championship. It was an organization, and its fans, exorcising generations of demons. The fans in attendance, every single one a die-hard follower of the team, got to experience something they never thought they would ever see and expressed the joy commensurate with the moment. One sign said it all: NOW I CAN DIE IN PEACE. It was one sign, but it represented the thoughts of every Rangers fan in that building.

—**A shocking upset:** Villanova over Georgetown. North Carolina State over Houston. Princeton over UCLA. There is perhaps no event in American sports more prone to the storybook upset than the NCAA Tournament. Anyone who witnesses an underdog shock the world is guaranteed to remember it.

—**Game 7:** Nothing can come close to the emotion that a winner-take-all game brings. When a seven-game series comes down to one night, where anything can happen, the tension on the field and in the stands is immeasurable, regardless of the sport or the city. These are the nights where the ultimate hero is unpredictable. Think about names such as Aaron Boone, Stephane Matteau, Jack Morris, or Willis Reed, and you'll know exactly what I mean.

—**Mega-events:** Let's face it. The allure of the Super Bowl or the Olympics or the World Cup is as much about the "event" as the actual game. There is something about being at the big games, where the world is watching, that raises the excitement level in a person and makes the night unforgettable, regardless of who won or lost. The thought of attending an event, and realizing that while you are there, hundreds of millions of people are sitting at home and watching, all wishing that they were in your seat, is enough to make even the most jaded of people think twice.

—**Events that have a very personal meaning:** It might be the first Super Bowl a person has covered, or the first baseball game a person ever attended. No one can measure the personal importance a specific event carries until reflecting back on it.

At the end of the day, it is that last qualification that carried the most weight through everyone's list. What makes this an enjoyable topic to think about and talk about, regardless of whether you are a broadcaster, a journalist, or a fan, is that everyone can relate to it, and everyone will weigh the events they have seen based on what those events meant to the person and the lasting impact that followed.

The one hundred lists you are about to read are the personal memories of broadcasters, journalists, and executives from the world of sports, plus a few die-hard fans from the world of entertainment. The lists span the gamut of sports, covering almost every sport and era imaginable, from the 1940s through the World Series of 2006. The stories are all first-person accounts.

The lists are in date order, so that no one would be forced to pick a favorite (in many cases, people had enough difficulty choosing just five). There are stories that will make you laugh and, yes, maybe even make you cry. But most importantly, many memories will be rousted, whether you were lucky enough to be in attendance at an event or you were watching it on television or listening on the radio.

What are the most memorable events you've ever seen? Let a hundred people share their answer to a question that has no real answer. All of these people remember "Being There. . . ."

Ernie Accorsi

Retired General Manager, New York Giants

Brooklyn Dodgers at Philadelphia Phillies, Shibe Park, Philadelphia, Pennsylvania, July 2, 1950

At the first baseball game I ever saw, I got to see Jackie Robinson steal home. It was a doubleheader in front of a sellout crowd between two teams that would battle down to the last day of the season for the pennant. In the first game, Robinson stole home. Later, he was called out on strikes and started jawing with the umpire from the dugout, eventually getting thrown out. Those were the days when the players would leave their gloves out on the field, and when Robinson went out to get his glove after being ejected, he held the game up for five minutes (although it seemed like an hour as a kid).

In the second game, the Phillies went ahead 8–0, but the Dodgers came back to tie it at one minute before 7:00, with a 7:00 curfew in place because of the Pennsylvania Blue Laws, when Pee Wee Reese homered. That game ended 8–8 and had to be replayed, and the Dodgers ended up winning. Because the Phillies blew the 8–0 lead, they had to win on the last day of the season to win the pennant. On a personal level for me, though, my dad wanted me to see Jackie Robinson play, and I got to see him steal home.

Cleveland Browns at Baltimore Colts, Memorial Stadium, Baltimore, Maryland, November 1, 1959

The two players who I think defined football in the fifties and early sixties both had career days that day. Jim Brown scored five touchdowns, while Johnny Unitas threw for 397 yards. It was a seesaw battle between the defending-champion Colts, who were on their way to another title, and the visiting Browns, won by Cleveland 38–31. If you were going to name the top five players in the history of the league, both of these guys would make the list.

The 1965 Masters, Augusta National Golf Club, Augusta, Georgia, April 8–11, 1965

I saw every shot of Jack Nicklaus's 64 on Saturday at The Masters, which shattered Ben Hogan's Masters record. After thirty-six holes, Nicklaus was tied with Arnold Palmer and Gary Player for the lead, but Jack blew the field away with the 64. At that time, those were the "Big Three" in golf, and Palmer was the defending champion, so everyone expected the weekend to be a classic Masters. The leaders weren't saved for later in the day then; all the tee times were the luck of the draw, and Nicklaus teed off early. He scrambled for a par on 1, and then drove the ball into the woods on 2, which is not a difficult hole. He had to chip out of the woods, and I wasn't standing that far from him for his next shot (the crowds weren't what they are today) when he hit this mortar shot to the tiny green that went straight up and plopped on the back of the green. No one hit irons like Nicklaus—they sounded like gunshots compared to everyone else. He made the birdie putt, and that was all he needed to get started. You could hear the echoing in the timbers, and the tournament was over. I normally would have gone back to watch Palmer, but when Nicklaus started making birdies, I just had to stay with him and watch every shot.

1967 NBA East Division Finals, Game 5, Boston Celtics at Philadelphia 76ers, Convention Hall, Philadelphia, Pennsylvania, April 11, 1967

A dynasty ended as the 76ers dethroned the Celtics after going 68–13 in the regular season, stopping Boston's run of ten titles in eleven seasons. Chamberlain stopped Russell that night, 140–116. The Convention Hall was really not built for basketball, and for the entire fourth quarter, the building just thundered, "Boston is dead! Boston is dead!" It was Russell against Chamberlain, and finally Chamberlain won . . . and never beat him again.

New York Football Writers Dinner, Americana Hotel, New York, New York, May 25, 1970

The night he received the George Halas Award for Courage at the New York Football Writers Dinner at the Americana Hotel, Gale Sayers gave the speech that was re-created in the movie *Brian's Song*. There was an added impact for me that night, because I went to college at Wake Forest with Brian Piccolo. In that era, no one ever printed in the paper that someone had cancer. Brian and I were very close friends in school; we lived just a couple doors apart in the dorm and used to hitchhike to Mass together. I had read in the paper that he had had surgery, but that was all I knew and all that was said, and I never thought any more about it.

The Football Writers Dinner in New York was always a big event, and all the coaches were required to come and meet with the writers during the day— I actually met Vince Lombardi for the very first time that day. Sayers had rushed for over 1,000 yards in 1969 after hurting his knee the year before, in an era where knee injuries usually meant the end of your career. When he got the award that night, he held it up and gave the famous speech where he said, "He has the heart of a giant and that rare form of courage that allows him to kid himself and his opponent—cancer. He has the mental attitude that makes me proud to have a friend who spells out the word 'courage' twenty-four hours a day, every day of his life. . . . I love Brian Piccolo, and I'd like all of you to love him, too. Tonight, when you hit your knees, please ask God to love him."

Well, I was shattered. I was twenty-seven, Brian Piccolo was twenty-six; you don't even think about mortality at that age. When Sayers told the audience Brian was at Sloan-Kettering Hospital, it sent chills down my spine because I knew what that meant. Afterwards, I went to tell Sayers that I went to college with Brian, and Vince Lombardi was in front of me. Lombardi said, "Gale, you are a great American," then choked up and started to cry. I couldn't say anything after that and just turned and walked away. I never said anything to Gale Sayers; how could I after Vince Lombardi? I eventually got up the courage to go visit Brian in the hospital, but that was how I found out about my friend's illness.

Bonus Story. . . .

Interview with Moonlight Graham, Charlotte, North Carolina, 1963

I never would have remembered this, but my mother kept a scrapbook from my first job at the *Charlotte News*. In 1993, it was the thirtieth anniversary of Kennedy's assassination, and I remembered writing an article about it— Davidson College was going to try to play a game that day when the entire world wasn't playing, and I blistered them. I was thinking about that and was home for Thanksgiving and asked my mom if she still had the scrapbook. It was in her attic, and I went looking for this column. While flipping through the scrapbook, I stumbled across a picture of Moonlight Graham. I had just seen

Field of Dreams, which is one of the best sports movies ever, and I looked at the photo and got chills. I asked myself, "I interviewed Moonlight Graham?"

When I read the story, it complied exactly with the movie. He played one game, then broke his leg and went to medical school. The reason the interview even happened was that I had just gotten the job at the *News* and since I was the new guy, they sent me to a reunion of a famous team from Charlotte that won twenty-five straight games in 1902 and caused the league to disband because no one could beat them. I never would have remembered interviewing him if I didn't accidentally find that article, though.

Rich Ackerman
Host, NBA Radio/WFAN Radio New York

Miami Dolphins at New York Jets, Giants Stadium, East Rutherford, New Jersey, September 21, 1986

It was a very warm September day at the Meadowlands. I had just started college and went to the game with my roommate, Kenny Albert. Jets vs. Dolphins is a great rivalry, and the crowd was really into it, as always. It was an offensive battle all day, and the teams went back and forth, up and down the field. There was a third-and-30 play where Dan Marino threw a pass that picked up 48 yards. That is the type of day it was; the teams just moved the ball at will. The lead changed hands six times in the game until the Dolphins went ahead, 45–38.

As the Jets drove back down the field, the big play was a hook and lateral to Mickey Shuler, which is ironic, since the Dolphins made that play famous in their playoff game against the Chargers. I loved Wesley Walker as a player, and he ended up scoring the game-tying touchdown with no time left on the clock, on a 21-yard pass from Ken O'Brien. I was sitting in the front of the upper deck and had a great vantage point for O'Brien's 43-yard game-winning pass to Walker early in overtime. He had already caught three touchdown passes on the day, and it was amazing that the Dolphins let him catch another. But they did, and I knew I had seen a game for the ages.

1986 World Series, Game 6, Boston Red Sox at New York Mets, Shea Stadium, Queens, New York, October 25, 1986

There is a lot of sentimental value to this game for me, as it would have been my father's fifty-fifth birthday and was his first birthday after he passed away. I went to the game with my brother and told him that it would have been our dad's birthday, so something was going to happen. I just had that feeling—I didn't know what it was going to be, but I just had that feeling. The Mets should have walked through the postseason but kept making everything close, first against Houston, now against the Red Sox. When Dave Henderson homered in the tenth inning, my heart just sank, and I had that empty feeling in my stomach. After the Sox added an insurance run, it was tough to think the Mets would come back.

When Keith Hernandez flew out to center for the second out in the bottom of the tenth on a ball he hit really hard, it all of a sudden felt like it just wasn't meant to be. The people next to us got up and left, and it really bugged me. I looked at my brother and asked, "What kind of traffic could they possibly be beating out of the stadium?" I remember seeing the scoreboard read "Congratulations, Red Sox," and that made me even angrier. The game wasn't over yet. It looked grim, but it wasn't over yet. As Gary Carter came up, all I wanted was for him to not strike out, which he had a penchant for doing. Carter singled, then Kevin Mitchell singled. Ray Knight floated one over Marty Barrett's head, and it wasn't over yet.

Mookie Wilson stepped up, and as with Carter, all I hoped was that he wouldn't strike out. On the wild pitch that tied the game, from where I was sitting, I couldn't tell if he was hit by the pitch or if it just got past the catcher—the baserunners told me all I needed to know, though. The game was tied, and we could all breathe a little easier. When Wilson hit the grounder to first, from my seat in Section 10 of the upper deck (which the first baseline would cut through if you extended it), I had a direct line to see what happened. My first reaction was that, with Buckner playing deep and having a bum ankle and Mookie's speed, Wilson had a chance to beat the play to first. From my angle, I was able to watch both guys, and the ball got past Buckner. I don't think anyone even considered that happening and was more focused on whether Mookie was going to win the race to first.

As Buckner moved over to make the play, though, he looked so awkward getting there and getting his glove down for the ball. When it got past him, the roar was something I'll never forget. If Shea Stadium had a roof, it would have been blown off. The upper deck was actually shaking. The way this game ended, I just don't think you'll ever see anything like it again. To come back like that, with the season on the line, and then that play . . . you couldn't script it if you tried. On the way out of the building, you couldn't find a single person who thought the Mets were going to lose Game 7. It was like a new lease on life and the comeback of comebacks.

Super Bowl XXIII, San Francisco 49ers vs. Cincinnati Bengals, Joe Robbie Stadium, Miami, Florida, January 22, 1989

This was the first Super Bowl I ever attended. There was a lot of stuff going on at the time, including a riot in Miami during the week, plus rumors of Jerry Rice hurting himself at a nightclub. I really didn't realize the enormity of the event, and it isn't even close to what it is today, until walking into the stadium. That was when it hit me how big this really was. It was a well-played game that unfortunately opened with two major injuries, to Tim Krumrie of the Bengals and Steve Wallace of the 49ers, who were both important parts of their teams. The crowd was split pretty evenly, although it seemed everyone was into the Ickey Shuffle.

On the final drive, Joe Montana had to go 92 yards, but for him that didn't seem like enough of a problem, since he had done it before. They moved the ball down the field toward the end zone that I just happened to be sitting right behind in the second row. It was just amazing to watch them move down the field with the precision they did. The winning pass to John Taylor was perfect—over the middle, right on the money—and right in front of me, to give the Niners a 20–16 victory. Here it was, my first Super Bowl, and I just got to see one of the best games I'll ever see, and the game-winning touchdown was scored right in front of me. I haven't been back to a Super Bowl since.

1994 Stanley Cup Finals, Game 7, Vancouver Canucks at New York Rangers, Madison Square Garden, New York, New York, June 14, 1994

I moved from Washington to Chicago in the spring of 1994 and had to follow the Rangers from afar all season. I was twenty-five at the time, so even though I grew up a Rangers fan, I didn't experience as much angst as others had. I think the thing that always got Rangers fans of my generation the most was watching the Islanders win four straight Stanley Cups, which just annoyed me to no end.

But when the Rangers made it through to the finals to face Vancouver, I felt pretty confident. The Canucks were a good team but didn't really intimidate anyone. I knew there was a ticket waiting for me in New York, if there was a chance to win the Cup, but I was still too new at my job to take any vacation time (I actually thought about putting a provision in my contract to allow me time off for just this situation but didn't—the Rangers had a history of not coming through). I passed on Game 5 but had to jump at the opportunity to go to Game 7 and was able to get home for two days and go. I was a nervous wreck the entire time I was in New York, though, and couldn't wait for the game to start.

It was really hot in New York that day, probably around 95 degrees and very humid. By the time I got to the Garden with my friend Dave Brooks, we were sweating through our clothes. There was just a ton of nervous energy outside the building, with half of the fans screaming and yelling, and the other half walking around just hoping the Rangers would win and avoid yet another heartbreak. It really didn't feel that great inside until the national anthem, and as John Amirante got the building going, that was when it started to feel good. It was so intense in the stands, it was as if we were all on the ice with the Rangers, and from the time the puck dropped until Brian Leetch's goal to make it 1–0, it felt like everyone was holding their breath waiting to see what would happen. It was one of the best hockey games I've ever seen. The game had a great pace and just kept moving, there was no chippiness, and guys were leaving everything on the ice. I was sitting right behind the net where Leetch scored that goal, and when it went in, the place roared but also exhaled, and from that moment on, everyone thought this was going to be the night.

The Rangers scored first and were playing from ahead, which was what they needed. I remember more about the night than I do about the game from that point, because I was basically just sitting there watching the clock the rest of the way. When the 3–1 lead was knocked down to 3–2, though, everyone in the stands started to get nervous again, thinking, "We've all come too far. Please don't do this to us again." Vancouver kept applying pressure, and it felt like the ice was tilted in their favor for some time, but Mike Richter kept coming up with save after save, and I just kept watching the clock, waiting for it to end before the Canucks scored.

In the final seconds, the Rangers iced the puck and the Canucks had one last chance, but Craig MacTavish won the faceoff, and that was it. I'm still not sure whether people were more happy or relieved. I know I was ecstatic; the Rangers had finally won the Stanley Cup. I jumped on my seat, and it felt like I jumped 10 feet in the air. The celebration in the building was one big Garden party. It couldn't have been a more jovial crowd, and everyone was intoxicated on the joy of winning the Cup. It went on for at least an hour, but you just didn't want to leave the arena that night. It was too good to end, and you wanted to soak in every last drop of it. Outside, the party continued, but it was so orderly, there wasn't a single incident. I flew back to Chicago eight hours later, which was bittersweet, because I wanted to stay and bask in the atmosphere as long as I could.

Boston Red Sox at New York Yankees, Yankee Stadium, Bronx, New York, May 28, 2000

I'm not a Yankees fan or a Red Sox fan but went to see a Memorial Day weekend Sunday night pitching matchup between Pedro Martinez and Roger Clemens. You could feel how intense it was in the air that night, and the Stadium was absolutely packed. It felt like a playoff game, not one in May. The pitchers matched zeroes all game; it was an old-fashioned pitcher's duel. No one was having much success, aside from Derek Jeter, who got hits his first two times up. There was one walk between the two pitchers and just nine hits in the game. Clemens struck out 13, Martinez 9. It was just mano a mano, and if one pitcher did something, the other would come right back and match it or top it.

You kept asking yourself who was going to blink first, and in the ninth, it was Clemens, who gave up a two-out single to Jeff Frye, followed by a two-run homer to Trot Nixon. Nixon absolutely crushed the ball, and there was no doubt it was gone when he made contact. The Yankees rallied in the bottom of the ninth after Chuck Knoblauch was hit by a pitch and Jeter singled to start the inning, and with two outs, Jorge Posada was hit by a pitch and the bases were loaded. I've seen plenty of Yankees comebacks before, and this is Yankees–Red Sox, of course, so you never know exactly what to expect, but Tino Martinez grounded out to end the game, with the Red Sox taking the 2–0 win. It wasn't the warmest night, and the chill in the air made it feel even more like October, but it wasn't. It was May, and it was one of the best regular-season baseball games I've ever seen.

Al Albert
Broadcaster

1975 Stanley Cup Semifinals, Game 7, New York Islanders at Philadelphia Flyers, The Spectrum, Philadelphia, Pennsylvania, May 13, 1975
The third-year expansion-team Islanders had made it to the NHL Semifinals against none other than the Broad Street Bullies, who bullied their way to a 3–0 lead in the series. In their previous series against Pittsburgh, the Islanders had become just the second team in NHL history to come back from a 3–0 deficit to win a series and were now on the verge of doing it again, as the series headed back to the Spectrum for Game 7.

The Flyers had to go deep to get themselves out of this mess. They were nearly invincible at home whenever they played the immortal recording of Kate Smith's rendition of "God Bless America." Before the start of the game, to the astonishment of the sold-out crowd, the lights were turned off, a spotlight shone on a red carpet on the ice, and there she was, Kate Smith, live and in person. The next two minutes were the most stirring and inspirational moments I've ever experienced at a sporting event—Kate Smith and all

17,000 Flyers fans belting out a deafening and soulful rendition of "God Bless America." This was not the recording. This was Kate Smith on the ice . . . the Flyer fans were flabbergasted and joined in lustily with their lucky charm. At the end, the ovation was thunderous and long. In an attempt to defuse the hysteria, Islander captain Eddie Westfall skated up to her and presented her with a dozen roses from the Islanders—but that didn't work.

The Flyers, so fired up, with the supercharged, roaring crowd behind them, came out and scored a goal in the first nineteen seconds. Minutes later they would add another, and the Islanders were smothered under the wave of emotion. Philadelphia went on to a 4–1 win. In the end, the Broad Street Bullies needed the assist from Kate Smith to get by the young Cinderella Islanders and went on to win the Stanley Cup.

1976 ABA All-Star Game, McNichols Sports Arena, Denver, Colorado, January 27, 1976

This was the night of Dr. J's "Dunk Heard 'Round the Basketball World" to capture the first ever Slam Dunk contest, which changed the face of the game. The moment is a snapshot in basketball history—Dr. J, running the length of the court, taking off at the foul line, seemingly shifting to slow motion, floating in the air down the lane, grasping the ball like a grapefruit held high in his right hand, and then coming down with such force at the basket that it moved every molecule in the building. There was an immediate explosion of sound and movement; a burst of energy; fans screaming, cheering, bodies reeling; high fives; smiles; slaps on the back; looks of amazement—from the fans and the players. Everyone saw it, everyone felt it . . . nobody could believe it!

After that, basketball was never the same. It changed the direction, perception, and marketing of the game. The Slam Dunk Contest was part of the last hurrah for the ABA, coupled with an All-Star Game that showcased the extraordinary talent in the league. There were just six teams remaining in the league, so the All-Star format had the first-place team at the time, the hometown Nuggets, against the stars of the rest of the league. The Nuggets, led by David Thompson, Dan Issel, and Bobby Jones, played against a star-studded team consisting of Dr. J, George Gervin, George McGinnis, Moses Malone, Artis Gilmore, Billy Knight, Larry Kenon, and Maurice Lucas. On a night celebrating the individual talents in the first-ever Dunk contest, it was a supreme display of team ball, as the Nuggets, in a playoff atmosphere in front of their loyal and loud fans, beat the All-Stars in a game that featured a growing list of future Basketball Hall-of-Famers. That night, and the sight of some of the most exciting players in the game all together on one court in ABA uniforms, may have accelerated the merger that occurred that off-season.

Denver Nuggets at Detroit Pistons, Cobo Hall, Detroit, Michigan, April 9, 1978

On the last day of the regular season, the Nuggets and Pistons played an afternoon game at Cobo Hall in Detroit with playoff positions all set. This one was for the scoring race. It was the second year after the merger and two ABAers, David Thompson and George Gervin, were ranked one and two in the NBA in scoring. Thompson, with a quick first step, incredible leaping ability, and hot outside shot, was unstoppable. He was double- and triple-teamed, and it didn't matter. He went up and over and around his defenders. He had 53 points at halftime. Would David pass Wilt Chamberlain's 100 points in a game? Once he hit 60, he began moving by one NBA great after another . . . Mikan, Fulks, West, Barry at 64, Maravich at 68 . . . then he became just the third player to hit the 70-point plateau and passed Baylor at 71 . . . ending with 73. At that point Wilt was the only player to have scored more points in a game in NBA history. Thompson took over the scoring lead from Gervin, who won it back later that night, going for 63 points in his final game, taking the title by .07 points, 27.22 to 27.15.

2002 NBA Playoffs Opening Round, Game 5, Indiana Pacers at New Jersey Nets, Continental Airlines Arena, East Rutherford, New Jersey, May 2, 2002

Reggie Miller, the legendary and repeated cause of nightmares at Madison Square Garden against the Knicks in the playoffs, took his act across the Hudson. The Pacers had squeaked their way into the eighth seed by winning their last five games of the regular season, then took that momentum and shocked the top-seeded Nets by winning the first game of the five-game series in New Jersey. It came down to a fifth and final game in New Jersey, and the Nets looked to have finally shaken loose of the Pacers, up three, in the closing seconds, and I'm planning my off-season vacation. Indiana had the ball on the run, and Reggie, from 40 feet, off balance, banked in the desperation three-pointer to send this classic into OT. The New York–metro-area fans saw Reggie do it again.

Reggie provided another Miller Miracle, but the Pacers ran out of gas in the second overtime, losing 120–109. The Nets were able to exhale and would go on to the NBA Finals, where they lost to the Lakers.

2005 NBA Eastern Conference Semifinals, Game 6, Detroit Pistons at Indiana Pacers, Conseco Fieldhouse, Indianapolis, Indiana, May 19, 2005

Bitter rivals Indiana and Detroit were in Indiana for Game 6 of the Eastern Conference Semifinals, with Detroit leading the series three games to two. Six months earlier, these two teams had engaged in a brawl at the Palace of Auburn Hills that spilled into the stands, leaving the Pacers decimated by suspensions. But Reggie Miller led a crippled Pacer team to a personal storybook ride in his eighteenth and final season, strapping the depleted team to his back and leading them to the playoffs, then taking them to Game 6 of the second round against the defending champs. The underdog Pacers gallantly attempted to send the series to a seventh game, but the Pistons took control of the game late.

Then, in the final minute, with the game over, the rest was storybook. Pacers' coach Rick Carlisle took out Reggie Miller for a final bow in front of the standing-room-only crowd at Conseco Fieldhouse. During an emotional and lengthy outburst from the adoring crowd, Reggie was embraced by his teammates. He stood on the floor, looking into the stands, thumping his heart towards the fans, holding back the tears, when Pistons coach Larry Brown called an extra timeout to enable the resounding tribute to Reggie to continue. Larry and his Pistons all came out to center court, standing and applauding Reggie. The bitter rivals had clashed in one of sports' ugliest incidents just months earlier, and here were the Pistons, joining the Pacers fans, paying a final tribute and demonstrating their great respect for another warrior.

Kenny Albert
Broadcaster, FOX Sports/MSG Network

California Angels at New York Yankees, Yankee Stadium, Bronx, New York, June 17, 1978

As a ten-year-old, I was in the stands at Yankee Stadium the night The Gator struck out eighteen Angels. Guidry raised his record to 11–0 in a 4-hit, 4–0 shutout. Randy Johnson and Steve Carlton are the only left-handers who have struck out more batters in a single game.

1992 Summer Olympics, Men's Basketball, Palau d'Esports de Badalona, Badalona, Spain, July 26–August 8, 1992

Four years after the stunning upset by the Soviet Union of the U.S. Olympic basketball team in Seoul, South Korea, in 1988, the United States sent a "Dream Team" of NBA stars to the Summer Olympics for the first time. Michael Jordan, Magic Johnson, Larry Bird, and Charles Barkley aligned together as teammates to try to avenge the loss suffered by the collegians. I had a front-row seat in Barcelona, Spain (handling statistics for NBC), as Team USA rolled through the Olympics with a perfect 8–0 record, from the opening 116–48 victory over Angola through the gold-medal-winning game against Croatia. I have had the privilege of working at four Olympics. I also handled research for NBC at the boxing venue in Seoul in 1988 and called men's and women's ice hockey play-by-play for NBC at the Winter Games in Salt Lake City, Utah (2002), and Torino, Italy (2006).

1994 Stanley Cup Finals, Game 7, Vancouver Canucks at New York Rangers, Madison Square Garden, New York, New York, June 14, 1994

I had the fortune of calling the series for NHL Radio. The Rangers' Cup hopes almost ended in the Conference Finals, as they trailed the New Jersey Devils three games to two. Captain Mark Messier "guaranteed" a Game 6 victory; then the Devils forced overtime with a goal in the final ten seconds of Game 7. Stephane Matteau sent the Rangers to the Finals with a goal in double over-time; Howie Rose's "Matteau, Matteau, Matteau" call on WFAN Radio will be remembered by New Yorkers for decades.

On to the finals, and the Rangers took a commanding three-games-to-one lead over the Vancouver Canucks. New York City was ready to celebrate on June 9; however, the Rangers lost Game 5 at home. The Canucks forced a decisive Game 7 by winning Game 6 at home, and the Rangers won the clincher in a 3–2 nail biter. A sign held up at the final buzzer by one Ranger fanatic said it all: NOW I CAN DIE IN PEACE. I will never forget the emotions of the series, especially during the final frantic moments. Madison Square Garden erupted with chants of "We Want The Cup" and "No More 1940," while the Rangers celebrated on the ice. When NHL Commissioner Gary Bettman handed the Stanley Cup to Messier, fifty-four years of frustration were erased.

California Angels at Baltimore Orioles, Camden Yards, Baltimore, Maryland, September 6, 1995

Cal Ripken plays in his 2,131st consecutive game, breaking the record set by the Iron Horse, Lou Gehrig, fifty-six years earlier. Having grown up in Aberdeen, Maryland, Ripken was one of Baltimore's own. The city of Baltimore has a small-town feel, especially at sporting venues, and the city celebrated as it never had before, as a native son reached a mark most sports experts thought would never be attainable. Eighty-one-year-old Joe DiMaggio, Gehrig's former teammate, gave a poignant speech during the ceremony.

2003 American League Championship Series, Game 7, Boston Red Sox at New York Yankees, Yankee Stadium, Bronx, New York, October 16, 2003, and 2004 American League Championship Series, Game 7, Boston Red Sox at New York Yankees, Yankee Stadium, Bronx, New York, October 20, 2004

I could feel the tension in the ballpark throughout my entire body. I will always cherish the opportunity I was given to handle the postseries interviews for FOX on the podium in the winning clubhouse both years (Joe Torre and Mariano Rivera in '03 following Aaron Boone's walk-off home run, Terry Francona and Tim Wakefield in '04) as Jackie Autry handed the hardware to the winners. Though I watched the first eight innings of both games from the photographers' box directly to the right of the Yankees' dugout, I did not see Boone's homer in person. I was watching on a 12-inch monitor in the hallway just outside the Yankees' clubhouse because I had to enter the winning clubhouse immediately to set up for interviews at the conclusion of the game. Seconds after Boone ended the series, I sprinted toward the clubhouse and was nearly knocked over by clubhouse attendants and other team personnel as they ran the other way toward the tunnel leading to the dugout so they could join in the celebration.

Marv Albert

Broadcaster, Turner Sports/YES Network

Recipient of Basketball Hall of Fame's Curt Gowdy Award, 1997

1970 NBA Finals Game 7, Los Angeles Lakers at New York Knicks, Madison Square Garden, New York, New York, May 8, 1970

This game is considered the largest audience for a sports event in New York radio history; the game was on tape delay on television, so unless you had a ticket, this was the only way to follow it live. I taped the pregame show, and at that point, most people did not think Knicks center Willis Reed was going to play after he injured his leg in Game 5 and missed Game 6. I interviewed Willis for the show just before he was about to get a cortisone shot and asked whether he was going to play, and he told me there was no way he would not be out there. During warm-ups, Willis was not on the floor and everyone in the building was more concerned with where he was more than anything else. The Lakers were looking around for him, as were his Knick teammates. The game was getting close to starting, but there was still no sign of him. Then, at 7:27, he dramatically came out of the tunnel to the court, and I said on the air, "Here comes Willis," followed by a deafening roar from the 19,000 in attendance. Everything in the building stopped and the crowd was going berserk. Wilt Chamberlain of the Lakers couldn't believe what was happening, and just stood there with his mouth wide open — apparently, his mindset was that he wasn't going to have to play against Willis. Both teams abruptly stopped warming up as Willis trotted onto the floor and hit a couple of practice jumpers, causing the crowd to go even crazier, all just moments before the game was about to start. Once the game actually got underway, he hit his first two jump shots, and I've never heard an NBA crowd that loud. Normally, a couple of early baskets wouldn't be that meaningful in the first quarter of an NBA game, but this seemed to provide a great deal of inspiration. As it turned out, Walt Frazier had one of the greatest games in Finals history, and undoubtedly one of the most forgotten great games ever, but Willis's mere presence in uniform gave everyone the feeling that there was no way the Knicks were going to lose. The Knicks won in a romp, 113–99, to take their first NBA championship.

1988 World Series Game 1, Oakland Athletics at Los Angeles Dodgers, Dodger Stadium, Los Angeles, California, October 15, 1988

Bob Costas and I cohosted the World Series pre- and postgame shows for NBC. We would each do a postgame interview and, this night, I was in Oakland's dugout as the game was coming to an end. The Athletics held a 4–3 lead in the ninth and were starting to celebrate, since it appeared that they were going to win the game. Hall-of-Fame closer Dennis Eckersley, who had 45 saves that season, was on the mound to shut the door, and I was standing right near then-Oakland manager Tony LaRussa when the injured Kirk Gibson came hobbling out of the dugout following a Mike Davis walk with two outs. The entire Oakland dugout was astonished that he was about to pinch-hit—he could barely walk due to a painful knee injury, so no one thought he could actually step up to the plate and produce. I was all set to interview Oakland's Jose Canseco once the final out was made, since he was the star of the game to that point, when Gibson remarkably homered into the rightfield pavilion to give the Dodgers a 5–4 win. The moment he made contact, Canseco knew the ball was gone, just from the crack of the bat. Of course, the crowd went wild at that point. As Bob interviewed Gibson after the game, Eckersley, who looked crushed after giving up the homer, agreed to talk with me without any hesitation. He looked at it as just one of those things that happens and you have to talk whether things went well or not. Gibson didn't make another plate appearance in the Series, but that home run will go down as one of the most extraordinary moments in the game's history, and it spurred the Dodgers to the Series win.

1992 Summer Olympics, Men's Basketball, Palau d'Esports de Badalona, Badalona, Spain, July 26–August 8, 1992

It was chilling for me just to watch the original Dream Team take the court for the first time in the Olympics. This was clearly the most incredible group of players ever assembled in a team sport, from Jordan to Bird to Magic to Stockton and Malone. Obviously, the games were blowouts, but to see this group performing together was daunting. When they took the floor, the crowd, which was comprised mostly of fans from overseas, went crazy. Once the tournament started, though, the games weren't even close, and the U.S. won every one by at least 32 points. It meant a lot to the team to win the gold medal, but the games themselves were actually difficult to broadcast since they were all so one-sided. Most of the excitement surrounding the team was off the court, usually centered around Charles Barkley, who was all over the city, soaking up the Olympic experience and the adulation, with throngs following him everywhere. Throughout the two weeks in Barcelona, it felt as if we were covering the exploits of the Beatles, not a basketball team.

1994 Stanley Cup Finals Game 7, Vancouver Canucks at New York Rangers, Madison Square Garden, New York, New York, June 14, 1994

As I was broadcasting the game, I remember gazing at the seats surrounding the radio booth in Madison Square Garden, which was located in the middle of the lower stands. As the clock wound down and the Rangers won their first Stanley Cup since 1940, I remember seeing people all around me in tears, reminding me how emotionally Ranger fans reacted to the team. While this was all going on, I thought back to my earlier days as a broadcaster for the team, when they were often contenders, with guys like Rod Gilbert, Jean Ratelle, Vic Hadfield, Eddie Giacomin, and others, but it was the era of the Montreal Canadiens, and Bobby Orr's Bruins, then the Philadelphia Flyers, and the Rangers were never quite good enough. It was fifty-four years between Ranger Stanley Cup wins, and chants of "1940" were prevalent for a long time. So, this night was more about the fans as the final seconds ticked off. Growing up as a Rangers fan, with firsthand knowledge of the frustrations from all of the disappointing conclusions to seasons, it felt like this day would never happen. When the buzzer sounded, I said on the air, "The New York Rangers have won the Stanley Cup, something most people thought they would never hear in their lifetime." I can recall looking to my left, where I saw a fan holding up the sign which read NOW I CAN DIE IN PEACE. That said it best of all, and I can only imagine how many people in the building that night shared in those sentiments.

1997 NBA Finals Game 5, Chicago Bulls at Utah Jazz, Delta Center, Salt Lake City, Utah, June 11, 1997

To me, this was one of the most remarkable individual performances I have ever seen. Michael Jordan reportedly had eaten some bad pizza and was weakened by food poisoning and a stomach virus. He could barely stand up before the pivotal Game 5 in Salt Lake City, with the series tied at two. He was dizzy and dehydrated to the point where I remember newspaper reports the next day describing him as being "deathly ill." I did a five-minute interview with him a few hours before the game as we always did, but he didn't give us any indication that he wasn't feeling right, so we didn't even know about that until after the game started. Of course we discussed it on the air for the television audience, but those in attendance had no idea of the extent of his physical condition—what they were watching really was amazing. As the game went on, Michael became weaker and weaker, but somehow he just kept going, and I remember we showed him, at times, being helped to the bench or being propped up by Scottie Pippen during timeouts. Despite his debilitating illness, he scored 38 points in the game, 15 of them in the fourth quarter, to lead the Bulls to a 90–88 win. It was incredible just to watch him preserve his energy and will himself to lead his team to its most important win of the season. Afterwards, Pippen said he had never seen Michael that sick and that he didn't think he'd even be able to put his uniform on. I have been fortunate to call a host of memorable Jordan games, but I've never seen anything quite like this one. The series would end two nights later in Chicago.

Steve Albert
Broadcaster, Showtime Championship Boxing

1970 NBA Finals, Game 7, Los Angeles Lakers at New York Knicks, Madison Square Garden, New York, New York, May 8, 1970

I was a student at Kent State, and when the shootings occurred, the entire campus had to evacuate. So I went home to Brooklyn. Knicks trainer Danny Whelan, who was so great to me when I was a team ball boy in high school, invited me back to be on the bench during the Knicks-Lakers Finals in 1970. Before Game 7, I was on the floor folding warm-ups and towels when Willis emerged from the tunnel. He hobbled out, and the crowd's roar just built to a crescendo. It became deafening. He hit his first couple of practice shots, and I'll always remember looking over at the Lakers players on the floor and focusing in on Wilt Chamberlain's face, in particular. You could see in their eyes that the game was over before it even started. It truly was a poignant moment indelibly etched in my memory. Willis scored the Knicks' first two baskets; he didn't score again, but his mere presence inspired the Knicks to a 113–99 victory and the franchise's first NBA championship.

1976 ABA Finals, Game 6, Denver Nuggets at New York Nets, Nassau Coliseum, Uniondale, New York, May 13, 1976

In Game 6, the Nets came from 22 points behind in the final seventeen minutes to beat the Nuggets for the last ABA Championship. It was an amazing finish by "Super" John Williamson, who scored 16 of his 28 points in the fourth quarter. Dr. J had a great game, too, with 31 points and 19 rebounds, but it was Williamson who really spearheaded the comeback. My brother Al was broadcasting the game for the Nuggets and was sitting at the other end of the courtside table. When the buzzer sounded and the Nets won 112–106, outscoring Denver 34–14 in the final period, the ecstatic fans stormed onto the court at the Nassau Coliseum, and as a result of the stampede, they jumped on the media table and cut Al off the air. Every phone line, every headset, every monitor was just ripped out of its socket. He was not a happy camper. Since I was the Nets announcer, out of respect, I guess, the fans left me alone and went around my area of the table, and I was able to finish the broadcast of the final game in ABA history.

Robbie Knievel Caesars Palace Fountains Jump, Caesars Palace, Las Vegas, Nevada, April 14, 1989

Robbie's father, Evel Knievel, attempted this jump and broke virtually every bone in his body. Robbie made it unscathed, though, and landed right on his tires without even skidding. I'll never forget a conversation I had before the jump, though, with the telecast's executive producer. He forewarned me that I should have in my mind three scenarios before the jump started so that I would be prepared for the potential outcomes—Robbie making the jump successfully, Robbie making the jump but crashing, or Robbie losing his life. That, without question, was the oddest broadcast I ever had to get ready for and actually call.

Mike Tyson vs. Evander Holyfield, MGM Grand Garden Arena, Las Vegas, Nevada, June 28, 1997

This was just a surreal moment. Walking to the arena from my hotel room that night in Las Vegas, I remember having a sinking feeling that something bizarre was going to happen. That was usually the feeling before a Mike Tyson fight, but I had a premonition that Tyson was going to do something unusual. I never thought, in my wildest imagination, however, that he would resort to cannibalism. At the start of the fateful third round, I noticed Holyfield motioning to referee Mills Lane that Tyson had failed to put in his mouthpiece, which makes you wonder if Tyson went into the round with the preconceived notion of taking a chomp out of Holyfield's ear.

Diego Corrales vs. Jose Luis Castillo, Mandalay Bay Events Center, Las Vegas, Nevada, May 7, 2005

This was one of the greatest fights in boxing history. It was just a dramatic, compelling fight—Corrales was knocked down twice in the tenth round by

Castillo but came back to win the fight that same round. It was an awesome, action-packed fight, just nonstop punching from the opening bell to the end of the fight, sort of like "Rock'em, Sock'em Robots." It was just punch after punch after punch. The fans were worked into a frenzy, and it brought heart, determination, and sheer guts to new, unimaginable heights in boxing.

Kevin Allen
Columnist, USA Today

1984 World Series, Game 5, San Diego Padres at Detroit Tigers, Tiger Stadium, Detroit, Michigan, October 14, 1984

I was a young reporter covering sports in my hometown of Detroit. The confrontation between Rich Gossage and Kirk Gibson in the eighth inning of this game really was the essence of sports; it was a power pitcher against a bulldog hitter. Tigers manager Sparky Anderson had signaled to Gibson that they were going to walk him, but Gibson just laughed and dug in. The pitch he hit was pure Gossage—a blistering fastball that was rocketed out of the ballpark. I remember Anderson telling me once that, in meaningless games, Gibson was probably a .200 hitter, but when the game was on the line, he was a completely different player. Most people that know me think this game is meaningful to me only because it was Detroit, but I had already crossed over the line by then and had learned to root for the story, not for my favorite team. And this was a great story—a guy from Michigan, who starred at Michigan State, hitting a big home run in the World Series for the Tigers.

1987 Stanley Cup Finals, Game 7, Philadelphia Flyers at Edmonton Oilers, Northlands Coliseum, Edmonton, Canada, May 31, 1987

Looking back now, I romanticize hockey in the 1980s. The teams that were put together, the way the game was played—it was a wide-open time in hockey history and about offense and big saves. The Edmonton Oilers were in the midst of dominating the game in the second half of the decade, and I spent all of my springs in Edmonton covering them. The finals against Philadelphia were a great series, with Flyer goalie Ron Hextall playing fantastically and leading his team to Game 7. At that time, the press seating in the Northlands Coliseum was in a catwalk extended out over the ice; it was a terrific vantage point—high, but you really got to see the play develop. It was a 2–1 game until Mark Messier, Kent Nilsson, and Glenn Anderson broke out of the offensive zone like a squadron of F-14s; by the time they reached their own blue line, they were already at Mach Three, and to this day, even though in my heart I know the game is much faster today, I will never be convinced that anyone has ever been faster than those three guys. It is still vivid in my mind, the tic-tac-toe play from Messier to Nilsson to Anderson, who scored. I remember sitting there thinking that it just doesn't get any better than that. And after that goal, you just knew the game was over and the Flyers weren't coming back, and they didn't, losing 3–1. I will always say it was the greatest goal I've ever seen.

42nd NHL All-Star Game, Chicago Stadium, Chicago, Illinois, January 19, 1991

Sports are so intertwined with life, and it really showed that day in Chicago. I really think this was the last time that the entire country was banded together regarding overseas affairs and supported the idea of America's serving as a peace officer in the Middle East and going in to clean up what had happened in Kuwait. The All-Star Game took place at this time in Chicago, of all places, where they already had a tradition of cheering through the national anthem. I had heard the fans there do it many times, but never like this. It was less about sports and more about politics and patriotism and life. I'm not sure everybody in that arena did it for the same reasons, but I am convinced that it affected everyone and that everyone felt moved by it all. Nothing about hockey translates too well on television, but that did. I can't even tell you who won the game. It just doesn't matter.

Pittsburgh Penguins at Philadelphia Flyers, The Spectrum, Philadelphia, Pennsylvania, March 2, 1993

People have a tendency to look at athletes as indestructible, and the players certainly do look at themselves that way. So when Mario Lemieux was diagnosed with non-Hodgkin's lymphoma, it was something that almost everyone can relate to, since we all know someone who has been diagnosed with cancer at some point. However, I think there was a gasp around the sports world when a superstar like Lemieux received that diagnosis. When he came back, though, what he did for sports wasn't nearly as important as what he did for cancer patients everywhere. He took his last treatment in the morning, then played that night in Philadelphia and had a goal and an assist. It reminded everyone that cancer could be beaten. This comeback transcended sports and was more about life.

1994 Winter Olympics Ice Hockey Finals, Sweden vs. Canada, Haakons Hall, Lillehammer, Norway, February 27, 1994

In hockey, the Olympics are a huge stage, with people watching that couldn't tell you anything about the National Hockey League. For that reason, Peter Forsberg's goal, in this setting, in a shootout to determine the gold medal, is just unbelievable. I've never felt as much tension in an arena as I did during this shootout. We found out afterward that, as the shootout went on, all the veterans in the game didn't want to shoot because the Swedish press is very difficult, and they felt that if they missed they would be hated for the rest of their lives.

Forsberg, though, didn't know what he didn't know. He was young and a fantastic player who thought he was invincible. And he pulled off a move where he left the puck behind him, pulled the goalie to the right, and then reached back and tapped the puck in. It was an amazing move, but on that stage, at that moment, with a billion people watching all over the world, it was unforgettable. They put Forsberg on a postage stamp in Sweden, and it set him up for life. He might have had the success he had afterward regardless, but I don't think anybody ever came to the National Hockey League with more confidence than Forsberg did, just based on what he did under the biggest spotlight of all.

Maury Allen
Author/Journalist

Interview with Casey Stengel, Polo Grounds, New York, New York, 1962

Casey Stengel was managing the Mets after all those great years in the Bronx with the Yankees. I had my first sit-down with him one afternoon on the bench at the Polo Grounds at 2:00. Two hours later, he was still going strong as batting practice started. Broadcaster Gabe Pressman came over for an interview with two cameras and five assistants. He said to Casey, "Let's talk about the Mets." Casey looked up at him, pointed to me, and strongly blew Pressman away by saying, "Can't you see I'm talking to my writers?"

Ron Hunt Trade, November 29, 1966

Ron Hunt had been the Mets' first homegrown star and was very sad about being traded. I didn't think being traded mattered all that much. He was still being paid. He started to list all the things he loved about playing in New York. This was a kid from Missouri, and he couldn't stand leaving New York, the Mets, and Casey Stengel. The more he talked, the more he cried. Finally, I started crying, the only time I ever cried over a baseball player being traded to another team.

1969 Major League Baseball All-Star Game, RFK Memorial Stadium, Washington, D.C., July 23, 1969

President Nixon invited the players and press to the White House while we were all in Washington. He talked about what a great baseball fan he was and how he loved the Chicago White Sox. He said if he had his life to live over he would have been a sportswriter. This was during the bitterness of the Vietnam War, and we went through the line to the President for a photo op. When I got to Nixon I told him, "I wish you had become a sportswriter." Joe Garagiola, standing nearby, almost fainted.

1969 World Series, Game 5, Baltimore Orioles at New York Mets, Shea Stadium, Queens, New York, October 16, 1969

As Cleon Jones caught the last fly ball out off the bat of Davey Johnson, later their 1986 World Series–winning manager, he kneeled down as if in thankful prayer. It was very touching because Baltimore manager Earl Weaver thought the Mets cheated their way to the Series when Jones was hit on the foot by a pitched ball. Then the Mets rallied for the win after manager Gil Hodges showed the umps the spot on the ball. Weaver said Hodges put it there. To this day, he hates Hodges for it and has worked to keep Hodges out of the Hall of Fame.

Muhammad Ali vs. Joe Frazier, Madison Square Garden, New York, New York, March 8, 1971

I was in press row at the Garden, about ten seats away from Frank Sinatra . . . me, a kid from Brooklyn, sitting near Sinatra while he took pictures for *Life* magazine. He didn't sing, but I saw his pictures later. Great stuff—he missed his calling. I still think Ali was the second-most-significant figure of twentieth-century America, just behind FDR.

Dave Anderson

Columnist, New York Times

Recipient of the Football Hall of Fame's Dick McCann Memorial
Award, 1998

1955 World Series, Game 7, Brooklyn Dodgers at New York Yankees, Yankee Stadium, Bronx, New York, October 4, 1955

The Dodgers had never won a World Series while representing Brooklyn until this Series—they played in plenty but never won one. There was a history of frustration, especially against the Yankees, who had won five straight Series between the teams. They had virtually the same team from 1947 on, since Jackie Robinson came up to the team with Duke Snider, with Roy Campanella joining them in 1948. The only position that really changed in this stretch was in leftfield, where there seemed to be a different player every year. Otherwise, virtually everyone else was the same through this whole stretch. So when the Dodgers ended the frustration against the Yankees, in Yankee Stadium, by shutting out the Yankees 2–0 behind Johnny Podres, there was a tremendous celebration. Brooklyn just exploded.

Super Bowl III, New York Jets vs. Baltimore Colts, Orange Bowl, Miami, Florida, January 12, 1969

I was the beat writer for the *New York Times* for the Jets that season. There were about a half dozen people that actually picked the Jets to win this game, and I was one of them. The reason I picked them was Joe Namath. My rule of thumb in big games like this is that the team with the best quarterback should win. Earl Morrall was a very good NFL quarterback for many years, but I thought Namath was an exceptional quarterback. I had done a piece for *True* magazine about Namath, and the topic was whether Namath could make it in the NFL. I believed it but needed someone to support that, so I talked to Vince Lombardi, who said Namath was "almost a perfect passer." Lombardi never said things like that about anyone unless he meant it. I also remember that at halftime, with the Jets ahead, people were saying what they were watching was amazing, to which I replied, "Not to me." And while Namath led the Jets that day to the 16–7 triumph, I thought Matt Snell should have been the MVP. But Namath being Namath, he got the award.

Muhammad Ali vs. Joe Frazier, Madison Square Garden, New York, New York, March 8, 1971

The Thriller in Manila was probably a much more brutal fight, but the first fight had the biggest legitimate hype of any fight we've ever had. You had two boxers, each of whom had a claim to the heavyweight championship—Ali had it before his exile; Frazier won it while Ali was away. They were also both undefeated. You aren't going to see that very often, if ever again. At that time, the Garden was still the Mecca of boxing, with a meaningful fight seemingly every month.

There was also a morality play going on, since people also forget that, at this point, Ali was not the most popular fighter around. A lot of people still resented the fact that he would not enter the army, and he was considered by many to be a villain, so Frazier was the guy everyone got behind, especially after he won the gold at the 1964 Olympics. He became very popular and was being insulted by Ali time and time again, so anyone that hated Ali was rooting for Frazier. It is amazing how many people think Ali should have been awarded the decision—Frazier beat the heck out of him. When Frazier knocked Ali down, I was sitting at ringside in the first row in the corner where it happened. I remember not just the punch but Ali falling like a tree right in front of me, and the sound when he hit the canvas was like a thunderclap.

1980 Winter Olympics Ice Hockey Semifinals, United States vs. Soviet Union, Olympic Ice Center, Lake Placid, New York, February 22, 1980

The thing that made the 1980 Winter Olympics so great was that it wasn't just a sports story. There was the Cold War, there was Jimmy Carter threatening to boycott the Moscow Olympics later that year, and you had the hostage crisis in Iran, so there was a lot going on at the time. It all had some effect on the thinking of this team as they went through the Olympics. You could see the United States and the Soviets on a collision course, and here was this great Soviet team, the best team in the world. It had beaten the NHL All-Stars just a year earlier, 6–0 in Madison Square Garden, and had blown out the U.S. team 10–3 in the final exhibition game before the Olympics.

The turning point came when Mark Johnson scored in the last second of the first period and Viktor Tikhonov responded by benching Vladislav Tretiak, the best goaltender in the world, to start the second period. Years later, when Slava Fetisov was playing for the New Jersey Devils, I talked to him about the game, and the big mystery to him was still how Tikhonov could bench Tretiak at that point. Of course, we all know what happened after that.

The 1986 Masters, Augusta National Golf Club, Augusta, Georgia, April 10–13, 1986

There have been many great Masters and many Jack Nicklaus tournaments, but for him to win at age forty-six with a 30 on the back nine on Sunday, and the eagle he made on 15, was just an amazing story. He hadn't won a major since 1980, and it was a very theatrical moment. No writer would have even dared to write this story. There was more theater and more emotion involved than at any other golf tournament I've ever covered.

Jim Armstrong
Columnist, Denver Post

1988 NFC Divisional Playoff, Philadelphia Eagles at Chicago Bears, Soldier Field, Chicago, Illinois, December 31, 1988

At least I think that was the Eagles and Bears down there, playing in the famous "Fog Bowl." Talk about surreal. You couldn't see an inch outside the press-box window. I remember going with the "Gorillas in the Mist" lead the next morning. Hey, it worked at the time.

Super Bowl XXIII, San Francisco 49ers vs. Cincinnati Bengals, Joe Robbie Stadium, Miami, Florida, January 22, 1989

For all the Super Bowls that have been played, how many have come down to a last-minute drive? Precious few. To me, that was the day Joe Montana cemented the "greatest of all time" tag for quarterbacks. Talk about cool under pressure. He said after the game that he told his teammates in the huddle that John Candy was in the stands.

Montreal Expos at Colorado Rockies, Mile High Stadium, Denver, Colorado, April 9, 1993

There were 80,227 people in the stands, creating a football-like atmosphere, as the Colorado Rockies made their Denver debut. To this day, I'm not sure if I've ever heard a louder crowd. So what happens? Rox leadoff hitter Eric Young homers to open the bottom of the first. Young later said he floated around the bases.

1993 World Series, Game 6, Philadelphia Phillies at Toronto Blue Jays, Skydome, Toronto, Canada, October 23, 1993

No, they didn't win, but I loved that Phillies team. They shaved once a year whether they needed to or not. I remember calling them "The Beast Team Money Can Buy."

Super Bowl XXXII, Denver Broncos vs. Green Bay Packers, Qualcomm Stadium, San Diego, California, January 25, 1998

The memorable part wasn't so much the action on the field. John Elway played relatively poorly. It was afterward where the great theater came in. Never has a player wanted to win a game more than Elway wanted to win that one. He, more than any athlete ever, had been tagged as the guy who couldn't win the big one. That's why Broncos owner Pat Bowlen held up the trophy and proclaimed, "This one's for John!"

Marty Aronoff
Sports Statistician

1978 NBA Finals, Game 7, Washington Bullets at Seattle SuperSonics, Seattle Center Coliseum, Seattle, Washington, June 7, 1978

Starting with the 1974–75 season, I did the statistics for the Washington Bullets telecasts and, prior to that, had been a Bullets' season-ticket holder after the franchise moved from Baltimore to Washington before the 1972–73 season. For the 1978 championship round between the Bullets and the Sonics, I was asked by CBS Sports to go on the road with announcers Brent Musburger, Rick Barry, and John Havlicek, thus becoming the first stats person CBS had ever traveled for an NBA event. Therefore it was with great personal and professional pleasure that I celebrated when Wes Unseld, Bob Dandridge, and Elvin Hayes led the Bullets to this decisive Game 7 victory in Seattle, 105–99.

1986 NBA Playoffs Opening Round, Game 2, Chicago Bulls at Boston Celtics, Boston Garden, Boston, Massachusetts, April 20, 1986

Just another first-round walkover by a Celtics team that went 67–15 in the regular season over a Bulls squad that barely squeaked into the playoffs with a 30–52 mark? Not exactly. This became the ultimate "one superstar vs. one great team" contest that I have ever witnessed. Michael Jordan, who had missed most of the regular season with a broken bone in his foot, scored an NBA playoff record 63 points against a Celtics team that would eventually win the championship that year over the Houston Rockets. Most basketball fans have seen the highlight from this game of Jordan going one-on-one with Larry Bird, "yo-yoing" the ball between his legs before driving for one of his many spectacular baskets that left the crowd in the Boston Garden, including this busy CBS Sports statistician, totally drained at game's end.

1987 NBA Finals, Game 4, Los Angeles Lakers at Boston Celtics, Boston Garden, Boston, Massachusetts, June 9, 1987

This game featured another Hall-of-Famer making a spectacular game-winning shot. With the Lakers trailing by one in the closing seconds, Magic Johnson took an inbounds pass, drove toward the top of the lane, and put up what he later called a "junior, junior skyhook" over the Celtics' great front line of Kevin McHale, Robert Parish, and Larry Bird. A stunned Boston Garden crowd, which just seconds earlier had been confident the Celts were going to tie the best-of-seven series at two games each, watched in disbelief as this rarely used shot by Magic swished through for a 107–106 lead. Bird had one final chance to win the game, but his long jumper from the left side hit the rim, and the Lakers took a commanding 3–1 series lead en route to a 4–2 championship victory. After the series Bird said, "Magic is a great, great player, the best I've ever seen."

1989 NBA Playoffs Opening Round, Game 5, Chicago Bulls at Cleveland Cavaliers, Richfield Coliseum, Richfield, Ohio, May 7, 1989

This was the famous Michael Jordan–over–Craig Ehlo 16-footer at the buzzer to win this series. The only person who jumped higher than Jordan was his head coach, Doug Collins, racing off the bench when MJ's shot from the top of the key swished through the net. What fans may not recall is that just two seconds before Jordan's shot, Ehlo made a great driving layup to give the Cavs a 100–99 lead and an apparent victory. However, Craig is only remembered as the unfortunate defender on Jordan's winner.

2003 American League Championship Series, Game 7, Boston Red Sox at New York Yankees, Yankee Stadium, Bronx, New York, October 16, 2003

My favorite sport growing up was baseball, and this contest was the ultimate thriller this grand old game can produce: Red Sox vs. the Yanks at the Stadium, extra innings in the deciding game, and an unlikely hero producing the game winner. Aaron Boone joined Bucky Dent as the most despised infielder to ever bury a Boston team when he blasted a Tim Wakefield knuckler into the leftfield stands at sixteen minutes after midnight for the 6–5 victory. How do I know the exact time? I dropped my pen and stat sheet, grabbed my camera, and took a dramatic photo of baseball history as Boone rounded second, with the Sox starting to leave the field and the Yankee Stadium scoreboard in the background. To an impartial sports fan with no rooting interest in the game, this contest presented everything a person who loves athletic competition as much as I do could hope for in a climactic event.

Brian Baldinger
Broadcaster, FOX Sports/NFL Network

New York Knicks vs. Chicago Bulls and Los Angeles Lakers at Philadelphia 76ers, The Spectrum, Philadelphia, Pennsylvania, January 5, 1968

I was living in Cherry Hill, New Jersey, and my dad took my brother and me to the Spectrum to see the 76ers and the Knicks each play in a doubleheader. The Sixers' starting lineup was Wilt Chamberlain, Chet Walker, Hal Greer, Wali Jones, and Billy Cunningham, while the Knicks had Willis Reed, Walt Frazier, Cazzie Russell, and lots of other greats. They also gave out NBA basketballs that day, and I remember I took that ball home and never stopped dribbling it.

1987 NBA Finals, Game 4, Los Angeles Lakers at Boston Celtics, Boston Garden, Boston, Massachusetts, June 9, 1987

I was playing for the Dallas Cowboys and went with a couple of buddies of mine in a private plane to check out the Lakers and Celtics in the game featuring Magic Johnson's "junior skyhook." Boston Garden that night was hot and filled with exactly the type of tension a Celtics-Lakers finals game would bring in those days. Larry Bird had a shot to win it at the end, but his shot hit the rim, bounced straight up, hit the rim again then fell out. The Lakers would go on to win the series, and Magic Johnson had written another chapter of his legacy.

1991 NCAA Men's Basketball Tournament Semifinals, UNLV vs. Duke, Hoosier Dome, Indianapolis, Indiana, March 30, 1991

I was living in Indianapolis and playing for the Colts at the time. I went to Duke and of course am a big Blue Devil basketball fan. UNLV was undefeated, but Bobby Hurley was outstanding, and Duke played the perfect game. Grant Hill was great and played better than you could ever expect a freshman to play in a game as big as this, while Christian Laettner was incredible and scored 28 points. UNLV was heavily favored and had blown Duke out the year before in the NCAAs, but the results were different this time around, with Duke winning 79–77.

Super Bowl XXXII, Denver Broncos vs. Green Bay Packers, Qualcomm Stadium, San Diego, California, January 25, 1998

I was trying to get into broadcasting and had started getting a little work in the business. I was able to get a press pass and went to San Diego and pretended like I was doing the game. I stood next to a post in the handicapped section, where I wouldn't interfere with anybody and took a notepad out and took notes for the entire game as if I was working it. I analyzed every single play as if I was actually calling the Super Bowl, because it was my ambition to do exactly that. Afterward, when the media descended on the field, I pretended to be interviewing John Elway, Terrell Davis, Brett Favre, and others, just like I would if I were on network television.

Super Bowl XXXIV, St. Louis Rams vs. Tennessee Titans, Georgia Dome, Atlanta, Georgia, January 30, 2000

I did this game for European television. The game had everything, from the Cinderella story of Kurt Warner to Dick Vermeil's winning a championship to Eddie George's putting the Titans on his back in the second half to the emergence of Steve McNair as a stud quarterback to the last play of the game ending on the 1-yard line, as the Rams won 23–16. And I got a chance to call it.

Carl Beane
Public Address Announcer, Fenway Park

Bobby Orr, Boston Bruins, Boston Garden, 1966–76

I've seen a lot of hockey players, but Bobby Orr was different. We've never seen a defenseman who could skate like him, with Doug Harvey probably coming the closest. Like Harvey, Orr really controlled the game, but he was a faster skater, a better passer, and, horror of horrors, a defenseman who was a goal scorer. He was the diamond on a hockey team that really captured the New England region. To this day, there are so many state-owned hockey rinks in Massachusetts because of the Bruins of the late sixties and early seventies, and Bobby Orr was the reason. He was just a very special player.

I saw him at the Garden one night against Atlanta, and he had the puck behind his own net and just casually came up ice, weaved his way through everybody, ended up going down the right side, around the net, faked everyone out, including the goalie, and flipped the puck up into the net. He just went through everybody. And his last couple of years he basically played with one knee, which was even more amazing.

1988 NBA Eastern Conference Semifinals, Game 7, Atlanta Hawks at Boston Celtics, Boston Garden, Boston, Massachusetts, May 22, 1988

Larry Bird against Dominique Wilkins. The way these guys traded baskets in the fourth quarter was amazing. It was the Shootout at the OK Corral. We knew Larry Bird well enough to know that he was an incredible competitor.

They were guarding each other, and Wilkins would make a shot, then Bird would answer. It became a personal game of HORSE in the middle of an NBA game. Sometimes you don't realize something like that is going on, but everyone picked up on it right away. The referees, the coaches, the other players, the crowd . . . everyone knew what was going on. It became a game of one-upmanship between a pair of players with completely different styles. It was fun to watch both teams just throw the playbook out the window, set up each of the players, and just get out of the way and amazing to watch two guys compete like that at that level.

1999 Major League Baseball All-Star Game, Fenway Park, Boston, Massachusetts, July 13, 1999

When they brought Ted Williams out on a cart and all the past and present players in attendance gathered around him, we all had the feeling that this was the last time we were going to see him, certainly the last time in Fenway Park. What a life he had—the greatest hitter that ever lived. What he accomplished, to see him there, and to see other great players, the ones who played both with and against him, all gather around him because they wanted to see him. The players of today, who wanted to touch him and talk to him and see him in person, all became little kids. We knew his health had been failing and this was the last time we were going to see him.

Over the years, having the chance to interview him numerous times, I found him to be a fascinating man. It wasn't just the baseball stories, but the war stories and learning about the difficulties he had growing up, virtually without parents. It gave us a little insight about why he might have been as cantankerous as he was and why he would sometimes get so angry at the dumbest things. But in major situations he would come through. He offered no excuses and no alibis for hitting just .200 in the 1946 World Series, his only appearance in the Series. He was a special man and one of my father's favorite players.

My favorite Ted Williams story is from the early eighties, when the Sox were at spring training in Winter Haven. I was there to cover spring training, and my youngest brother, Butch, was working for an airline and arranged to fly my father down to Winter Haven, where I would meet him. We were walking toward the cafeteria and passed former umpire Hank Soar, Johnny Pesky, Bobby Doerr, and Ted Williams sitting near the cafeteria. Bobby Doerr and I have been friends for many years, and after we said hi, Ted asked, "Who's this character with you?" I said it was my father, Al, and he looked at my father and asked, "Is this your son, Al Beane? Well, I'm sorry. That is too bad." He then dismissed me and told me to leave my father with them. So here is my dad, whose all-time favorite player was Bobby Doerr, along with his other favorites

Johnny Pesky and Ted Williams, hanging out with them. After a bit, I came back, and Ted said, "I thought I told you to get lost. He's fine with us. Take off." In his gruff and bombastic way, he made the point that my dad was just one of the guys with them. It was a memory my father had the rest of his life.

2001 AFC Division Playoff, Oakland Raiders at New England Patriots, Foxboro Stadium, Foxboro, Massachusetts, January 19, 2002

This game is remembered more for the "Tuck Rule" call, but the kicks that Adam Vinatieri made in the snow were amazing. The first one, which tied the game, was impossible, while the one that won the game, 16–13, was almost impossible. Those two kicks, considering the conditions in the old Foxboro Stadium, which was a terrible stadium, were really the reason the Patriots made it to the Super Bowl and started their run of three titles in four seasons. Those two kicks started their legacy and really got people's attention that the Patriots might just be about to start something special.

2004 World Series, Game 1, St. Louis Cardinals at Boston Red Sox, Fenway Park, Boston, Massachusetts, October 23, 2004

This is something that is personally very significant for me, since, as the PA announcer at Fenway Park, I got to do all the introductions at the start of the Red Sox' first World Series since 1986. All my friends and family got to hear me, and the pageantry of the whole evening still makes me go, "Wow." It made me a part of Boston and Fenway Park history, and no matter what happens from here on out, a kid from Agawam was in the history book. I was sitting in the booth, waiting for my cue, thinking of my father, who passed away in 1990 and was an ardent Red Sox fan and who instilled my love of baseball. I also thought of my best friend, Bobby Eldridge, whose mother, Janet, was a huge fan, and all the other Sox fans I knew who were no longer with us. What a cool moment it was.

Len Berman
Broadcaster, NBC Sports/WNBC-TV New York

1975 World Series, Game 7, Cincinnati Reds at Boston Red Sox, Fenway Park, Boston, Massachusetts, October 22, 1975

Yet another heartbreak for Red Sox fans as the Reds beat the Red Sox, 4–3. What a collection on the field . . . Rose, Bench, Morgan, Yaz. I'll never forget interviewing Yaz in the locker room after the game. He said, "I can't wait for spring training to start." Who knew it would take twenty-nine more years for Boston to win a World Series.

1976 NBA Finals, Game 5, Phoenix Suns at Boston Celtics, Boston Garden, Boston, Massachusetts, June 4, 1976

I watched the first quarter, then left to do a newscast on WBZ-TV in Boston. I returned to Boston Garden in time for the end of regulation. It was like entering a time warp, featuring a frenzied crowd and clutch shots by John Havlicek and Garfield Heard. Boston finally won it in triple overtime, 128–126, and captured the NBA title two days later. It was the only game my parents ever saw in Boston Garden. They probably figured they were all like that.

Super Bowl XXV, Buffalo Bills vs. New York Giants, Tampa Stadium, Tampa, Florida, January 27, 1991

Wide right. The game was played in Tampa during the first Gulf War. Whitney Houston sang the national anthem, with all the fans waving small American flags, and there wasn't a dry eye in the house. After the game, nobody was around Scott Norwood, who had missed the field goal that could have won it for Buffalo. So I just walked up and did a TV interview. I thought it was odd that most reporters were ignoring the biggest story of the game.

1994 Stanley Cup Finals, Game 7, Vancouver Canucks at New York Rangers, Madison Square Garden, New York, New York, June 14, 1994

Nobody thought it would ever happen in our lifetime. I had gone to Ranger games at the Old Garden on my GO card and stood in the second balcony. Teams in other cities had won recent championships, and there had been rioting, but not that night in New York. It was incredibly peaceful, as was the parade on Broadway that followed. Truly a once-in-a-lifetime event.

1996 World Series, Game 6, Atlanta Braves at New York Yankees, Yankee Stadium, Bronx, New York, October 26, 1996

The Yanks broke their eighteen-year drought between championships. I remember walking under the stands and came upon Tim Raines and his wife crying and drinking champagne. "Respecting" their private moment, I shoved a microphone in their faces and had them share it with the world!

Craig Bolerjack
Broadcaster, CBS Sports

Cleveland Indians at Kansas City Royals, Royals Stadium, Kansas City, Missouri, September 29, 1993

I grew up in Kansas City watching George Brett play and then had a chance to cover him as one of my first broadcasting assignments out of college (I graduated from Kansas State in 1981 and got a job in Topeka, Kansas, doing weekend sports). The love the city had for Brett was amazing, and I just had to fly home to see him play his last home game. The way his career ended was a

Cinderella-style story that you only read about. He singled in his final at bat to drive in the eventual winning run, and after the game, he went back to home plate, lay down, and kissed it. All I could think was "Wow!!!"

To me, as a sports lover, I just appreciated that moment so much because it was the culmination of a lot of things—his hard work and day-to-day grind. He came to the park and played hard every day and was the ultimate professional. He represented what happens when you give yourself to your profession. Brett was the total definition of a pro, and what he gave back in that one moment made the entire Royals Stadium crowd realize just how much they were going to miss him. I still have the ticket to this day and walked out of the stadium knowing that I was part of something that, for me personally, brought things full circle.

1994 Winter Olympics, Ladies' Figure Skating, Hamar OL-Amfi, Hamar, Norway, February 23–25, 1994

Salt Lake had just been awarded the 2002 Olympics, so my station sent me to Lillehammer in 1994 to cover the athletes from the area. After everything that happened at the U.S. Championships between the two skaters, Nancy Kerrigan and Tonya Harding, there was so much drama following them, it was like a soap opera. I knew the press conference was going to be big but was still surprised at the enormity and the number of cameras from all over the world there to cover it. It really felt like this was a bigger story than the Olympics itself. It might have actually been the first reality TV show, given how closely and how much everyone was covering the story, if you think about it. Here were Kerrigan and Harding, after everything happened, on the stage together, and all you could think while standing there was, "How is this really going to unfold?" You didn't know what to expect. Obviously, it went off without a hitch. I was standing around 10 feet away from Harding by the exit as she left and had a camera in my pocket, so I took a couple photos, just to freeze that moment in time. The whole press conference, though, was surreal.

1997 NBA Finals, Game 5, Chicago Bulls at Utah Jazz, Delta Center, Salt Lake City, Utah, June 11, 1997

I covered both the 1997 and 1998 finals between the Bulls and Jazz for KSL in Salt Lake City and saw lots of great basketball in those twelve games, but this game was just one of those that you never forget. Before the game, the rumor was flying around that Michael Jordan had the flu and a 103-degree fever, and sure enough, on the bench, he was slumped over, leaning on Scottie Pippen. It really made you feel like the Jazz had that game, since we weren't sure whether he could even play. Well, he played, all right. Whenever he was on the bench, as the game went on, he would slump more and more, but as soon as the buzzer sounded, up he got and it was time to play. That was what Michael Jordan did. His ability to dominate in that state and win fascinates me to this day. He was incredibly tough mentally, and if his team couldn't do it, he would.

2001 NCAA Tournament, First Round, BSU Pavilion, Boise, Idaho, March 15, 2001

I was calling four games for CBS with James Worthy on the first day of the NCAA Tournament in Boise, and the four games were decided by a total of seven points. Georgia State upset Wisconsin, 50–49; Maryland beat George Mason, 83–80; Georgetown topped Arkansas, 63–61; and in a shocker, fifteenth-seed Hampton upset Iowa State, 58–57. If you get one good game on the first day, you look at it as a successful day. If you get two, it is an absolute joy. A third is not even thinkable. So four is just a once-in-a-lifetime opportunity. The capper was Hampton's upset of second-seed Iowa State. When the game ended, James and I looked at each other and realized, "This is insane!" I didn't want the day to end and was ready to call four more games, even after already calling four in the last ten hours. I just did not want the day to end.

As the day went on, we realized we were becoming a part of something special but had no idea how special. We knew going into the last game that if it ended as a two-point game or less, it would be an NCAA Tournament record for closest four games in one regional. I remember the Georgetown game was delayed in the second half for a good ten minutes because the buzzer got stuck and one of the shot clocks got stuck. It was a day full of weird things happening. The winning shot in the Georgetown game had to be decided via replay because of a shot-clock malfunction. It was a very special day, capped off by the Iowa State loss. I'll never forget Cyclone coach Larry Eustachy coming up to me before the game and saying, "I just don't know if the kids have it today." Obviously, he sensed that his club was not on, but little did he know at the time that he correctly predicted his team's demise.

Cincinnati Bengals at Cleveland Browns, Cleveland Browns Stadium, Cleveland, Ohio, November 28, 2004

On paper, this was not exactly the most intriguing matchup of the day, as both franchises were in a down period, so no one expected what we ended up seeing—a 58–48 shootout that was the second-highest scoring game in NFL history. It was remarkable how both teams marched up and down the field this day, though. I've seen high-scoring quarters before, but in this game, it never stopped. It was just a parade of passing and rushing and special teams play (329 rushing yards, 637 passing yards, 478 kick-and-punt-return yards). Both defenses were porous all day. The crowd got so into it, we got really into it in the booth, and the offense just kept coming. For a play-by-play guy, a game like this is heaven. Every play was big; there was no grinding it out. Every play had impact and felt like it had playoff implications. It was another day when I really didn't want the game to end.

Mike Breen
Broadcaster, ESPN/MSG Network

1986 World Series, Game 6, Boston Red Sox at New York Mets, Shea Stadium, Queens, New York, October 25, 1986

The press box was so crowded that the Mets were just putting people wherever they could find seats. I was working for NBC Radio at the time, and they happened to seat me in the Red Sox radio booth, where there was enough room for the broadcasters to sit in the front, while others sat in the back. I was really young and had just started working in the business, so I hadn't really learned the proper etiquette yet. Being a Mets fan my whole life, I was dejected because it appeared that they were going to lose the World Series. So when the ball went through Bill Buckner's legs, I lost all journalistic perspective and started jumping up and down like everyone in the stands. I can't remember if it was the producer or one of the Red Sox radio guys, but one of them turned around and shot me the dirtiest look. I should not have been acting that way, and I quickly quieted myself down. But it was such an unexpected great moment for a Mets fan that I believe even the most hardened journalist would have had a difficult time not reacting.

USC at Notre Dame, Notre Dame Stadium, Notre Dame, Indiana, October 24, 1987

I was in my mid-twenties and was dating my future wife, when we went to Notre Dame to visit a friend of hers who went to school there. Notre Dame was playing USC that weekend, and we were able to get tickets to the game. At halftime, the USC Trojan Marching Band was the entertainment. Of course, when they came out to play, the Notre Dame fans booed them. But the band was so impressive that the boos quickly stopped. As they continued to play, fans that were leaving their seats to indulge in their own halftime activities almost immediately started to return to their seats. The boos now became cheers. In their grand finale, as they turned to leave the field, the USC Marching Band played the Notre Dame fight song, and the place exploded. It was so unexpected—the visiting band of the hated USC Trojans playing the Notre Dame fight song as they marched off the field.

1994 NBA Finals, Game 5, Houston Rockets at New York Knicks, Madison Square Garden, New York, New York, June 17, 1994

NBC was broadcasting the NBA at the time, and during the game, the O.J. Simpson White Ford Bronco chase was going on. On our TV monitor NBC put up a split screen of the game and the O.J. chase; then, at some point, it just became O.J. I found it too distracting while broadcasting the game, so I asked our statistician, Harry Robinson, to shut the monitor off. When he went to turn the TV off, all the fans sitting around the booth objected and asked if I would leave it on. The radio booth at Madison Square Garden is right in the middle of the stands, and you become friendly with the people sitting around you all the time, so we turned it back on for them. I remember thinking, here was the biggest game I had ever broadcast, and people are more interested in watching O.J. Simpson and a white Ford Bronco. It was a very bizarre experience.

1996 Summer Olympics, Women's Basketball Finals, Georgia Dome, Atlanta, Georgia, August 3, 1996

The American women had lost in the 1994 World Championships to Brazil and were no longer considered the best team in the world, so they completely changed how they prepared for the Olympics. They hired Trish VanDerveer from Stanford, who took a leave of absence to coach the team. All the women on the team toured around the country and the world for a year and a half to become a cohesive unit and make sure they won the gold. They didn't lose a game the entire time they were together while preparing for the Games in Atlanta, so the pressure on them to win the gold was enormous; any loss would have been a huge disappointment.

They won the Olympics going away, destroying Brazil in the finals. After the game in the Georgia Dome, they gave the medals out immediately, since this was the final event of the Games. When the national anthem played, it felt like every one of the 40,000 fans in the building sang the anthem. I've never been in a building where so many people sang the national anthem. You could see that the players became very affected by the outpouring of patriotism and began crying. I still get chills thinking about it.

2002 FIBA World Championships Finals, Yugoslavia vs. Argentina, Conseco Fieldhouse, Indianapolis, Indiana, September 8, 2002

NBC was scheduled to broadcast the semifinals and finals, with the expectation that the United States would be in one of the two semifinals. Well, that didn't happen, as the Americans were knocked out in the quarterfinals, leaving us to broadcast the rest of the tournament without Team USA on American television. Argentina and Yugoslavia won the two semifinal games to make it to the championship and were clearly the two best teams in the world at this point. The finals were in Conseco Fieldhouse in Indianapolis, thousands and thousands of miles from either country, yet there was a huge core of fans from both Yugoslavia and Argentina.

One of the great things about international basketball is how emotional and passionate the fans are. The fans and the players are so emotional and so passionate. They chant and sing all game long as they cheer their country on.

Yugoslavia won the game, and at the final buzzer, the players on the Yugoslavian team, along with their fans, were all crying with tears of joy. The players and fans from Argentina were all crying but with tears of disappointment. It was one of the best-played games and certainly the most emotional game I've ever seen, from both a player's and a fan's standpoint.

Christine Brennan
Columnist, USA Today

Ohio State at Michigan, Michigan Stadium, Ann Arbor, Michigan, November 22, 1969

Ohio State was undefeated, the defending national champion, and a heavy favorite. Michigan had a more modest 7–2 record under first-year coach Bo Schembechler. I was a huge sports fan as an eleven-year-old, so my father took two of my younger siblings and me to the game. It was the first Big Ten game I ever attended, and what a game it was. Lucky kids that we were, we witnessed one of the greatest upsets in the history of the college game. My dad couldn't stand the arrogance of Ohio State's Woody Hayes, who seemed to presume his team would win. They didn't. Final score: Michigan 24, Ohio State 12.

1988 Summer Olympics, Men's 100 Meters Final, Jamsil Olympic Stadium, Seoul, South Korea, September 24, 1988

Ben Johnson ran 9.79 seconds, Carl Lewis, 9.92. Johnson crossed the finish line well ahead of Lewis, with his right arm thrust into the air, his index finger extended to the sky. I watched from press row, no more than 25 feet from the track. Three days later, I received a phone call in the middle of the night with the news that Johnson had tested positive for steroids and was being stripped of his gold medal, which later was given to Lewis. With that, performance-enhancing drugs became one of the major topics in sports. This was the beginning of our nation's awareness of chemical cheating by elite athletes, a problem that would spread from the Olympics to many other sports, including Major League Baseball.

1991 IAAF World Outdoor Championships in Athletics, National Olympic Stadium, Tokyo, Japan, August 30, 1991

I was sitting in the press tribune watching the long-jump competition on the far side of the track. Mike Powell and Carl Lewis engaged in a majestic duel, with Lewis uncorking his four best jumps ever. But in the end, Powell had the single best jump of all, leaping 29 feet, 4½ inches, breaking the oldest and most legendary record in track and field: Bob Beamon's 29 feet, 2½ inches, set at the 1968 Summer Olympics. I remember the tantalizing wait after Powell's jump, perhaps fifteen seconds, before the scoreboard registered the length of the jump. Powell leaped for joy when he saw what he had done.

1994 Winter Olympics, Ladies' Figure Skating, Hamar OL-Amfi, Hamar, Norway, February 23–25, 1994

Popularly known as the Tonya-Nancy saga, the two nights of figure skating at the 1994 Games were utterly surreal. After the drama of the January 6 attack on Nancy Kerrigan by associates of Tonya Harding, it was impossible to believe anything more bizarre could occur. But it did. Harding at first failed to show up on the ice when her name was called for the long program, then she was allowed a do-over after her skate lace broke. Kerrigan skated later and did very well but finished second to Oksana Baiul, while Harding dropped to eighth. The short program two days earlier was the sixth-highest-rated TV show in history. Not just sports. All TV, ever.

1999 Women's World Cup Finals, United States vs. China, Rose Bowl, Pasadena, California, July 10, 1999

As a high school athlete, I played games in mostly empty gyms. Girls' sports went virtually unnoticed in the 1970s. But more than twenty years later, on a glorious, sun-splashed day in Southern California, I was covering the United States–China game, looking out of the Rose Bowl press box at 90,185 spectators, the largest crowd to ever witness a women's athletic event anywhere in the world. An intense game ended in a scoreless tie, leading to a series of penalty kicks. When Brandi Chastain made the last one and whipped her shirt over her head, she and her nineteen U.S. teammates had become the very popular personification of Title IX, the law that changed the playing fields of America.

Rob Burnett

President, Worldwide Pants/Executive Producer,
The Knights of Prosperity

Detroit Red Wings at New York Rangers, Madison Square Garden, New York, New York, November 2, 1975

I was twelve years old, and the New York Rangers had already become my religion, largely because my dad had season tickets at center ice right next to the Rangers' entrance. I used to hang over the railing in my oversized Rangers jersey, waiting for that moment when my heroes would appear, and Madison Square Garden would ignite with joy. That moment was always defined by the first glimpse of the Rangers' silver-haired goaltender, Ed Giacomin, who was always first in line. He was the match, the fuse, and the bomb all in one.

Then, on October 31, 1975: disaster. After ten years of minding the Rangers' net (virtually my entire conscious life), Giacomin was dropped by the Rangers and was picked up on waivers by the Detroit Red Wings. I was heartbroken. As fate would have it, the Red Wings were to play the Rangers in

Madison Square Garden just two days later. I decided to do the unthinkable: "Dad, I'm going to root for the Red Wings." Turned out, I was not alone. When Giacomin took the ice, the crowd burst into its familiar chant: "EDDIE! EDDIE! EDDIE!" and continued to cheer for the Red Wings the entire game. To this day it remains the most moving tribute I have ever witnessed in sports.

1978 NASL Conference Semifinals, New York Cosmos vs. Minnesota Kicks, Giants Stadium, East Rutherford, New Jersey, August 16, 1978

What is cool? For some, it's James Bond. For others, it's Clint Eastwood. For me, it is New York Cosmos sweeper Carlos Alberto. Specifically, it was a single moment in the 1978 North American Soccer League semifinal game between the Cosmos and the Minnesota Kicks. In the late seventies, still in the afterglow of Pele's exporting himself to America, the Cosmos routinely filled Giants Stadium with 70,000 ravenous soccer fans. On this night, the Cosmos found themselves in a game-deciding shootout (the more exciting cousin of penalty kicks, where the shooter started at the 35-yard line and had five seconds to score). The first several Cosmos attempts were foiled by Minnesota goalie Tino Lettieri, who would charge the shooters the minute the whistle blew, cutting the angle and creating panic.

Then came Carlos. The whistle blew, and Tino sprinted off his line. Carlos calmly flipped the ball up to his waist with his foot. I was at the game with three of my high school soccer mates, and to a man we gasped. "What's he doing?" "Did he hear the whistle?" "Does he realize it's ON?" The ball bounced lazily on the Astroturf. Carlos hit it up again with his thigh, all the while with Tino charging at him with pure evil in his eyes. The ball bounced on the Astroturf once more, and then, with complete nonchalance, Carlos arced the ball high over the head of Tino, now a good 20 yards away from the goal. As the ball landed in the goal, I turned to my buddies and said, "Did we just witness the coolest thing that a human can do?" They all nodded yes. Now, almost thirty years later, Carlos is still, as the young'uns like to say, the man.

1986 World Series, Game 6, Boston Red Sox at New York Mets, Shea Stadium, Queens, New York, October 25, 1986

I was sitting in the leftfield bleachers with a buddy from high school, doing that special thing that die-hard sports fans do: scavenging for optimism in the most dire of realities. Every sport has its version: "If we recover two onside kicks and then get a safety . . ." "If we hit a three-pointer and get fouled, then miss the foul shot on purpose and. . . ." You know how they go. Well, this was baseball, which, because there is no clock, is the sport where hope lingers longest. The Mets were trailing 5–3 with two outs and no one on in the bottom of the tenth. I turned to my buddy and said, "Is it absolutely impossible?" Before he could answer, the Mets got their first of three singles, making the score 5–4. Then Mookie came up, and you know the rest. The moment when the ball squirted through Bill Buckner's legs will be frozen in my mind forever. You knew that you were watching history being written in permanent ink. You knew you were witnessing the moment where lives would be forever changed.

1994 Stanley Cup Finals, Game 7, Vancouver Canucks at New York Rangers, Madison Square Garden, New York, New York, June 14, 1994

I attended all of the Ranger playoff games that year. I felt I owed it to myself for suffering through decades of the Rangers' heartbreakingly futile stabs at the Stanley Cup. So loyal was I that I actually went to Madison Square Garden for Game 6, which was played in Vancouver. That's right—for five bucks you could watch the game on the Jumbotron with thousands of other equally obsessed Rangers fans. For Game 7 I took my brother and a well-chosen friend. I wanted to be surrounded by diehards. And of course I was: 17,000 of them, all just like us. As the clock wound down and the Rangers clung to a 3–2 lead, Madison Square Garden wasn't a stadium; it was a church. A really loud church to be sure, but a church nonetheless, with 17,000 people unified in a single prayer. When that prayer was answered, and the Rangers won the Stanley Cup, my brother and I looked at each other with complete bewilderment. It was like we were watching a movie we had seen a hundred times before, but suddenly there was a different, much, much better ending.

2006 World Cup, USA vs. Italy, Fritz-Walter-Stadion, Kaiserslautern, Germany, June 17, 2006

A few years ago a childhood friend of mine was diagnosed with ALS (Lou Gehrig's disease). We've been friends since we were six, and a good part of that friendship took place on soccer fields. For the record, he was always better than I was (off the field, too, but that's for another book). Last summer he mentioned that he had always wanted to go to the World Cup, so our two families flew to

Germany for the USA vs. Italy game in Kaiserslautern. The game was at 9:00 P.M., and, not taking chances, we arrived at noon.

By the looks of things, we were late. The entire town was bathed in blue for Italy, and red, white, and blue for the United States. It was the Super Bowl on steroids—a nine-hour celebration of singing and dancing with people from all over the world. Inside the stadium, my buddy and I were escorted to the handicapped seating area, which was practically on the field. He's in a special wheelchair, which can rise up, and I'll never forget seeing him "rise" for the national anthem. The game did not disappoint, with the underdog Americans fighting for a 1–1 tie. At the end of the game one of the American players came over and gave my buddy's son his jersey, capping an already unforgettable day.

Andres Cantor
Broadcaster, Futbol de Primera

Sugar Ray Leonard vs. Roberto Duran, Louisiana Superdome, New Orleans, Louisiana, November 25, 1980

My career as a journalist started with *El Grafico*, which is Argentina's equivalent of *Sports Illustrated*. While I was a student at USC, they would send me to cover different events around the United States, from boxing to big news events. The Leonard-Duran match in New Orleans was a rematch from the bout Duran won in Montreal and, at the time, was the biggest fight of the year, with both fighters in their prime, not to mention among the greatest of all time in their weight division. The hype the fight generated was enormous, not just in the United States but all over the world. The Superdome was an extraordinary venue for a fight. Most of the big fights were usually in Las Vegas, so the location made it feel more like an event than a boxing match.

As the fight unfolded, it was an awkward fight, and then, all of a sudden, Duran just quit in the middle of the ring. No one really knew what was going on—he just simply waved his hand and said the now famous words, "No mas, no mas." It really threw everything into a state of confusion, with the biggest and most hyped fight of the year ending this way. Afterward, in the locker room, I was part of the assembled media as he said that he just didn't want to fight any more and that Leonard was driving him crazy during the fight. That was it. We all expected him to say he was hurt or that something serious had happened, but his reason was just that he didn't want to fight any more. Here was a guy nicknamed "Hands of Stone," one of the gutsiest fighters of all time, openly saying he quit because he wanted to quit. It was just a bizarre way for such an anticipated event to end.

1984 Summer Olympics, Opening Ceremonies, Los Angeles Coliseum, Los Angeles, California, July 28, 1984

I was living in LA and was part of the crew assigned to cover the Olympics for *Editorial Atlantida*, which owned *El Grafico* and other magazines. The most memorable moment of the Games for me was during the Opening Ceremonies, when Bill Suitor came flying through the air into the stadium, powered by a jet pack on his back. We all looked up over the arches of the Los Angeles Coliseum, and all of a sudden, here comes this guy flying and circling without any apparent gear other than a backpack, all dressed in white. There were no visible cables or anything else supporting him, and back in 1984 it really was a shock to see something like that. There were rumors that there was going to be a surprise element at the Opening Ceremonies, but everyone in the stadium was just in awe of this and couldn't figure out how he was flying around. He circled the stadium like a bird.

The other event that stands out for me, for obvious reasons, was the Soccer Final in the Rose Bowl. Soccer was not nearly as popular as it is today, but there were still a hundred thousand people in the stadium. For a soccer enthusiast, it was a thrill to see so many people in attendance. Soccer in the Olympics is not as big a show or event as the World Cup and isn't one of the more important events for national teams. But even with no Pele or Maradona, the Rose Bowl was still filled to capacity.

1978 World Cup Final, Argentina vs. Netherlands, Estadio Monumental, Buenos Aires, Argentina, June 25, 1978, and 1986 World Cup Final, Argentina vs. West Germany, Estadio Azteca, Mexico City, Mexico, June 29, 1986

I was fifteen years old in 1978 and remember being literally the first person into the stadium that day. The doors opened at noon for a game that started at 7:00, and I got there early because I had general admission tickets for the grandstand, which did not assure you a seat. The two grandstands were filled to capacity four hours before the game began, and if they say that part of the stadium holds twelve thousand people, I can assure you there were sixteen thousand there that day. I went up to the top row, because, since it was standing room only, if you stood in the middle you could get crushed. I had attended all of the Argentina games to this point, and this one was just unparalleled, since it is one of the great thrills for a soccer fan to see his home team with the World Cup, especially when it is as dramatic as this was. Argentina was up 1–0; Holland tied it, then almost won it in the last thirty seconds of regulation play when they had a header hit the post. I will never forget the silence when the game almost ended on that play and Holland came within inches of winning. Soccer is a religion in my home country, so when the Argentina team won it in overtime, it was one of the greatest thrills I will ever experience.

Eight years later, I was covering the World Cup in Mexico for *Editorial Atlantida* and got to see all of Argentina's games again. The quarterfinal game against England featured Maradona's "Hand of God" goal and was the most precious moment I've ever witnessed in all of my years covering soccer. Maradona's goal has become famous, but not being there live, not too many people could figure out how he scored until the day after, when the pictures came out. But when it happened, no one made much of a fuss about the play, since it wasn't clear.

On his second goal, he went about 65 yards, slaloming around defenders left and right. It was a work of genius and unlike anything I had ever seen before. With the game being against England, there were a lot of political connotations, since it wasn't too long after the Falkland Islands war, so after Maradona scored, I had tears in my eyes. We all knew we had witnessed one of the defining moments in the history of the World Cup.

1994 World Cup, United States, June 17–July 17, 1994

I had called the World Cup in Italy in 1990 for Univision, and when 1994 rolled around, they again gave me the responsibility of being their play-by-play announcer for all of the matches. It was a dream come true for a soccer nut like myself for the World Cup to come to the United States, and this was the match that kicked the whole thing off. I started getting ready for the World Cup around six months before it began, but one month before the opener, I was diagnosed with a herniated disc in my back and could barely walk. The day before the opening match in Chicago, we went to Soldier Field to scout the location and decide whether I could do the opening and still have enough time to get to the booth, or whether someone needed to fill in while I made the trip upstairs, since I was having so much trouble walking. I was able to get it done on my own, though. The game was between Germany and Bolivia, and I don't know if my excitement that day was because of the anticipation of the event and the impact it would have on soccer in America, but it was one of the most amazing and exciting days of my career.

After the game, since I was calling all the games, I had to get back to Miami as soon as possible for a game the next morning because that was where our studio was, but since there were no available commercial flights, they chartered a private jet for me. I remember getting to O'Hare, and everyone was paralyzed in front of the televisions in the terminal . . . it was the O.J. Simpson car chase. I also stopped to watch, but my first reaction was anger, because I realized that this was now the biggest story of the day, not the opening of the World Cup. That didn't stop us from standing in the terminal and watching, though. Of course, the pilot of the jet kept us updated on what transpired after we got on the plane.

The entire 1994 World Cup was the defining moment in my career, and I ended up getting a lot of attention for my play-by-play style, including an appearance on David Letterman's show. As emotional as the game was in Chicago, the finals at the Rose Bowl had a completely different type of emotion. After we signed off, I remember hugging my longtime partner Norberto Longo, who passed away in 2003 (we were the Al Michaels and John Madden of Hispanic television soccer), and I told him, "We just finished a f—ing great World Cup." He was a veteran of television, and it must have been difficult for him to see me get all of the attention I got during the month, but he was a true gentleman in the way he handled it.

2006 World Cup Finals, Italy vs. France, Olympiastadion, Berlin, Germany, July 9, 2006

Seeing France win the World Cup in 1998 was an awesome moment, and I remember every single moment of the match. In 2002 my experience was very personal, as I was now the president of my own radio company, Futbol de Primera, and was able to call all my own shots throughout the World Cup. Coupled with Argentina's biggest rival, Brazil, being in the final, it was a very special tournament for me. But the most recent World Cup, in Germany, was unforgettable for me on many levels. Futbol de Primera again produced the 2006 World Cup, and my partner, Alejandro Gutman, and I brought a veritable Who's Who of soccer with us to Germany to participate in the broadcasts. Among the sixty high-profile people were Colombian superstar Carlos Valderrama, Mexican legends Carlos Hermosillo and Benjamin Galindo, famed coaches Carlos Bilardo and Bora Milutinovic, former World Cup referee Javier Castrilli, and many others. Very humbly, I can say that it was the best group ever assembled for a World Cup broadcast on either TV or radio.

Of course, with two European teams in the final, it was harder for me to get as excited as if a Latin American team had been there. My radio style is quite different from my television style, and I basically don't stop talking for the entire duration of the game, with an energy level considerably higher than I have on television. The game between France and Italy went to penalty kicks, so I was exhausted when it was all over. During the World Cup, there were a couple days when I called two games in two cities on the same day and had a driver take me from one city to the next, going 110 on the Autobahn to get me there on time for the next kick. So on that last day, I was pretty worn out.

Of course, the defining moment from that game was the Zidane headbutt. In the stadium, though, I don't think anyone saw it. They usually don't show replays of controversial calls on the screen in the stadium during the game, but one member of my crew, a very experienced World Cup coach, said that he saw the replay on the big screen. Nobody saw what happened in real time, though. The ball had moved toward the other end of the field, and everyone was focused on the play, while this was happening around 70 yards behind the ball. I still believe to this day that, despite the denials, the fourth official only called the referee to show the red card to Zidane after seeing the replay on television, which came over a minute after the actual play took place.

An hour and a half after the game ended, I left the stadium to meet my family outside, and the first thing they all asked me was, "What happened with Zidane?" To me, Zidane is the best player of his generation and an artist who ranks in the all-time Top 5, and what he did was indefensible. I wish I didn't have to say what I said about the play, but I also had to do my job and couldn't defend his actions.

Linda Cohn
Broadcaster, ESPN

1984 Patrick Division Semifinals, Game 5, New York Rangers at New York Islanders, Nassau Coliseum, Uniondale, New York, April 10, 1984

I grew up a Rangers fan on Long Island, and this was during the glory years of the New York Islanders. My first job was with WALK Radio on Long Island, which at the time was the Islanders' station, and since I loved hockey, I basically volunteered to cover the team, even though I really hated them—I was just looking for the experience covering sports. With all the success the Islanders had had at that time, winning four straight Stanley Cups, their fans were pretty spoiled. The Islanders were winning 3–2 in the last minute of Game 5 of the opening-round series, and fans were starting to leave, since they just assumed the game was over at that point, when Don Maloney (who would later go on to become general manager of the Islanders in the nineties) batted a puck past Billy Smith to tie the game.

You have to be on your best behavior in the press box, of course, but I'm sitting there, watching all these fans that were leaving, and that reinforced the belief of Rangers fans that Islanders fans were overly confident and spoiled. Of course, the Islanders' Ken Morrow ended up winning the game in overtime on a shot that Rangers' goalie Glen Hanlon barely saw or moved on. I still remember that tirade, though. For a moment, I was a fan again, instead of a member of the media, but it was my first big test as a journalist about letting my emotions get the best of me.

1994 Stanley Cup Finals, Game 7, Vancouver Canucks at New York Rangers, Madison Square Garden, New York, New York, June 14, 1994

To me, being an obsessive New York Rangers fan since I was around eleven, the 1994 Ranger playoff run was just amazing. If I had been at Game 7 of the Devils series, with Stephane Matteau's goal to send the Rangers to the finals, that actually would have superceded this one. In the finals, the Rangers were up three games to one, and I was at Game 5, which they lost, but the series ended up coming back to New York for the final game. There was no way in the world I was going to miss it. I was able to get a press pass and went to the Garden by myself and basically hung out in the blue seats. I wanted to experience this from somewhere other than a press box. I was just hanging with the diehards.

Any Rangers fan will tell you the same thing. To have that feeling of not wanting to be anywhere else, that to me is something that not too many people can experience. It is so close to your heart and, with the Rangers, that is the way it is with me. What made things even more special for me was that, after they won, I went to find a phone to call my dad. At that time, he was living in Florida—he was the one that started me on hockey and the Rangers. To be able to pick up the phone and spend that moment with him was beyond words.

After things ended on the ice, I was on a mission to be a part of the celebration. I just had to have more. Using my reporter's instincts, I managed to find out where the Rangers were having their postgame celebration at the Garden. I was invited into the party to celebrate the Rangers' first Cup in fifty-four years with the team and their friends and family. If that wasn't enough, as I'm looking around wide-eyed like a little kid, I see the Stanley Cup and people drinking from it. The night just kept getting better and better. A couple of guys recognized me and invited me to take a drink from the Cup. A photographer saw this and took a picture. I have the picture hanging up in my office at ESPN and at home, just to remind myself of that magical night.

2000 World Series, Game 2, New York Mets at New York Yankees, Yankee Stadium, Bronx, New York, October 22, 2000

I was at the game as a fan with my husband in the worst seats possible—in leftfield, all the way at the very top. I was with a great group of fans up there, though. And even from up there, a million miles away, we could see that Roger Clemens intentionally threw the bat at Mike Piazza. The response in the stands was what you would predict. The Yankees fans were saying there was no way it was intentional, while Mets fans like me were convinced it was. After the game, in the car ride home, I needed to hear the press conferences. I needed to hear from Roger Clemens why he threw the bat. I needed to hear Joe Torre talk about it. I needed the therapy of hearing what these guys were saying to get me through it. I wanted to be in the press room, but I was there as a fan that day, and you can't have it all.

2003 NCAA Men's Basketball Tournament Finals, Syracuse vs. Kansas, Louisiana Superdome, New Orleans, Louisiana, April 7, 2003

I went to Oswego State in New York, where there was no men's basketball team, so I never got to experience what college basketball was all about. Earlier in Syracuse's championship season, I found out that Jim Boeheim was a big fan of mine, and we ended up becoming friends. I also became friendly with his wife, Julie, so when they made their run to the Final Four, it was hard not to be excited for them. I was at the Final Four for ESPN and was the only one on our crew who predicted that Syracuse would win it all (of course, I might have been picking with my heart a little).

When the championship game rolled around, Julie had an extra seat and invited me to sit with her. So between that and going to Oswego, forty-five minutes from Syracuse and always being compared negatively on every level, there was a personal attachment, and it was very easy to be happy for them. It was an incredible game, which on paper beforehand didn't look good for Syracuse, but they won because of the intangibles. And that is one of those things about sports that you can't help but love. Not only will I remember how great Carmelo Anthony was that day but also a guy they called "Helicopter" for good reason. Hakeem Warrick's block on Michael Lee's three-point attempt right in front of where we were sitting saved the game for the Orange. Unlike the teams I grew up rooting for, I became a Syracuse fan later in life and for personal reasons, but this moment was just as special.

2006 NHL Eastern Conference Quarterfinals, Game 3, New Jersey Devils at New York Rangers, Madison Square Garden, New York, New York, April 26, 2006

This was the Rangers' first home playoff game in nine years, but there was another story to go along with that. When Jaromir Jagr took the ice before the game, returning from an injury in Game 1, the Garden was the loudest it had been since the Rangers' Cup win in 1994. When Jagr appeared on the video screen as he walked to the ice, I couldn't believe the feeling in the building. Then, sixty-eight seconds into the game, it went quiet, as the Devils took a lead they wouldn't relinquish. There was just so much going on in such a short amount of time. As sports fans, we can sometimes realize there is more going on than what meets the eye, so when the camaraderie between the fans and the players died down, you realized what a bittersweet moment it really was. That it came at the 68-second mark, which just happens to be Jagr's uniform number, was surreal.

Stephen Collins

Actor, 7th Heaven

New York Giants Home Game, Polo Grounds, New York, New York, mid-1950s

I grew up in a village called Hastings-on-Hudson, New York, just outside the Bronx. One summer in the mid-1950s, we got word that Alvin Dark—the shortstop and captain of the New York Giants—had rented a house on our block. It's hard to imagine today, but this was a time when baseball was rarely on television outside the World Series and an occasional local game, and very few kids in America ever got an opportunity to meet a big-league baseball player. It was a huge, almost unimaginable thing for a kid in those days.

The day Al Dark moved in, every kid in the neighborhood was camped out in front of his house on the small, narrow, one-way street he was moving to, and we all brought our bats and balls and gloves, hoping he'd sign. Sure enough, after an endless wait (although I was so young it might have been fifteen minutes and might have been an hour and a half), Alvin came to the door. It was around 6:30, following a day game. He got to the door, and someone asked how they did, and he said, "We beat the Cubs. I got a couple of hits. It was a good day." I practically fainted at hearing him talk. Here was an actual major leaguer standing right in front of me talking to all of us, and that still didn't seem possible.

Over the next few months, my parents got to know him and his wife a little, and they invited us to go to a ball game with them. Mrs. Dark drove us to the game, which went into extra innings and ran very late. We got into the Darks' car to drive back, and Alvin was behind the wheel in the players' section of the Polo Grounds parking lot. I was very young and had started falling asleep in the backseat, when Alvin rolled down the window and said, "G'night, Willie. G'night, Whitey." I tried to crane my neck to see these Giants who were, apparently, right outside. But there was no moon that night, and no lights in the parking area. I couldn't see anything, but still, I knew that

Willie Mays and Whitey Lockman were just outside the car, walking by. It was like hearing, "G'night, God." At that point, I think I almost immediately fell asleep, happier than at any previous moment in my life. I once told this story to a friend, Tom Klimasz, who's a sports producer at KTLA in Los Angeles. A few years later, on my birthday, Tom showed up on the set of *7th Heaven* with an autographed picture of Alvin Dark. It said, "Stephen, I've always been a fan of yours." It absolutely blew me away.

California Angels at New York Yankees, Yankee Stadium, Bronx, New York, August 22, 1976

Frank Tanana was pitching a two-hitter at Yankee Stadium for the California Angels and had an 8–0 lead heading to the bottom of the ninth. One thing I love about New York sports fans is that they don't normally leave games early, but this day, at least half the crowd of over fifty-two thousand was already gone. The fans were just disgusted, and the Yankees really had nothing that day. Thurman Munson led off the ninth and made the first out—and then something amazing happened: Lou Piniella singled to start an impossible rally that didn't end until Roy White homered to tie the game at 8. It was all eventually for naught, as the Angels scored three times in the eleventh to win, 11–8—the worst anticlimax possible. But to see the home team score eight runs in the bottom of the ninth to tie the game, when they'd been flat on their backs until then, was just awesome.

When White homered to tie the game, what was left of the crowd reacted as if the Yanks had just won the seventh game of the World Series. After they scored the first few runs and got close, there was a feeling of inevitability that they were actually going to tie or win the game. The thing I love about baseball is that the game is never, ever over, and this game proved it. Unlike any other sport, a team can always come back, regardless of the score or how late it is in the game. The best thing about baseball is that there's no clock. Because of that, anything can happen. And not very often—but just often enough—it does.

1986 World Series, Game 6, Boston Red Sox at New York Mets, Shea Stadium, Queens, New York, October 25, 1986

Ever since this night, I've always felt that if I never got to go to see another game, I could retire as a fan after this one. It brought everything into play that baseball has to offer. I was there with my father, and after the Mets fell behind in the seventh, Dad turned to me and commented that it didn't look too good. I was completely acting when I replied, "Dad, you gotta believe. Come on!" He looked at me as only a father can, with an expression that said, "Where have I gone wrong?" Knowing he was feeling that way, I just kept telling him over and over that it was going to happen, that the Mets were going to pull it out. They tied the game an inning later, prompting my dad to raise his eyebrows a little. It went into extra innings. Then Dave Henderson homered for the Sox in the tenth, and they added an insurance run, and Dad was doing it again, saying it had been a great season, but now it was really over. And I just started saying it again and again, that the Mets were going to pull it out. Dad's expression was even more blatant this time: "You're pathetic. Grow up."

In the bottom of the tenth, with the Mets three outs from losing the World Series, I was still insistent. "You gotta believe, Dad; you gotta believe." Even with two outs and nobody on, I kept saying it, even though I no longer really believed it and can't imagine that Dad actually thought I did, either. Then came the miracle: the Mets rallied, each batter getting on after two strikes, and when Mookie's little dribbler finally scooted through Buckner's legs, nobody jumped higher in the air than my father. He turned and looked at me as if I were Nostradamus. He couldn't believe it. He started asking me, "How did you know? How did you know? You *knew*!" As beautiful as it was that the game turned out the way it did, the moment when he jumped and started dancing around with everyone else in the stadium—that was the best part. We took the subway back to Manhattan after the game, and the ride on the "7" train was just pure celebration, every single person shouting, high-fiving, and recounting each moment of the game. And my Dad was in the thick of it, a new believer.

1988 National League Championship Series, Game 4, Los Angeles Dodgers at New York Mets, Shea Stadium, Queens, New York, October 9, 1988

A horrible moment to be a Mets fan, but memorable nonetheless. I was at Shea Stadium with my buddy Christopher Guest, a lifelong friend and fan. Dwight Gooden was pitching for the Mets that night, but this wasn't vintage Gooden. Not even close. He gave up two runs in the top of the first and somehow struggled through eight innings holding a 4–2 lead. He'd given up an uncharacteristic five walks and clearly didn't have his best stuff.

The ninth inning started, and we all expected to see Randy Myers, but to my chagrin, Davey Johnson left Gooden in the game. I had a feeling of doom when Doc took the mound. "What's Johnson thinking? How could he possibly send Gooden out to start the ninth?" And then, of course, it happened. After a leadoff walk, Mike Scioscia, who'd hit just three home runs all season, parked one over the rightfield fence. The Dodgers won in the twelfth inning, 5–4. This loss kept the Mets from going up three games to one, and now the series was tied at two. The Dodgers went on to win it in seven. When Scioscia hit that homer, I looked at Chris, and we just had that feeling that it was all going to go bad from there. Part of being a baseball fan is that you suffer through your team's lowest moments, and that night certainly ranks up there with the worst.

2006 National League Division Series, Game 3, New York Mets at Los Angeles Dodgers, Dodger Stadium, Los Angeles, California, October 7, 2006

I had never had the chance to see the Mets clinch a playoff series until the fall of 2006, when they wrapped things up against the Dodgers in LA. This was a much better game than it appears on paper. The Mets took an early 4–0 lead, the Dodgers came back and took a 5–4 lead in the fifth, then the Mets scored the game's last five runs to take a 9–5 victory and sweep the Dodgers in three straight games. The Dodgers kept mounting threats after the Mets went ahead, so it wasn't an easy win. The odd thing was watching the Mets clinch as the visiting team. It's not a great experience for the fan of the visiting team, since the overwhelming majority of fans are walking away dejectedly as you're trying to enjoy the celebration on the field. The Mets really only celebrated for a couple of moments, before respectfully disappearing into their dugout.

I did note two things about the Dodger fans, though. They are much more into the game than they used to be and aren't the same fans that are known for leaving early. On the other hand, it astounded me that, after what the Dodgers did late in the season just to make the playoffs, the fans didn't stick around and ask for an end-of-the-season curtain call. The stands emptied in minutes, and it clearly wasn't on anyone's mind to bring the Dodgers back out after what really was a surprisingly good year. The New Yorker in me couldn't help but think, "You just had to get into your car and beat the traffic rather than salute a great season."

Bill Conlin
Columnist, Philadelphia Daily News

Leotis Martin vs. Sonny Banks, Philadelphia Arena, Philadelphia, Pennsylvania, May 10, 1965

This was the first boxing match I ever covered and my first day on the job for the *Daily News*. Jack Fried, the *Bulletin* boxing writer for more than twenty years, did a "Who Struck John" piece that never mentioned Banks was taken unconscious to the hospital. His 12-inch story ran five pages inside the section. The headline on the *Daily News* front page was "Boxer Banks Near Death." He died later that day.

1966 NCAA Men's Basketball Tournament Finals, Kentucky vs. Texas Western, Cole Field House, College Park, Maryland, March 19, 1966

My last NCAA final as a basketball beat writer was the famous 1966 Texas Western vs. Kentucky game in College Park, Maryland. David Israel wrote a line he heard by another writer (it might have been Tony Kornheiser) about the game's being basketball's Brown vs. Board of Education, and it made him famous. But he wrote it days after the game. In his book on the game, Frank Fitzpatrick credits me for being the only game story writer who featured the obvious social implications in his lead and made it the central theme of the piece.

1975 World Series, Game 6, Cincinnati Reds at Boston Red Sox, Fenway Park, Boston, Massachusetts, October 21, 1975, and 1986 World Series, Game 6, Boston Red Sox at New York Mets, Shea Stadium, Queens, New York, October 25, 1986

By using incredibly bad timing, I was on press elevators trying to get to the interview rooms when two of the most dramatic moments in World Series history happened: Carlton Fisk's 1975 Game 6 homer and Bill Buckner's epic boot.

1991 Pan Am Games Bowling, Havana, Cuba, August 2–18, 1991

Yo, Fidel, you're in my seat! Due to a ticketing mix-up, four U.S. writers who decided to cover the novelty of bowling in the Pan Am Games were shocked to learn that Fidel Castro had decided to present the gold medal and had arrived with his entourage unannounced. Panicky officials escorted us to seats in a nearby section. I got so close to his beard with my camcorder, it went out of focus, and the clip was shown on ESPN's *Sports Reporters.*

1994 Winter Olympics, Ladies' Figure Skating, Hamar OL-Amfi, Hamar, Norway, February 23–25, 1994

Why me? Why us? I did a byline search about a year after the Tonya Harding–Nancy Kerrigan Chronicles and discovered I had written more pieces about those two than any other subject in my career. It was lowlighted by the practice session at a rink in Hamar with a fire-department-listed capacity of eighty-seven standees. There were at least three hundred media crammed in there to watch their first practice session since the kneecapping. I referred to Tonya's costume as resembling a cheap motel shower curtain.

Seth Davis

Staff Writer, Sports Illustrated/*Broadcaster,*
CBS Sports

New York Giants at Washington Redskins, RFK Memorial Stadium, Washington, D.C., November 20, 1985

I would not exactly call this one of my "greatest" moments, but it happens to be one of the most memorable injuries in the history of sports. As a high schooler growing up in Maryland, I was a huge Washington Redskins fan. We were lucky enough to have season tickets to RFK Stadium, and the Monday Night game between the Skins and the New York Giants on November 20, 1985, promised, as always, to be a great game. It was a great game— Washington ended up winning 23–21—but the excitement of the victory was overshadowed by the drama at the beginning of the second quarter, when Giants linebacker Lawrence Taylor broke Joe Theismann's leg on a sack.

When Taylor first got up, leaving Theismann on the ground, it was hard to tell from inside the stadium just how hurt the quarterback was. Like most everyone else who was there that night, I quickly found my way to a seat where someone was holding a portable television. Then I saw what America saw: Theismann's lower right leg literally shattered under Taylor's weight, in full view of a field-level camera. When that replay was broadcast, you could hear the fans in the stadium react with horror. Instantly, we all knew that Theismann's season was over. As it turned out, that was also the last play of his career.

I've seen the Redskins play in four Super Bowls, three of which they won, but whenever I tell people I was in RFK Stadium the night Joe Theismann broke his leg on Monday Night Football, they really raise their eyebrows. Whether you were in the stadium or watching on television, it was just one of those moments you never forget.

1991 NCAA Men's Basketball Tournament Semifinals, UNLV vs. Duke, Hoosier Dome, Indianapolis, Indiana, March 30, 1991

What could be better than being a college student and having your team make the Final Four? This: being at the game . . . with all your close buddies . . . to see your team win . . . in one of the greatest and most historically significant games in the history of the sport. Surely, most of the Duke Nation could not have expected the Blue Devils would defeat UNLV at the 1991 Final Four in Indianapolis. Not only was Vegas undefeated and largely untested for most of the season, but the Rebels had walloped Duke by 30 points in the national championship game the year before. Many of my fellow students had actually traveled to Indianapolis with the intention of scalping their tickets instead of actually going to the game. Woe unto those who missed what happened.

From the opening tip, it was apparent that this would be no blowout. Duke was aggressive, competitive, and sharp, while UNLV seemed surprised to have to play such a tight game. The critical play came with a few minutes remaining, when UNLV point guard Greg Anthony fouled out. That left Vegas without its most important leader, and the Rebels could not make the decisive plays down the stretch—most notably when Larry Johnson turned down an open three-pointer, deciding instead to hand the ball off to Anderson Hunt, whose off-balance jumper clanged harmlessly off the rim.

There is nothing like experiencing that kind of win when you are still a student, because many of the players on the floor are your friends and class-mates. I remember two images from the postgame delirium. From my vantage point in the stands behind the basket, I could see Bobby Hurley jump on the back of junior center Clay Buckley, who was a member of my fraternity and a close friend, as they ran off the court. Second, I clearly remember seeing Greg Koubek, a senior forward who was a social affiliate of my fraternity's, spot a pack of my buddies sitting courtside. Greg stopped and gave them a group hug before exiting the floor.

The win not only propelled Duke to the championship, which they won two days later over Kansas, but sent Coach K's program on its way to success that has not been seen in college basketball since John Wooden roamed the sidelines at UCLA. It was a great game, an exciting game, and an important game . . . and I was there.

California Angels at Baltimore Orioles, Camden Yards, Baltimore, Maryland, September 6, 1995

It's hard to describe the palpable excitement that a lifelong Baltimore Orioles fan like me had as the day approached when Cal Ripken Jr. would break Lou Gehrig's epic consecutive-games streak. If there was one streak in all of sports that would never be broken, least of all by a shortstop, this was the one. But as the days grew closer, the Orioles honored Ripken's historic march with a huge banner that hung from the famous warehouse that frames the rightfield bleachers at Camden Yards. At the moment that day's game became official, the banner would change, indicating the new number of his streak. Waiting for Ripken to break the record wasn't like watching Mark McGwire try to break Roger Maris's home-run record. You never knew when, or even if, Maris's record was going to fall, but all of us knew exactly which date Rip-ken was pegged to step into the pages of history.

A friend had gotten a ticket for me to watch Ripken's record-breaking game from deep in the leftfield bleachers. They weren't great seats, but we were in the stadium, and that was great enough. When the game became official and the new banner unfurled, Ripken came out of the Orioles' dugout fo repeated ovations. That, however, was not enough to satisfy the fans. So he did an entire lap around the field, shaking hands with fans as he jogged. The impromptu gesture was so long that my hands hurt from clapping. Finally, it was over, and the game resumed–whereupon Ripken bolted a home run right into my section in leftfield. It was the perfect punctuation mark to a most memorable night at the ballpark.

1997 U.S. Open, Congressional Country Club, Bethesda, Maryland, June 12–15, 1997

As a young golf writer at *Sports Illustrated*, I didn't have a whole lot going for me when I told my editors I wanted to help cover the 1997 U.S. Open at Congressional Country Club in Bethesda, Maryland. I did, however, have one ace in the hole: My father, Lanny, was working for President Clinton at the time as a special counsel. I knew Clinton was a huge golf fan, so it was natural to assume that he would want to attend the tournament. If the President goes, I told my editors, maybe I'd have a chance to interview him. They agreed it was worth a try. My chance came during Sunday's final round. My father had arranged for me to join the President in his box overlooking the 17th and 18th greens. As the leaders made the turn, I arrived in the President's box, pulled out my tape recorder, and interviewed him for five to seven minutes. He was perfectly friendly and charming during the interview, but he hardly said anything newsworthy. When the interview was over, I just stood off to the side, waiting for someone to ask me to leave. But no one did.

So I stayed in Clinton's box for ninety minutes as we watched the Open come to its conclusion. For someone who had a free world to run, Clinton, dressed casually in a short-sleeved button-down shirt and navy slacks, was extremely knowledgeable about golf. He kept up a running commentary on what was happening (he had played the course a few times and passed along his perspectives on it) and who was playing. I remember as Ernie Els walked under his box, Clinton said, "Look at him; he looks like a linebacker." He was rooting hard for Tom Lehman, saying, "You can just tell he's a man of great character." And as the last group walked to the 17th green, Clinton looked like a kid as he shifted in his chair and said, "This is it. It's showtime!"

I scribbled notes the entire time and passed along my reporter's file to Rick Reilly, who used the scene to lead off his game story in that week's magazine.

As far as the reader knew, Reilly had been the one sitting at the feet of presidential power. The folks back at *SI*, however, knew who got them the get. I knew it, too. It was an experience I'll always treasure and never forget.

The 2005 Masters, Augusta National Golf Club, Augusta, Georgia, April 7–10, 2005

In many ways, the Masters is the worst event for a golf writer to cover. Unlike every other tournament (as well as the other three majors), the Masters does not issue passes to writers that allow them access "inside the ropes." Thus, we are forced to watch the action with the common folk, dashing ahead of the players we want to see to get a strategically conducive viewing spot, then craning our necks and standing on our tiptoes to catch a glimpse of the ball in flight. The one exception is the grandstands, where the last rows are reserved for the, ahem, "working press." For the final round of the 2005 Masters, I decided to use this small perk and follow Tiger Woods around the course. After watching Tiger hit his tee shot to the 16th green, I scampered ahead and was on the ground next to the green when he rolled in his epic birdie chip shot. Through all the fans—sorry, "patrons"—I could barely see the ball on the green but knew exactly what was happening by the roar of the crowd. Once that shot went in, giving Tiger a two-shot lead over Chris DiMarco with two holes to play, I figured it was safe to scoot up to the 18th hole to watch the inevitable conclusion.

Little did I know that Tiger would uncharacteristically bogey the final two holes, sending his duel with DiMarco to a sudden-death playoff. From my vantage point sitting in the small, cramped press tower next to the 18th green, I could clearly see Tiger smile as he shook hands with DiMarco once they finished the seventy-second hole. My only problem was that I knew that in the past the playoffs at the Masters went to the tenth hole. Thus, my stellar view was apparently going for naught.

To my delight, I quickly learned that for the first time the format had changed to have the players return to the 18th tee for the playoff. I could have spit on Tiger's head as he rolled in his tournament-clinching birdie putt. I remember Tiger stepping into his trademark fist pump when the ball was still rolling toward the cup. That was pretty cool. I also distinctly remember Woods, following that celebration, looking back toward the 18th fairway with a huge, amazed smile. It was as if he was photographing the moment in his mind. I know I was.

Matt Devlin
Broadcaster, Turner Sports/Charlotte Bobcats

Boston College at Miami, Orange Bowl, Miami, Florida, November 23, 1984

I was a junior in high school in Nashville, and my brother was attending Boston College. BC was playing Miami the day after Thanksgiving. So my family decided to have Thanksgiving in Florida and see the game. I'll never forget the moment it happened. It was raining that day, and many fans had already started to filter out of the stadium. There were a decent number of BC fans there, and most of them stayed until the end, because anyone who knew Doug Flutie knew about the "Flutie Magic." Well, there it was, no time left on the clock, Flutie escapes a tackle, launches the ball, a pack of defenders jump for it, and I'll never forget this moment of silence. There was just a hushed tone throughout the entire Orange Bowl, no one sure of what the call would be.

We were sitting in a big crew of BC fans; I didn't know any of them, but I remember a priest sitting nearby, and a couple of students sitting close to us, all huddled together in the rain, waiting for the sign. When the ref signaled for the touchdown, and Gerard Phelan jumped up with the ball, we all just exploded, screaming and hugging and jumping on each other. It was probably one of the best moments ever in college football, and to be there was amazing.

St. Louis Cardinals at Philadelphia Phillies, Veterans Stadium, Philadelphia, Pennsylvania, August 1, 1997

I was doing radio for the minor league New Haven Ravens and got a call to fill in for Joe Buck on KMOX Radio with Mike Shannon while Joe went to do a FOX game over the weekend. After spending seven years in the minor leagues, to get a call to do a major league game and also do it on KMOX Radio is a dream come true for any announcer. So to get that call, and for my major league debut to coincide with Mark McGwire's first game with the Cardinals, was certainly a memorable moment for me personally. The game was in Philadelphia on a Friday night, and I remember seeing him walk in a little late after flying in from Oakland. It wasn't as much of a media frenzy as one would have expected, though, since the game was on the road.

2004 Summer Olympics, Men's Athletics, Olympic Stadium, Athens, Greece, August 20–28, 2004

When I think of the Summer Olympics, I think of two things—basketball and track and field. So, to do track and field at an Olympics was a thrill for me. Jeremy Wariner is someone that came in with a great deal of hype out of Baylor, one of the great track programs in the country. The question, though, was whether he would be able to come through. The sweep of the medals by Americans in the 400 meters was monumental in track and field and for the United States. The other thing that stood out was Justin Gatlin winning the 100. Asafa Powell and Maurice Greene were the guys to beat in that race, and Gatlin did just that (Powell didn't medal, Greene finished third behind Portugal's Francis Obikwelu). Those two races, along with the U.S. men sweeping the 200 meters, were just so memorable for me. The 100 is a special race and always will be, and that race had the emergence of Gatlin and the beginning of a great rivalry between him and Powell.

2006 NBA Playoffs Opening Round, Game 5, Denver Nuggets at Los Angeles Clippers, Staples Center, Los Angeles, California, May 1, 2006

The Clippers have never spent money on players, so I was curious, why now? They've had players before that they just let walk away, but over the last couple of years that had changed. And I wanted to know why. Before the game, I had a conversation with Clippers' owner Donald Sterling and asked him, "Why did you trust Mike Dunleavy to go out and put this team together, getting Sam Cassell and spending for Cuttino Mobley? Why Mike Dunleavy?" He told me about a conversation with a fellow Brooklyn guy, Al Davis, who said, "This is your guy. This is the guy who can turn it around for you." So he put his trust in Dunleavy, who laid out a plan that was implemented, and it worked out. The Clippers had never advanced to the second round of the playoffs since moving from Buffalo to California and were an organization that had come to represent one thing and one thing only—losing. People around the NBA would say that if you traded for a Clipper player, it took a year to get the Clipper out of them. Yet with Cassell, Elton Brand, Mobley, Corey Maggette, Chris Kaman, they developed a mix of players that just worked. They were able to handle Denver and move forward in the playoffs for the first time in thirty years. People in LA were actually talking about the Clippers for a change. Billy Crystal, Penny Marshall, and all of the Clipper fans that have been there since Day One finally got to see a winner.

2006 NBA Playoffs Opening Round, Game 5, Washington Wizards at Cleveland Cavaliers, Quicken Loans Arena, Cleveland, Ohio, May 3, 2006

I was doing the game for TNT, and LeBron James hit the game-winning shot for Cleveland in overtime. Why is this significant? To me, LeBron James signifies a rebirth in the game of basketball. He is a phenomenal talent and possesses everything that it takes to be a champion. His will and drive to be a champion is what is going to make him one of the most special players to ever play in the NBA. For him to go into the playoffs for the first time, at the age of twenty-one and hit not one but two game-winning shots in the first round is really significant. This game, and every game in this series as well as the next one against Detroit, gave everyone a glimpse of what is going to be an extraordinary force for years to come.

When I was working in Memphis, I remember Hubie Brown telling me, "Reputations are made or broken in the playoffs." When the playoffs started, there were lots of questions surrounding LeBron and whether he could rise to the occasion. He answered every one of them. He had the ball in his hands, everyone knew it was going to him, he drove the baseline and came up strong, right at the bucket, and laid it in for the win. That really signified to me that he is "the guy" and the future of the NBA.

Jim Durham
Broadcaster, ESPN

1989 NBA Playoffs Opening Round, Game 5, Chicago Bulls at Cleveland Cavaliers, Richfield Coliseum, Richfield, Ohio, May 7, 1989

For the Bulls, this game, featuring Michael Jordan's famous shot over Craig Ehlo, began their first steps toward greatness, leading to five straight trips to the Eastern Conference Finals for Chicago and their first of two three-peat NBA Championships.

1992 Summer Olympics, Men's Basketball, Palau d'Esports de Badalona, Badalona, Spain, July 26–August 8, 1992

The United States was supposed to win and did, by large numbers. This team was idolized by the world, though. Most games, players on the opposition spent time getting autographs. But it was the point when the rest of the world knew what the benchmark was for closing the gap to getting competitive.

2000 NBA Western Conference Finals, Game 7, Portland Trail Blazers at Los Angeles Lakers, Staples Center, Los Angeles, California, June 4, 2000

The Lakers came back from 15 points down in the fourth quarter against a very good Portland team, with Kobe and Shaq teaming up to spark the rally to the 89–84 win. And on they would go for their first title in their three-peat reign.

2005 World Series, Game 2, Houston Astros at Chicago White Sox, U.S. Cellular Field, Chicago, Illinois, October 23, 2005

Two home runs by the White Sox—a grand slam by Paul Konerko in the seventh and a game-winning blast by Scott Podsednik in the ninth. After the game, over forty thousand fans refused to leave the ballpark, celebrating in the rain. The Sox went up two games to none, paving the way for a World Series sweep. After eighty-eight years, Chicago had its World Championship.

2006 Western Conference Semifinals, Game 7, Dallas Mavericks at San Antonio Spurs, SBC Center, San Antonio, Texas, May 22, 2006

Dallas over San Antonio, 119–111. Someone asked me how I'd rate this game in terms of the greatest I'd ever seen. So I thought about it. Let's see . . . a road team winning a Game 7. That doesn't happen very often. And it unseated the defending champs in the process. And it went to overtime, to boot. I have to rank it up there in my top five.

Ian Eagle
Broadcaster, CBS Sports/YES Network

1986 National League Championship Series, Game 3, Houston Astros at New York Mets, Shea Stadium, Queens, New York, October 11, 1986

I was a month into my freshman year at Syracuse University. I grew up in Forest Hills, New York, just ten minutes from Shea Stadium. During my impressionable years as a baseball fan, the Yankees were winning championships, while the Mets were fielding the worst team in baseball. Yet, as any good fan does, you stick with your team, take the abuse, and hope and pray for better days. 1986 was a special year, as any Mets fan will tell you. It was a dream season, with players that had personality, a lot of heart, and what appeared to be a championship destiny.

As a fan, I had concerns about the Houston series. Mike Scott had been a thorn in the Mets' side, and although I felt the Mets were on a collision course for the World Series that year, I knew the Astros were no pushover. Syracuse is about a four-and-a-half-hour drive from Queens, and I was fortunate to have a car on campus and knew that I had to attend one of these games. It was on a Saturday afternoon, and I woke up early in the morning and went directly to the game with a buddy of mine who had secured two tickets.

Sitting down the line in rightfield, I was exhausted and didn't like the way the game started. The Astros scored four early runs off Ron Darling, and the Mets weren't doing much against Bob Knepper. With the series tied at a game apiece, my confidence was slipping. But in the sixth, Kevin Mitchell got it started (it wouldn't be the last time he would start a big rally), and the Mets tied the game. Shea was rocking. It was amazing for me, attending Mets games starting in 1976, growing accustomed to having any seat you wanted, that Shea could actually have that kind of ambience. It felt like a Jets game. The Astros came back in the seventh, and the nervousness set right back in, but this team had a way about them, this cockiness, and it rubbed off on the fans. You never believed they were done.

The ninth inning proved it. Wally Backman got on with a bunt, a passed ball sent him to second, and with one out, fan favorite Lenny Dykstra ended the game with a homer. It was, for a die-hard Mets fan, like I had gone to heaven. The reaction in the stands, which then spilled out into the parking lot . . . I knew I had a long drive in front of me to get back to school, but I didn't want to leave.

1991 U.S. Open, Fourth Round, Jimmy Connors vs. Aaron Krickstein, National Tennis Center, Flushing, New York, September 2, 1991

Growing up in Forest Hills, the former home of the U.S. Open, tennis played a large role in my life. I played competitively as a kid and in high school and was also a ball boy for many years at the stadium in Forest Hills. Jimmy Connors actually chewed me out during a Tournament of Champions match one year in the early eighties. I was never a huge Connors fan, maybe because of that experience.

By the time 1991 rolled around, Connors's career was winding down, and on the only day I was able to get to the Open that year, he was taking on a young star named Aaron Krickstein in the round of sixteen. Connors had owned Krickstein during their careers, but the symbolism appeared to be pretty obvious that this was a passing of the torch. Connors had a love-hate relationship with the New York fans. I was there when he won the Open in 1982 and 1983 over Ivan Lendl, but Connors had never reached the level of adoration that others had in New York. In those matches, he had the backing of the fans more because of their dislike of Lendl.

It all changed against Krickstein. At the age of 39, Connors won over the crowd. He was trailing 2–5 in the fifth and deciding set, and even I was feeling sorry for the southpaw, as all of his hard work and sweat in a grueling match would go for naught. Krickstein was ready for his signature win, but Connors had something up his sleeve and rallied to beat Krickstein in a fifth-set tiebreaker. I had been to a lot of tennis matches in my life but had never seen a crowd that emotionally invested in a match like they were that day.

1994 Stanley Cup Finals, Game 7, Vancouver Canucks at New York Rangers, Madison Square Garden, New York, New York, June 14, 1994

Growing up, I admittedly wasn't the biggest hockey fan, but I did have an interest in the New York Rangers. When they went to the finals in 1979, I knew it was a big happening in New York, with the team having the potential of finally ending the "1940" chants.

In 1994, I was working at WFAN radio, which was the Rangers' flagship station. Living in New York City allowed me to get to the Garden frequently, and both the Rangers and Knicks were having banner years. When the playoffs rolled around, I finally got to see what hockey fans had always bragged about, experiencing the ambience of playoff hockey. I was doing some radio shows during the Rangers' run with Kenny Albert, who is as knowledgeable about hockey as anyone there is, while I helped provide the layman's perspective. It is hard to look back now and not focus on Game 7 of the Devils series as the standout moment, and I was fortunate enough to be there for that as well, but to watch the fans of New York react the way they did the night the Stanley Cup was won was almost a religious experience.

I sat in the stands for the first two periods, and although I thought there was an air of overconfidence in the building that night, it quickly dissolved when the game started. All the die-hard fans in attendance were not taking anything for granted. In the third period, I moved over to the radio booth and watched from there with Marv Albert and Sal Messina calling the game. I had as perfect a view of the ice as you could possibly imagine. That is exactly where I was when time ran out, and I took a moment as the scene unfolded on the ice to absorb my surroundings and witness the pure joy on everyone's faces. Generations of Rangers fans finally had their moment in the sun, and that evening was an outpouring of emotion for anyone in attendance.

1998 NBA Finals, Game 6, Chicago Bulls at Utah Jazz, Delta Center, Salt Lake City, Utah, June 14, 1998

I did play-by-play at the 1998 finals for a United Kingdom feed with former Nets broadcaster Mike O'Koren. There were rumblings at the time that this could be Michael Jordan's last go-around. In this series, it was the same old Jordan, and the Bulls looked like they were going to wrap up the title in five games, but Karl Malone had a vintage performance in Chicago to force a sixth game back in Salt Lake City.

Our location was literally in the stands among the screaming, rabid Jazz fans in the corner of the Delta Center. It was the loudest I had ever heard an arena in the NBA. If the Jazz could force Jordan into a seventh game, something he had never had to face before in the finals, then maybe the Jazz could rewrite history. What people forget is that the final shot in this game would never have happened if not for a defensive play by Jordan, knocking the ball away from Malone on the previous possession.

During the timeout, there was no doubt who was getting the ball. We had seen the matchup all series long, with Jordan against Bryon Russell. Crossover dribble, a little shove, he drills the jumper, 87–86 Bulls. On tape, we all see the push, but at the time, as play was going on, there was no way any official would have called an offensive foul on Jordan. The way he did it made it feel as if it was part of the flow of the play. To this day, I have no idea how I called it on the air (I never got the tape from Great Britain). The Delta Center went silent, and Michael Jordan's legacy was intact in what turned out to be his final game as a Chicago Bull.

2002 NBA Playoffs Opening Round, Game 5, Indiana Pacers at New Jersey Nets, Continental Airlines Arena, East Rutherford, New Jersey, May 2, 2002

This one is a personal favorite because of what it meant to the Nets organization, lifting them out of NBA Siberia and the shadows of the Knicks. When the Nets finished the regular season with the best record in the Eastern Conference, NBA observers looked at it as a fluke. The Nets had not been to the playoffs since 1994, and most people expected the team to fall on their faces once the postseason began. This was the last year of the best-of-five format in the first round, and the Nets were in a battle with the Indiana Pacers.

I worked the game with the great Bill Raftery, who had been calling Nets games for twenty years. The Jason Kidd era meant the beginning of a new persona, and that night it was truly born. The Nets had the game won in regulation, but rookie Richard Jefferson missed two free throws that could have iced it, and Reggie Miller made a desperation halfcourt heave off the glass as time expired to force overtime. The twenty thousand fans in attendance thought, "This franchise is cursed." In the first OT, Indiana jumped out, only to see the Nets respond, as Kidd willed the team into the second OT. Miller's heroics normally would take place just across the river against the Knicks at Madison Square Garden, but on this night, it was Kidd who created the lasting memory.

I had never felt tension for a sports team like I felt that night. All of the past failures, people who had worked for the franchise since their first day in the NBA, to see some of the looks on their faces at the end of regulation brought into focus just how much this night meant for an organization that desperately needed a highlight moment. When I got home that night, I couldn't sleep. I didn't realize until the next day what kind of impact that win had. It was, by far, the most reaction I had ever gotten after a broadcast . . . phone calls, e-mails, messages. For the first time, the Nets were the story, and they had a classic game to prove it.

Helene Elliott

Columnist, Los Angeles Times

Recipient of Hockey Hall of Fame's Elmer Ferguson
Memorial Award, 2005

1980 Winter Olympics, Ice Hockey Semifinals, United States vs. Soviet Union, Olympic Ice Center, Lake Placid, New York, February 22, 1980

When you look back at it now, you have to remember there was no CNN or Internet. So with Lake Placid being so isolated, no one had any idea what kind of impact this game had away from the Adirondacks, outside of some telegrams. When you would hear about people filling up walls with these telegrams, you had to step back and ask, "Wow, that many people really care about what is going on here?" The game wasn't on live, and it really was difficult to know what was going on in the outside world. When the United States beat the Czechs, you really started to get that feeling that something good was going on. But heading into the game against the Soviets, the hope was just that the United States could win the bronze if they were lucky, especially after they got creamed in an exhibition game just a couple of weeks earlier.

Before the Americans played the Soviets, a Canada team featuring future NHLers like Glenn Anderson and Randy Gregg faced them and led for a bit before losing, which showed that there just might be a little vulnerability in that team. No one expected what happened, of course. Herb Brooks was such a genius, preparing the team so well and taking advantage of their speed and youthful enthusiasm. Everyone knows how crazy Herb got with the media and how he wouldn't allow his players to talk during the tournament, but I found a side entrance where the players would come out, so I would stand outside in the cold and wait for them there (although I also found out that ink in pens freezes at a certain temperature). Herbie did it for a reason, though, and created an "us against them" mentality for the team—against him as much as against the opponent. Obviously, it worked. And one thing that is forgotten is how productive all these players have been in life. He didn't just mold them as hockey players; he affected them as people, too.

1983 Stanley Cup Finals, New York Islanders vs. Edmonton Oilers, Nassau Coliseum, Uniondale, New York, and Northlands Coliseum, Edmonton, Canada, May 10–17, 1983

Everyone had heard about the Oilers at this point, and especially Wayne Gretzky, who was putting up astronomical scoring numbers and doing remarkable things. The Islanders had been through a lot, though, and had won three straight Stanley Cups. After one of the games on Long Island, they set up a press-conference area for after the game. The Oilers lost, so Gretzky went first, and Billy Smith, the Islander goalie who would be named playoff MVP, was going after. Smith had been saying disparaging things about Gretzky all series, calling him "Whine" Gretzky and saying that Gretzky "would have to introduce himself to his own defensemen." As Smith entered and Gretzky left, Gretzky stopped and stuck out his hand to shake. Smith stopped, and I thought he was going to just ignore it. But he begrudgingly stuck his hand out real quick and just kept going. Smith is one of those guys who always refused to take part in the ceremonial postseries handshake. You could sense, though, that it was just a matter of time before the Oilers would do something special. They did exactly that the next year, and they made it easy to forget just how good those Islander teams, that won nineteen straight playoff series, really were.

1994 Stanley Cup Finals, Game 7, Vancouver Canucks at New York Rangers, Madison Square Garden, New York, New York, June 14, 1994

The Rangers were hapless for so many years, with the derisive "1940" chant following them everywhere. It felt like they would never win a Cup. But in 1994 you could see the Rangers were just loading up to try to win it all. To be in the Garden for Game 7, as it became apparent they were finally going to win the Cup, was a huge thrill. I'll always remember the sign someone was holding up that read, NOW I CAN DIE IN PEACE, and that summed it up perfectly. It was something that a lot of people thought they would never live to see. And now it was actually happening.

2002 Winter Olympics, Ladies' Figure Skating, Delta Center, Salt Lake City, Utah, February 21, 2002

Sarah Hughes was certainly not the favorite to win in Salt Lake City and was the third member of the U.S. team in the Olympics. She had a good season leading up to the U.S. Championships but didn't skate particularly well at that competition. I remember talking to her and her coach afterwards, and they were discussing how she was going to have to upgrade the difficulty in her program and redo some of the music. The best I thought she could do was maybe have a chance at a medal to complete a 1-2-3 U.S. sweep with Michelle Kwan and Sasha Cohen.

As Salt Lake City approached, I think she had the perfect attitude, which was, "I have nothing to lose; let the chips fall where they may." She then went out and skated a program that was incredibly difficult, featuring triple-triple jumps, and finished all the choreography and footwork perfectly. It was the kind of performance that every athlete, not just figure skaters, dream about, where they can look back and say that there wasn't a single thing they would do differently. She just skimmed along the ice and nailed all of her jumps and made it look so easy, like she was floating. And then Kwan self-destructed. And Irina Slutskaya didn't skate well. A lot of things had to happen under the old figure-skating rules for Hughes to win the gold, and incredibly enough, all of them did. It was so wonderful to see Hughes, who did it the right way, get rewarded after skating the program of her life.

2002 World Series, Game 7, San Francisco Giants at Anaheim Angels, Anaheim Stadium, Anaheim, California, October 27, 2002

This Angels organization had seemingly been doomed and cursed for many years. After ten seasons away from covering them, I came back and found a great group of guys in the locker room. I was at my college reunion for Game 6 and figured they were done and finished that night and that I wouldn't see them win a title in my lifetime. I was excited to find out there was going to be a Game 7 and was lucky enough to be there for the winner. Gene Autry owned the team for many years, and everyone there was fond of saying, "Win one for the Cowboy." It is too bad the Cowboy wasn't around to finally see it. So many people suffered for that organization for so long, you had to feel good for them. The press box was so crowded that night that I was assigned a seat in an auxiliary press box but decided to sit on a step in the main press box instead so I could have a better view.

Mike Emrick
Broadcaster, NBC Sports/MSG Network

1987 Stanley Cup Finals, Game 7, Philadelphia Flyers at Edmonton Oilers, Northlands Coliseum, Edmonton, Canada, May 31, 1987

In 1987, the Oilers were loaded with eventual Hall-of-Famers and six of the best players in the world. Paul Coffey, Grant Fuhr, Wayne Gretzky, and Jari Kurri are already in the Hall, and Glenn Anderson and Mark Messier are likely to be. The Flyers had come from three games to one down and won twice to force a seventh game, with J. J. Daigneault getting the clincher in a 3–1 home win at the old Spectrum in Game 6 with a late left-point blast into the top right above Fuhr.

Back in Edmonton, with tickets being scalped for a then-phenomenal thousand dollars each, the Flyers actually scored first. But, despite the brilliance of eventual Conn Smythe winner Ron Hextall, the Oilers had too much. Anderson's shot from about 50 feet made it 3–1 Oilers in the third. That was enough. The Oilers would win their fourth Cup in five years the next season, and then players would begin to leave. The Flyers, under Mike Keenan, may have overachieved to get to the finals and push the series that far . . . but they still could have won the game entering the third period.

1994 Winter Olympics, Ice Hockey Finals, Sweden vs. Canada, Haakons Hall, Lillehammer, Norway, February 27, 1994

This was a Swedish roster that had lots of experience. Though Tommy Salo was twenty-three, there were five thirty-year-olds on the team—and remember, pros weren't allowed yet. This was the last time "amateurs" were exclusively on the rosters, although Tomas Jonsson, 33, was a multiple Stanley Cup winner with the New York Islanders and Mats Naslund, who competed on the 1980 Olympic team, was back after his pro career at age 34 (don't ask me how he got reclassified). The Canadian roster, coached by Tom Renney, had Chris Kontos and Wally Schreiber as the thirty-year-olds, a twenty-one-year-old backup to Corey Hirsch in Manny Legace, teenager Paul Kariya, and Petr Nedved, who had defected from Czechoslovakia six years earlier at seventeen.

The shootout was dramatic, with Nedved shooting first and scoring on Salo. Hirsch stopped ex-Calgary Flame Hakan Loob, who once scored 50 goals in a season in the NHL. Then Kariya scored—that is often forgotten. Magnus Svensson answered. Both Dwayne Norris of Canada and Naslund failed. Now, fourth inning out of five. Greg Parks did not score, but Forsberg did, tying it up for the final inning. Both Greg Johnson and Roger Hansson failed. Now it was time for sudden death. It went to the second sudden-death inning when Forsberg scored on an incongruous, one-handed, apparent-afterthought shot, while Salo blocked Kariya's shot. Had it gone another inning, the shooters would have been Tomas Jonsson for Sweden and Jean Yves Roy for Canada. Sweden had never won Olympic gold in hockey, and they emptied the bench to mob Salo. Kariya was very disconsolate but had played a remarkable game, something we would see more of after his time at the University of Maine was over.

1994 NHL Eastern Conference Quarterfinals, Game 6, New Jersey Devils at Buffalo Sabres, Buffalo Memorial Auditorium, Buffalo, New York, April 27, 1994

It was a magnificent battle into four overtimes in Game 6 at the old hot Aud in Buffalo, Martin Brodeur vs. Dominik Hasek. Stephane Richer had a breakaway in one of the OTs and hit the goalpost behind Hasek. There were a number of great chances, but, as often happens, the game slowed as players were fatigued. The only goal in over two games of hockey in one night came off an offensive-zone, right-circle faceoff win and a wrister by Dave Hannan. Final was 1–0 Buffalo; shots were 50 for Buffalo on Brodeur, 70 for New Jersey on Hasek . . . not counting two posts, one in regulation time, by Richer.

1996 World Cup of Hockey Final, United States vs. Canada, Bell Centre, Montreal, Canada, September 14, 1996

The outcome of this game was unexpected. Mike Richter played goal for the United States and was acrobatic and all other adjectives while shutting down Canada's huge guns, including stopping Eric Lindros point-blank. Then the U.S. exploded in the third with goals by Tony Amonte and Brett Hull to win their first Canada Cup/World Cup Championship ever by a 5–2 score.

1998 Winter Olympics, Women's Ice Hockey Finals, United States vs. Canada, The Big Hat, Nagano, Japan, February 17, 1998

This was the first time the U.S. women had defeated Canada in a game for a medal in nearly two decades of trying. It was the first time that women's hockey was an Olympic sport. With the outcome still in doubt in the final minute after Canada pulled the goalie, the Americans got the perfect combination . . . a big save by Sara Teuting, followed by Sandra Whyte's scoring into the empty net to secure a 3–1 U.S. win.

Michael Farber
Senior Writer, Sports Illustrated
Recipient of Hockey Hall of Fame's Elmer Ferguson
Memorial Award, 2003

New York Yankees at Boston Red Sox, Fenway Park, Boston, Massachusetts, October 2, 1978

I had just been made a columnist for the *Bergen Record*, and they thought it would be neat for me to go to Boston and spend the last week of the season there. I was in my hotel room on Sunday, after it was determined that the one-game playoff between the Red Sox and Yankees was necessary, and turned on the radio and found a sports talk show, where Mike Torrez was the topic of discussion. One caller was ripping Torrez, who was scheduled to be Boston's starter in Monday's playoff game. The host defended Torrez by saying, "Torrez pitched the Yankees to the World Series last year," to which the quick-witted caller replied, "Yeah, and he is going to do it again tomorrow." That was the mindset in Boston heading into the game.

There were two plays I remember from that game. First was Lou Piniella's play in rightfield, where he was blinded by the sun and couldn't see the ball coming at him, but was still able to hold Dwight Evans at first, making a game-saving play. And of course, there was the Bucky Dent homer. I remember him coming back to the plate after breaking his bat and getting a new one from Mickey Rivers. The ball didn't look well hit, but all of a sudden it was in the netting. Dent was almost out of place in that lineup, with all of the stars on this team, but there he was with this huge hit. You never expected him to be the guy who would be the hero of this team.

I looked at the Red Sox bench after the homer, and it struck me that the "B" on their caps looked an awful lot like the "B" on the Brooklyn Dodgers cap and that this was a team just destined for bad things to happen to them. As much as it meant to the Yankees, it would have meant so much more in

New England. I always felt a little disappointed about that but then thought back and realized that caller was right after all.

1980 Winter Olympics, Ice Hockey Semifinals, United States vs. Soviet Union, Olympic Ice Center, Lake Placid, New York, February 22, 1980

The Lake Placid Olympics were the first Olympics I covered, and they were very strange for me personally. I had moved to Canada in April 1979, to work for the *Montreal Gazette*, so this was just ten months later. As we watched the team develop throughout the tournament, starting with the tie against Sweden that got everyone a little interested, no one really knew what to make of it. I had seen the Soviet team at Madison Square Garden the previous February at the Challenge Cup, where they beat an NHL All-Star team 6–0, so this team just did not seem beatable to me.

The first moment you thought that something historic might happen was when Vladislav Tretiak didn't come back for the second period, which made no sense to anyone. It completely altered the equation and was one of those inexplicable things that got everyone thinking. Because I had just moved, I was a man with either two countries or no country, so I just didn't feel the political ties or patriotism that so many around me felt—I was watching this as a hockey game. And it just struck me as the most extraordinary thing. With around thirteen minutes to go in the third period, I looked up at the clock, and at that point, I really felt the United States was going to win this game and that I was watching history. It felt like time stood still and that every time I looked at the clock, it still said thirteen minutes. It was just surreal. And yet, there was this feeling now that this was going to happen. I've always wondered if this would have happened if this game was played in any other country, but it speaks to the nature of the game that it actually did. Looking at it from strictly a hockey perspective, putting aside the political climate surrounding those Games, it was totally stunning.

1988 Summer Olympics, Men's 100 Meters Final, Jamsil Olympic Stadium, Seoul, South Korea, September 24, 1988

How many events actually live up to the hype or even exceed it? This one did, and I'm not talking about the subsequent drug-testing results. I'm talking about the 9.79 seconds, which I still say might have been the most thrilling ten seconds of my life. Ben Johnson and Carl Lewis clearly didn't like each other and truly believed the other was cheating. This event is the elemental event in all of sport—every country does it. It really is sport at its most basic. That is why it has such worldwide appeal and why Ben Johnson, to this day, remains the most famous Canadian, more so than even Celine Dion or Pierre Trudeau.

I was so excited to be there that, after filing the first part of my copy, I moved from my seat in the press area to a spot by the barrier just off the track at around the 85-meter mark, which was right about the spot where Johnson turned his head and looked for Lewis, didn't see him, and a smile crossed his face. I could see that all happen, even though these guys were going pretty fast. He clearly has the race won by a wide margin, then you look at the clock and it says 9.79 . . . it was just incredible. He had gone faster than any man had before and faster than most people thought was possible, and it could have been even faster if he hadn't looked back for Lewis. Of course, the aftermath with his positive steroid test was just appalling.

1992 Summer Olympics, Women's Single Sculls, Lake Banyoles, Banyoles, Spain, August 2, 1992

Silken Laumann is a Canadian woman who was just dominant in the sport of rowing. In May of 1992, leading up to the Olympics, she was in a horrific training accident involving a boat that crossed her path. The collision basically destroyed her thigh—it looked like she had been bitten by a shark and had a huge jagged scar on her leg. But she kept working at it and decided to give it a go at the Olympics. She had to walk with crutches, and we watched her get into the boat with the crutches and a leg that had been mangled. She had been the favorite in the race, but obviously was not any longer. She rowed a terrific race and with around 500 meters remaining was still fighting for third. An American rower passed her, but she was able to come back and regain third place with around 200 meters to go and hung on for the bronze. It was the single most courageous event I had ever seen in the sport. After the medal ceremony, she sat under a tree, totally drained and white, and talked about it, while almost seemingly falling asleep from being so exhausted. In its own way, this was almost more miraculous than what I saw in Lake Placid.

Philadelphia Phillies at Montreal Expos, Olympic Stadium, Montreal, Canada, September 17, 1993

The Expos had been down for many years, but it was mid-September and this season they were still playing meaningful games. Montreal was always a great place to watch games—it was a fun atmosphere, and the fans that were there were really into the game. Curtis Pride was a guy who had some speed and could hit a little bit but was never going to be an everyday player. What distinguished him from every other player, though, was that he was deaf. This night, he was sent to the plate to pinch-hit in the seventh and got a game-tying two-run double, his first hit in the major leagues. The ovation was so loud— and this was not exactly a stadium with great acoustics—that he could feel the vibration through his feet and into his chest. As he later explained through his limited speech, he could hear it through his chest. It was the loudest ovation I have ever heard in a baseball stadium, and that includes following Kirk Gibson's home run. I've never heard anything like it, and it was so unbelievably moving that the fans wanted him to understand and this was the one way they could do that. The 45,757 fans gave him his hearing back for a moment, and it was just incredibly moving.

Roy Firestone
Broadcaster

Super Bowl III, New York Jets vs. Baltimore Colts, Orange Bowl, Miami, Florida, January 12, 1969

I was there with my brother, and we sat a few rows behind Ted Kennedy, just months before Chappaquiddick. Obviously, we all know the story—no one thought the Jets could possibly beat the Colts. I was there when Joe Namath guaranteed that they were going to win the game, and then he went out and completed 17 out of 28 passes for 206 yards and was named MVP. He also didn't throw a touchdown. We thought the Jets had no chance, but they had a big day offensively with 337 yards. They also forced five turnovers. It was, at the time and I think it still is, the greatest upset in team sports history. The Colts were overwhelming favorites, and the AFL had been blown out in the first two AFL-NFL World Championship Games.

Matt Snell scored the first TD of the game right in front of us, and I remember turning to my brother and saying, "Boy, this is going to make the Colts mad." As he scored the touchdown, in the photo on the front page of the *Miami Herald*, my brother and I are just over his right shoulder jumping up and down. That front page, which had the headline "Joe Guaranteed It," is blown up in the Hall of Fame. Namath had a house in Fort Lauderdale at the time, and there was a restaurant there named Broadway Joe's. The day after the game, they had a party at the restaurant, and there were probably twenty thousand people there trying to get in, because they thought he was going to be there.

Sugar Ray Leonard vs. Marvin Hagler, Caesars Palace, Las Vegas, Nevada, April 6, 1987

I seem to sit near huge celebrities at many of these events, and this night I actually sat right behind Frank Sinatra, who was taking pictures of the fight. He was fairly conversational during the evening and kept saying, "The kid's going to win this thing." Of course, Leonard was no kid at the time. I know Ray very, very well, and when they were negotiating the fight, he took Hagler out for dinner and got him a little drunk, then started bargaining by asking for everything he didn't want. He would ask for fifteen rounds, and Hagler would say no, let's do twelve, which is what Ray really wanted all along. He did the same thing with the gloves, asking for the heavy, twelve-ounce gloves, when he really wanted the ten-ounce ones.

All this trickery worked to his benefit in the end, of course. Leonard had never fought as a middleweight and had only fought once in five years, but here he was about to take on the most notoriously tough, and possibly the best, middleweight of all time. If you think about it, it was preposterous for him to even take on this fight, let alone have a chance of winning it. People thought Leonard was going to get knocked out in the first round, but not only did he weather that round, his style almost mocked Hagler, which might have thrown him off a little. Hagler had trouble keeping up with the smaller Leonard, though, and was basically chasing him the whole fight.

Leonard kept moving laterally, and even though Hagler, in general, landed better punches, Ray landed more and flashier blows. Neither fighter was cut or knocked down, and Leonard was warned repeatedly by the referee for holding, but he walked out a winner via split decision. At the end, Sinatra turned around and reminded everyone about his prediction. I ran into Hagler in the parking lot of Caesars afterwards, and all he kept saying was, "They took it away from me. They took it away from me." Over and over, that was all he could say, to the point where I thought he was almost hyperventilating; it didn't even sound like conversation. He knew me, and I told him that it was okay and that he'd get a rematch, but he just kept walking by himself, saying, "They took it away."

1988 World Series, Game 1, Oakland Athletics at Los Angeles Dodgers, Dodger Stadium, Los Angeles, California, October 15, 1988

I was getting ready to leave Dodger Stadium to beat the traffic, and if it hadn't been for my then-wife telling me that it wasn't okay to leave yet, I would have missed what is probably the greatest moment in Los Angeles sports history. As it ended up, I was standing in the tunnel and headed to the concourse. The Dodgers weren't supposed to beat the A's and had one of the worst lineups of any World Series team. No one could hit Dennis Eckersley at the time, and Kirk Gibson could barely walk, let alone swing a bat. This ended up being his only at bat in the World Series, which, if you think about it, is truly remarkable. I'll never forget Vin Scully's famous call, "The one man who can make a difference here is the man who is not going to play tonight."

And upon hearing that, Gibson started to get what I call "competitively angry" and finally walked over to Tommy Lasorda and asked to play. What also made it unusual was that Mike Davis, who was the runner in front of Gibson, walked to get on base. Eckersley rarely walked anyone (in the eight seasons starting in 1988, he walked an average of just over nine hitters per season), so that was a mini-miracle by itself. The actual game was nothing special up to this point, but this at bat took forever, as Gibson just kept fouling pitches off and looked so bad as he did it—at one point he actually fell down while fouling a pitch off.

The best part, though, was that all along you really had that feeling something was happening, because the buzz during that at bat just kept growing. You knew he couldn't get a base hit, because there was no way he would be able to run to first base if he did. He wasn't going to bunt. Then, he got a back-door slider and hit it to right field, and from the moment the ball hit the bat, you knew it was out. It has been talked about many times, but if you watch carefully, in the rightfield parking lot, you can see the brake lights going on from all the cars that were on their way out, as if those drivers slammed on the brakes and said, "I missed it." I was almost one of those people.

1996 Summer Olympics, Opening Ceremonies, Centennial Olympic Stadium, Atlanta, Georgia, July 19, 1996

The Opening Ceremonies at the Olympics are always filled with lots of pageantry, and this was no different. It was time for the torch to be lit, and my five-year-old son, who was just blown away by the entire evening, saw in the corner at the other side of the field, a man dressed all in white coming out of the tunnel, and as people noticed, the stadium started to roar. It was Muhammad Ali. The torch relay made its way to him, and Janet Evans passed it off. Ali had to climb a number of steps before igniting the Olympic Cauldron, which was a big deal, given his health. But he walked up to the top of the stadium holding this very heavy torch. I remember he had a problem lighting the torch at first, since he was shaking from his Parkinson's Disease, and Evans was on her way up to help him, but he waved her off.

My son could see his hand shaking feverishly and turned to ask me, "Why is The Greatest shaking? Is he scared?" I told him that he had a sickness called Parkinson's, and he then asked, "If he is sick, why did he come?" My reply was simple, "Because he has dignity." My son learned that word that night. Ali wanted to do this and wanted to do it on his terms so that he can show people he has pride in who he is. And do the best he can in the moment. My son will never forget that night as long as he lives, and I put that as one of the highlights of not just my sporting life but my human life.

1984 Orange Bowl, Miami vs. Nebraska, Orange Bowl, Miami, Florida, January 1, 1984, and 2003 Fiesta Bowl, Ohio State vs. Miami, Sun Devil Stadium, Tempe, Arizona, January 3, 2003

I am a graduate of Miami, and there are two Hurricanes games that really stand out for me. The first was the game that put Miami football on the map. When they entered this game, they were probably as big an underdog as the Jets were in Super Bowl III, with the one difference being that Miami was playing in its home stadium. I think this game changed the speed at which college football is played to this day. Here's the irony: I was on the field at the Orange Bowl during warm-ups and halftime with . . . Joe Namath. He was there because he was friends with Miami coach Howard Schnellenberger, who was his offensive coordinator at Alabama.

Nebraska coach Tom Osborne was trying to win his first national title and get out from the shadow of Bob Devaney. He had a great quarterback in Turner Gill, plus a Heisman-winning running back in Mike Rozier, plus wide receiver Irving Fryar, and an amazing offensive lineman in Dean Steinkuhler; this offense was loaded, and there was talk that this Nebraska team could have been the greatest college football team of all time. Nebraska rolled over their opposition during the regular season by an average final score of 53–16, with only two games even close, while Miami lost their opener to Florida 28–3 and struggled against the likes of East Carolina. A lot of people believed the only reason Miami was even on the field that night was because it was in the Orange Bowl. With the other results of the day, though, this game ended up being for the national championship.

Nebraska got the ball first and on their first play got 28 yards. Right away, it looked like it was going to be a joke. But somehow the Miami defense held, and Nebraska had to try a field goal, which the Hurricanes blocked (Nebraska had actually attempted just four field goals all season to that point). The place went crazy, and it gave Miami a little confidence. On Miami's first play, quarterback Bernie Kosar hit Stanley Shakespeare on the Nebraska 35, and the stadium starting going nuts. Miami kicked a field goal to take the lead, and every time the Cornhuskers would get the ball, they would shoot themselves in the foot. The next thing you knew, it was 17–0 Miami in the first quarter! Miami fans started to think it was going to be a walk in the park, but then things started to fall apart for them, and Nebraska turned it on and came all the way back. But Kosar would rebound, and Alonzo Highsmith would run for a touchdown to give Miami the lead back, with an extra point that would bounce off the uprights and through.

No one realized it at the time, but that extra point that bounced through would end up being the difference in the game. Miami would go up 31–17, but Nebraska came back again, making it 31–24. After Miami missed a field goal that would have put them up by ten, Gill brought the Huskers down the field and, with 1:12 remaining, found Fryar in the end zone, only to have

Fryar drop the pass, then collapse to the ground in a moment of grief. On the next play, Gill fumbled the ball after getting hit, but Steinkuhler picked it up and ran for positive yards. This set up fourth-and-eight on the Miami 29, and what followed might be the most forgotten play of spectacular quality in college football history.

With the Orange Bowl crowd on their feet, Gill ran the option and, at the last possible second, pitched the ball to Jeff Smith, who tore up the right side and scored with four seconds remaining to make it 31–30. Without hesitation, and I give him a lot of credit for this, Osborne decided to go for two points. There was no overtime in those days, so if Nebraska had kicked the extra point, the game would have ended in a tie and the Cornhuskers would have been the national champions. But they went for the two-point conversion, because they wanted to win the title with an undefeated and untied record. For the rest of my life, I will respect Osborne for this. But Gill's pass was knocked down at the last second, and Miami won the title. I remember turning to Namath and saying, "Joe, this is the second greatest game you'll ever see at the Orange Bowl."

The other Hurricanes game was also for the national championship, and I think this was probably the greatest college football game ever played with the title at stake. It was also the first college football game I ever took my children to, so there is a personal attachment to the game for me. My kids had never experienced the pageantry that an event like this brings. The game was so thrilling and went back and forth and eventually went two overtimes and featured a play in the first overtime where we thought the game was over when a pass was batted down, only for a pass interference penalty to be called on the play (although that didn't stop fireworks from prematurely going off).

My kids and I were running around, celebrating and giving high fives, only to learn Miami hadn't won yet. It took so long for the play to get straightened out that we were ready to leave before finding out about the penalty. Ohio State running back Maurice Clarett scored the winning touchdown but also made the biggest defensive play of the game, stripping a Miami player after an interception and getting the ball back for Ohio State. The game ended incredibly late for a West Coast game, and I had never seen anything quite like it. I really believe it was the most exciting college sporting event I've ever been to, and to have my kids there made it even more special. It was so intense, though, that at one point one of my sons looked at me and said, "I don't care who wins, Dad. I'm so tired

I want to go home." He was just so exhausted. It was a four-hour nailbiter. We stood the entire game, from beginning to end, not too far behind Miami legends like Warren Sapp and Ray Lewis and others. We were in the middle of an Ohio State section, and in a stadium with around seventy-five thousand people, probably sixty-five thousand of them were Buckeyes fans.

Stan Fischler
Broadcaster, MSG Network

St. Louis Cardinals at Brooklyn Dodgers, Ebbets Field, Brooklyn, New York, May 20, 1942

Before the game, a very interesting episode took place involving my grandmother, a thermos bottle, and me. The Dodgers were the defending National League champs and had a great rivalry with the Cardinals. There was also a great rivalry between my best friend Howie Sparer and me; he was a Dodger fan, and I was a Cardinal fan. My grandmother took care of me during the day while my parents worked, and she always made me a sandwich before I would go anywhere. I had a Superman lunchbox and thermos. Instead of the usual chocolate drink she normally gave me, this day, I asked for some soda instead. It was a hot day, so she said no and told me it would explode. But when her back was turned, I filled it with soda anyway, grabbed the sandwich, loaded up the lunchbox, and left.

While I was on the trolley to Ebbets Field, though, I realized that grandmothers are never wrong and I was going to make a mess on the trolley. I got more and more nervous, hoping the thermos wouldn't explode on the trolley.

Finally, I got to Ebbets Field and ran to the pavilion entrance to meet Howie, and we got to our seats as fast as we could so I could open the thermos before it exploded. I opened the lunchbox, grabbed the thermos, and opened it like James Bond would disarm a bomb—very gingerly and carefully. I pulled the cork off and nothing happened. The soda didn't explode, and I enjoyed the best soda or champagne I ever had in my life.

As for the game, it was a battle between 20-game winners: Mort Cooper for the Cardinals and Whit Wyatt for the Dodgers. We were sitting in the front row of the bleachers in centerfield and saw a phenomenal pitchers' duel. The park was so small; these seats made you feel like you were looking over the pitcher's shoulder. Cooper allowed just two hits, and the Cardinals won, 1–0. I won, Howie lost, and I was happy for the rest of the summer.

Homestead Grays at Brooklyn Bushwicks, Dexter Park, Brooklyn, New York, 1944

When the Dodgers went on the road, my father would take me on Sundays to Dexter Park, which was on the border of Brooklyn and Queens. For a kid from Brooklyn, going all the way out to Dexter Park was like going to another planet. When you got there, it was like being in the country, with a semipro baseball stadium in the middle of it. The park was owned by Max Rosner, who put in the first stadium lights, before Major League Baseball ever did.

The home team was called the Bushwicks, and they would play double-headers every Sunday against other semipro teams. They also played the teams from the Negro National League, which gave me a chance to see guys like Jackie Robinson and Roy Campanella play. But the best of all was getting to see the Homestead Grays, featuring the legendary Josh Gibson, who came to Dexter Park every year. Most of the fans from East New York, who were white, sat on the first base side, which was the side in the sun in the afternoon. The third base side was where the African-American fans sat, as well as the white fans that weren't from East New York, such as us. Dexter Park also featured the best outfield billboard of all time, which read, "Don't Kill the Umpire. Maybe It's Your Eyes. See Cohen the Optician."

The way Dexter Park was configured, rightfield was about 320 feet, and beyond the billboards were homes with backyards featuring platforms to watch the games. In right-centerfield, there was a big scoreboard with all of the big-league scores on it. In left-center was a huge embankment, with a beer garden and picnic area at the top. On the embankment, which was well over 400 feet from home plate, in large clamshells, it spelled out Dexter Park, and anybody who hit the ball over the embankment had a home run.

In the eighth inning of the game, Gibson came up and hit the most tremendous line drive I've ever seen. It went over the embankment into the beer garden. Gibson rounded first and was headed toward second when, to everybody's amazement, he stopped and sat down on second base, turning a home run into a double, as if to say, "I've proven my point."

1955 World Series, Game 3, New York Yankees at Brooklyn Dodgers, Ebbets Field, Brooklyn, New York, September 30, 1955

I was working for the New York *Journal-American* in 1955. The Dodgers lost the first two games of the World Series to the Yankees in the Bronx before the Series shifted to Brooklyn. Even though I wrote a sports column for the *Journal*, I was gifted by legendary Dodger PR man Irving Rudd for Game 3; he got me a pair of box seats on the third base line—the best seats I've ever had for a game in my life.

I started becoming a Dodger fan in 1950, so by this point I was a very big fan and sweated through all the heartbreak, such as Bobby Thomson in 1951 and losing to the Yankees in the Series on a regular basis. It looked like the same thing was going to happen again in '55. Suddenly, the Dodgers erupted, and it felt like all of their pent-up anger was going into their bats. Duke Snider hit some of the longest shots I've ever seen and just took over. The Dodgers just beat the Yankees up, 8–3, and that was the catalyst for their finally taking the Series. It was just a perfect day that day, though. It was a perfect fall day, I had great seats, and the Dodgers had just destroyed the hated Yankees.

1987 Patrick Division Semifinals, Game 7, New York Islanders at Washington Capitals, Capital Centre, Landover, Maryland, April 18, 1987

It was Game 7 of the opening round, and I was doing between periods for the game for SportsChannel with Jiggs McDonald and Eddie Westfall. It looked like the Islanders were going to lose, and I was in our studio at ice level, which had a window that enabled us to see the ice. Washington goalie Bob Mason was outstanding that night, and it seemed like the Caps had things wrapped up. So I got ready for what we thought was going to be a sad postgame show, when all of a sudden Bryan Trottier scored to tie the game and send it into overtime.

I've never seen overtime quite like this. It defied the law of averages, with so many close calls on both ends. Islander goalie Kelly Hrudey was playing out of his mind, making incredible save after incredible save. The referee was Andy Van Hellemond, who reffed at this point as if he was wearing blinders. He wanted the players, not the officiating, to determine the outcome of the game. Guys were getting away with tackles, where Van Hellemond would look twice but then just skate away. Through all of this, though, no one could score, and one overtime turned into multiple overtimes. I decided to watch the overtime from the studio, since the game could end at literally any moment. I was sitting on a chair and was so busy making saves along with Kelly Hrudey that at one point I fell out of my chair.

Finally, in the fourth overtime, Islander defenseman Gord Dineen left the blue line in the offensive zone to chase a puck behind the net (a stupid play, by the way), got it, and threw it out to Pat LaFontaine, who did a pirouette and fired a shot. At first, you couldn't tell if it went in, because Mason spread his legs out and it looked like he had the whole net covered. But the red light went on and the Islanders had won, 3–2. When it was over, I needed to grab the star of the game as quickly as possible. After the celebration, LaFontaine came off, and I waved to him. He came right in, as exhausted as he was, and we did the interview.

2003 Stanley Cup Finals, Game 7, Mighty Ducks of Anaheim at New Jersey Devils, Continental Airlines Arena, East Rutherford, New Jersey, June 9, 2003

This was a remarkable series, especially considering no one expected the Devils to beat Ottawa in the Eastern Conference Finals and make it as far as they did. The Devils won the first two games, and everyone was starting to get cocky, thinking they were going to sweep the Mighty Ducks. But Anaheim won the next two at home to even the series. The home teams won each of the next two games, sending things back to New Jersey for Game 7. The Devils had brought up a nondescript kid from the minors named Michael Rupp, whom nobody expected anything from. But in this game Rupp took a regular shift and scored the first goal of the game. He then added an assist, then another assist, and the Meadowlands was going crazy. Martin Brodeur pitched a 3–0 shutout for the Devils, and Michael Rupp became the most unlikely hero I've ever seen. After the Devils won the Cup, Lou Lamoriello, the architect of the team, stayed in the walkway underneath the stands and, as each player came off the ice, he embraced each one of them.

Mike Francesa
Co-Host, Mike and the Mad Dog, *WFAN Radio New York*

1982 NCAA Men's Basketball Tournament Finals, North Carolina vs. Georgetown, Louisiana Superdome, New Orleans, Louisiana, March 29, 1982

This was the first Final Four I did for CBS. I was courtside standing next to Brent Musburger on the baseline, getting ready to go on after the game, so Michael Jordan's shot happened right in front of us. This is still the best college game I've ever seen in my life. From early on, with Patrick Ewing goaltending every shot, the level of play on the floor with Jordan, Ewing, Sam Perkins, James Worthy, Sleepy Floyd . . . the level of players in that game made this the best game at the highest level of play I've ever seen. It was the game that really started the Jordan legend.

1983 NCAA Men's Basketball Tournament Finals, North Carolina State vs. Houston, University Arena, Albuquerque, New Mexico, April 4, 1983

This game was bizarre. On Saturday in Albuquerque, Houston really unleashed Phi Slamma Jamma against Louisville. Everyone talked about how that was the "Space Age" game, that it was played a mile above the rim and everyone was dunking, and now NC State had no chance to beat Houston. I was in the interview room with Jim Valvano on Sunday, and because Jim was a Long Island guy, I knew him. He told me that day that he really thought they had a chance to win.

NC State went right at them in the first half and had a 7-point lead at the break, but Phi Slamma Jamma came out in the second half and was devastating. Houston, though, missed a lot of free throws, which kept Valvano's team in the game instead of blowing them out. Of course, we all know what happened at the end. I've never seen such a stunned building after NC State won. It took everyone a few seconds to realize what had happened. It really was a very strange night.

Boston College at Miami, Orange Bowl, Miami, Florida, November 23, 1984

CBS actually made this game between Boston College and Miami, with the thought that putting Doug Flutie and Bernie Kosar together could be one of the great shootouts. Never in my mind did I think it would be this crazy. Here was Miami, which played no defense, and the craziness surrounding Boston College and the "Flutie Magic" from that season. It was Jimmy Johnson's first season as coach of the Hurricanes, and he inherited the coaching staff that season. The team played terribly down the stretch, and he has stated that the defensive coaches had actually left the coaching booth and were in the elevator to the field when the play happened. This has been disputed by those coaches over the years. It was just one of the most remarkable plays ever. I was in the TV booth just standing there watching and wondering if Gerard Phelan actually made the catch. A lot of people will say they were at this game. . . . I was working it and got to see one of the truly special college players of all time.

Super Bowl XXV, Buffalo Bills vs. New York Giants, Tampa Stadium, Tampa, Florida, January 27, 1991

The Gulf War made for a very interesting backdrop to this game, plus you had to factor in the "three-peat" game the weekend before when the Giants knocked off the 49ers in San Francisco. The Niners were so confident they sent their equipment and staff ahead to Tampa before even playing the Giants (there was only one week off before the Super Bowl that year). It was a great scene in Tampa on Monday when they were moving the Niners' equipment out and the Giants' stuff in.

Now here come the Bills, who beat the Raiders 51–3 in the AFC Championship Game and were a team a lot of people thought was unbeatable. Many wondered if the Giants could contain the Bills' unstoppable offense. To an extent, the Giants did, but the best defense was actually their offense, which stayed on the field for forty minutes. The big sequence was Jeff Hostetler not fumbling in the end zone on the safety, then the Giants getting the ball back and scoring a touchdown right before the half to get back in the game, 12–10.

At the half, I went downstairs, and you could tell all the Giants fans knew they were going to win the game, and I did, too. I always thought Scott Norwood took a very bad rap for missing the field goal at the end of the game. That length field goal, on a grass field that is a little dewy at that time of night, under those circumstances, that is a long kick and a lot more difficult than people made it out to be. It wasn't like he had to kick a 30-yarder. That was a long kick. I think he took a lot more abuse than he should have. "Wide Right" is one of the great moments I'll ever remember. The scene in that stadium from a patriotic standpoint, with Whitney Houston singing the national anthem, and the planes flying overhead made this incredibly memorable.

1996 World Series, Game 6, Atlanta Braves at New York Yankees, Yankee Stadium, Bronx, New York, October 26, 1996

There are so many Yankee games I can list. I was there when Chris Chambliss homered in 1976, sending the Yankees to the World Series for the first time since I was a little boy. But as the years go by, having had the chance to go to all of these Yankee playoff games, I find this one the most incredible. I was sitting down by the dugout, and there is one play that stands out above all others. Joe Girardi, who was much maligned at the time, tripled—I've been in Yankee Stadium hundreds of times, and that was nearly the loudest roar I ever heard in Yankee Stadium. And I was there for Mickey Mantle. I really believe that *was* the loudest I've ever heard it—it actually shook. I think everyone finally felt the Yankees were going to win the Series. It had been so long since they won, and the Yankees had to come back after being embarrassed by the Braves in New York in the first two games. It really was symbolic of the whole season for the Yankees. It all culminated in that triple and the explosion that followed. I always like to look around the stadium in moments like this, and I've never seen it shake like this, not even in 2001 with the two game-winning homers.

Jay Glazer
Broadcaster, FOX Sports

Andrew Golota vs. Riddick Bowe, Madison Square Garden, New York, New York, July 11, 1996

I was sitting in the fifth row that night, when a riot broke out in the Garden after the fight ended in controversy. It was the craziest thing I've ever experienced. Lou Duva passed out in the ring, but because there was so much fighting going on in the seats, they couldn't get him out. Eventually, they put him on a stretcher and passed him through the crowd, and I actually had to help pass the stretcher along to the next person. Everywhere I looked, I saw fights. I was just trying to duck out of the seating area without getting into a fight myself, because it got to the point where people were simply looking around for fights with anyone they could find. It was like a maze, and you had to keep moving around just to avoid getting hit, like a running back trying to find a hole.

Super Bowl XXXI, Green Bay Packers vs. New England Patriots, Louisiana Superdome, New Orleans, Louisiana, January 26, 1997

This was the first Super Bowl I ever attended, and I just couldn't take enough pictures while I was there. I was friends with a bunch of guys on the Patriots, and that, along with guys like Brett Favre, Bill Parcells, and others being involved, made it special. I was working for the *New York Post* at the time and paid my own way there and stayed with people I didn't even know—I made calls to people who had friends there to find a place where I could crash at night. My goal while I was there was just to meet people and make contacts, and that is exactly what happened.

New York Jets at Green Bay Packers, Lambeau Field, Green Bay, Wisconsin, August 4, 2000

The first time I was given the chance to do sidelines for an NFL game was by CBS at Lambeau Field. I was standing there just in awe, and called my dad just so I could tell him that I was standing in Lambeau Field. I was twenty-nine and couldn't believe where I was. For me, even though I grew up a Giants fan in New York, there is just something special about Lambeau Field.

PRIDE Final Conflict 2005, Saitama Super Arena, Saitama, Japan, August 28, 2005

This is one of the greatest spectacles in sports. Forty-thousand-plus people fill the arena to watch the PRIDE Fighting Championships, which is Mixed Martial Arts. Every single person in the building takes it very seriously. During the fights, nobody talks out of respect for the samurai. Imagine being at a football game with forty thousand people and no one is talking . . . it is surreal. When someone throws a kick, you can hear it in the upper deck. Every single fight on the card is produced like it is the halftime show at the Super Bowl, with huge movie screens, fireworks, and pyrotechnics. The fighters enter on a stage that rises up, like when Ivan Drago enters in *Rocky IV*, and fire shoots out, music blares, drummers start beating on these enormous drums, all while the fighters walk down a ramp that is around 50 yards long, and the crowd goes insane. There are no breaks between the fights like in boxing over here. It is the excitement of a big event, but times ten, once for each fight on the card.

2006 Palio di Siena, Piazza del Campo, Siena, Italy, July 2, 2006

Every year in Siena, Italy, they hold a horse race unlike any other I've ever seen. Siena is a medieval city amidst the castles and wineries of Tuscany, and this is the oldest horse race there is. A quarter of a million people pack the city every year for the event. The rules are very simple—there are none, except for when it comes to drugging or kidnapping an opposing jockey, which can only be done the night before the race. Each of the horses in the race represents one Contrada (neighborhood) of the city. During the race, the horses are going around the track, but the jockeys are beating the hell out of each other, and many of the horses end up finishing without a rider. The race lasts only around two minutes and takes place within the city walls in Siena's main piazza, the Piazza del Campo, which is lined with restaurants and cafes that close for the day. They erect stands in the piazza, but there is only room for around five thousand people in the stands, meaning everyone else is basically in the middle of the piazza, or on roofs of the buildings.

Before the race, jockeys are seen making deals and trying to bribe each other. The winning Contrada's horse is allowed to eat at the table with the villagers, and the people from that village suck on pacifiers as a sign of being reborn. The moment the race ends, people exit the stands, which are immediately broken down, and within a half hour, all the restaurants reopen and a big party starts to celebrate and toast the winning Contrada. This day was easily one of the most incredible experiences I've ever had, sports or not.

Bonus story. . . .

2006 World Cup Finals Viewing, Circus Maximus, Rome, Italy, July 9, 2006

I got the chance to be in the Circus Maximus in Rome, where they had the chariot races in gladiator times, with a half million Italians, as their country won the World Cup. I was so into it, I shaved my head and painted my head and face the colors of the Italian flag. There wasn't one single incident of violence the entire time. People were drinking and celebrating all day. There were three huge screens built to watch the event.

In the U.S., we know how big the Super Bowl is, but imagine a Super Bowl in which *everyone* is rooting for one team, as opposed to one third being for one team, one third being for the other, and the final third only being there for the event. This was half a million people cheering for their country in a sport that they are passionate about. Our hotel was 6 miles away, but we had to walk back afterwards, because besides the half million people inside, there were another five million more people outside celebrating.

Jim Gray
Broadcaster, ESPN

1984 Summer Olympics, Men's 100 Meters Final, Los Angeles Coliseum, Los Angeles, California, August 4, 1984

The buildup leading to Carl Lewis's first attempt at a gold medal at the 1984 Olympics was unbelievable. Everybody knew he was going to win, and his agent had proclaimed that he would be "bigger than Michael Jackson." And even after all of the hype, Lewis delivered. It was such a tense environment in the Coliseum in anticipation of those ten seconds. Then the gun went off, and it was all up to Lewis, and he crossed the finish line as the winner. I've been involved in seven Olympics, and I've never seen a moment like that. I witnessed every one of his medals, but this one had an aura about it that really makes it stand above the others. It was like a prizefight—when Muhammad Ali walked into the ring, it was unbelievable, and the feeling this night was just like that, maybe even bigger.

Marvin Hagler vs. Thomas Hearns, Caesars Palace, Las Vegas, Nevada, April 15, 1985

This fight was everything you ever could have imagined. It was ferocious, brutal, magical, artistic, scientific, violent . . . and incredible. I don't think I've ever been at a fight where the entire crowd was on its feet for the entire time.

The 1997 Masters, Augusta National Golf Club, Augusta, Georgia, April 10–13, 1997

This was a bit personal for me, because I had done one of Tiger's first interviews. I've known Tiger since he was eight years old, when I went out to interview him and his father, Earl. To see what that youngster, whom I had known for years, had committed himself to—and then accomplished—just can't be described. It is one thing to win the Amateur Championship (and win it again and again), but it is another thing to win the Masters. To see him accomplish that, and to see the joy that he and his dad had, and to see many of the game's African-American pioneers like Lee Elder on the course to watch, and to see some of the African Americans who worked at Augusta, all witnessing something they never thought they would see was unlike anything I've ever seen. I was there with my dad, and I know he'll never forget it. To see Tiger embrace his father, it was a great scene that had societal impact. It was just something very special.

Mike Tyson vs. Evander Holyfield, MGM Grand Garden Arena, Las Vegas, Nevada, June 28, 1997

I've done many of Mike Tyson's fights, so it had gotten to the point where I knew to expect the unexpected. When he was involved, it was a carnival, a circus, and a train wreck just waiting to happen. It was always an awesome display of talent and an awesome show of power. But even with expecting the unexpected and thinking you've seen everything and with nothing like this even in the realm of going through someone's mind, let alone acting it out and doing it, he did it. And even after doing it once, and being told not to do it, he did it again.

It is easy to miss something like this when it happens, but I actually saw him do it both times. The first time, I thought to myself, "He just bit that man's ear." Immediately, you knew something had happened, because Holyfield jumped up and was bleeding. Referee Mills Lane showed a lot of bravery standing up to Tyson and allowing the fight to continue, then stopping it after the second incident. Tyson's behavior after the fight, including the interview I did with him outside his locker room (we couldn't do it in the ring because of the near riot he had started), was just astonishing.

1998 NBA Finals, Game 6, Chicago Bulls at Utah Jazz, Delta Center, Salt Lake City, Utah, June 14, 1998

We all thought at the time that this was Michael's last shot in the NBA, although that would change when he came back with Washington. The shot won the sixth championship for the Bulls and signaled the breakup of the team, which we all knew was coming and were reporting. Jordan's shot was one of those moments where you knew you were watching something special that was coming to an end, so there was the elation of being able to see it but also the depression of thinking this was the last time we would see him play basketball and the last time we would see this great team together. The relief, the joy, the depression, the silence of the building after the Jazz lost . . . it was an amazing circumstance once everything was factored in. There were tears flowing in Utah that night because Karl Malone and John Stockton and the Jazz had lost, but while they were presenting the trophy to the Bulls, the tears very well might have been for Michael Jordan's farewell.

Jay Greenberg
Columnist, New York Post

Soviet Red Army at Philadelphia Flyers, The Spectrum, Philadelphia, Pennsylvania, January 11, 1976
The Flyers were amused by the irony that they, the NHL's black sheep, were suddenly the last defense of the league's honor. But when the mighty Soviet Red Army finished up a so-far undefeated challenge of four NHL teams at the Spectrum on January 11, 1976, the Broad Street Bullies solemnly accepted the responsibility.

The 1972 Summit Series, the first meeting between NHL stars and the Soviet National Team that had dominated the amateur teams nations had been sending to the Olympics, had ended with Team Canada rallying from a 3–1–1 deficit to win in the final minute in Game 8 at Moscow. A series with the same format, with World Hockey Association stars substituted, had been won by the Soviets, 4–1–3, in 1974.

Two years later, this was the first meeting of the USSR's best club team (made up of all but one line of the national team) meeting the two-time defending Stanley Cup champions. Montreal outshot the Red Army 38–13 on New Year's Eve but had only gained a 3–3 tie, sandwiched between convincing Russian Army victories at Madison Square Garden and Boston Garden. "It was the biggest game in Flyer history," Fred Shero would say later. "We had to win or else."

If the Cold War peaked with the Cuban Missile Crisis in 1962, the Spectrum that afternoon staged one of its last great ideological battles. It was a political rally as much as a hockey game, with a pregame atmosphere as charged as I have ever felt.

Ten minutes into the game, not from the start as people remember, the Bullies started hitting. "It wasn't really planned," defenseman Tom Bladon recalled later. "We were just wound up because of the pressure on us. I think it was more emotional than anything."

Three jarring Philadelphia hits preceded one by Ed Van Impe, who left the penalty box to elbow Soviet star Valeri Kharlamov. Kharlamov, whose leg had been broken by Flyer captain Bobby Clarke in the 1972 series, lay on his knees, head in his gloves while coach Konstantin Loktev waved disgustedly at NHL referee Lloyd Gilmour. Kharlamov was helped to the bench, but Loktev dallied putting his players on the ice. When Gilmour motioned a delay-of-game penalty, the coach waved his team into the locker room. They stayed seventeen minutes while NHL President Clarence Campbell appealed to Vyacheslav Koloskov, the head of the Soviet Hockey Federation. Koloskov convinced Loktev to bring his team back, not without first unsuccessfully trying to negotiate his way out of the delay penalty.

Seventeen seconds after play resumed, Reggie Leach tipped a Bill Barber power play drive past goalie Vladislav Tretiak, and the Spectrum exploded. The Flyers made it 3–0 before the Soviets had registered three shots on goal. And the final shot totals, 49–13, were more indicative of the rout than the 4–1 final score. "They were scared," recalled Bladon. "Plain and simple."

But the Soviets also were flustered by the Flyers' absolute domination of the boards, part of their plan to keep passes out of the middle, where the swift and almost robotlike Soviet players could turn them into dizzying counters. The Flyers' plan that day wasn't just their elbows, and they exercised it perfectly to save the league's honor.

"The greatest coaching job I have ever seen," Flyers owner Ed Snider told Fred Shero in front of the media afterwards. Shero, usually reserved in victory, if not downright critical, agreed it was his finest hour. "We are the world champions, and 99 percent of the NHL didn't think we could do it," he said. Shero exaggerated the skepticism, hardly the pride. The Soviets felt different kinds of bumps from everybody else at the Spectrum that day: goosebumps.

1979 NHL Stanley Cup Semifinals, Game 7, Boston Bruins at Montreal Canadiens, Montreal Forum, Montreal, Canada, May 10, 1979

Because I have never seen a sadder locker room than the Boston Bruins' on May 10, 1979, at the Montreal Forum, I will adopt that as my definition for the most compelling sports event I have ever attended. No game I have ever witnessed live had a bigger buildup, leading to a more twisted and painful ending.

Even when the Bruins won the Stanley Cup in 1970 and 1972, their only two in the last sixty-five years, they hadn't beaten the Canadiens, who robbed them of a dynasty with a first-round upset in 1971. Retooled later in the decade as an ultimate working team, the Bruins had twice again banged their heads against probably the greatest Canadien dynasty of their many, losing in four straight in the 1977 finals, then in six in 1978.

It was a Boston team that looked old and tired by the 1978–79 season's end, dropping to third in the overall points standing that determined seedings in those years. Colorful coach Don Cherry, not getting along with GM Harry Sinden, was on his way out. But to no one's huge surprise the Bruins, almost on memory, were making one last run.

The three-time defending champion Canadiens, too, were not quite what they had been, having been beaten out for the overall points title by the New York Islanders. Thus, the series between two of the sport's oldest and proudest franchises this time was in the semifinals. But when the New York Rangers upset the Islanders, and the Bruins forced Game 7 with a 5–2 win at Boston Garden, only New York was not clued in to the probability that this year's final would be an anticlimax.

The Bruins, losers of their last fourteen games on the most famous sheet of ice in the sport, had the hardest game they would ever have to win within their grasp, too. Guy Lafleur, the best player in the NHL, scored a goal and set up another within 2:04 in the third period to bring the champions back to a 3–3 tie. But Rick Middleton took a pass from Jean Ratelle behind the goal, raced Ken Dryden to the opposite post, and tucked the lead goal in off the goalie's blocker with 3:59 to go. The air went out of the Forum with a shriek. "I thought it was over," Montreal coach Scotty Bowman confessed.

Then it happened, though to this day Cherry won't say exactly what happened. But the Bruins put too many men on the ice for estimates of up to twenty seconds, too long for linesman John D'Amico to ignore, even in a time when officials were loathe to call anything in close third periods. Lafleur took the puck in his own end, raced to the top of the right circle, and fired a perfect slap shot just inside the far post behind goalie Gilles Gilbert with only 1:14 left to play. Sitting in the auxiliary press box high in the Forum's end, where I was covering the game for the *Philadelphia Daily News*, I could feel it shake, literally. "What happened were the kinds of situations that Lafleur thrives upon," said Dryden. "It was going to be his game to decide."

The Bruins were not dead. Dryden stopped point-blank chances by Don Marcotte and Terry O'Reilly in overtime until Yvon Lambert got a step on Brad Park, took a feed from Mario Tremblay, and, in one motion, shoved it past Gilbert before tumbling into the goalie. The Canadiens, their excruciating tension broken, rushed out to pick up Lambert. The Bruins sat transfixed on their bench for the longest time, before going to the locker room to sit and stare some more.

"I've never seen a team try so hard, give so much, come so close, and not get it," said goalie Gerry Cheevers. "I look at these guys, and I just want to cry. I just want to cry." A lot of the Bruins, tough guys like Terry O'Reilly, did on the charter flight home. The drained Canadiens lost Game 1 to the Rangers, fell behind in Game 2, but won their fourth straight Cup in five. The Bruins didn't make another final for eleven years and still haven't won another Cup.

I didn't see the ghosts of the Forum the night the Bruins suffered the cruelest loss I have ever witnessed. But I felt them.

Philadelphia Flyers at Boston Bruins, Boston Garden, Boston, Massachusetts, December 22, 1979

Twenty-eight straight games, since the third game of the 1979–80 season, the Philadelphia Flyers had gone without losing, and without public acknowledgment that they really cared about the NHL consecutive unbeaten record of 29 set only two seasons earlier by the Canadiens.

But then the Flyers had played a tight, hanging-on kind of third period to save a 1–1 tie at Madison Square Garden in Game No. 27. "We've been saying it's not affecting us," said Coach Pat Quinn, "but you know that's a crock. You might play a hundred years and never get another chance at something like this." Indeed, it looked like it was all passing before their eyes four days later at the Spectrum, where the mediocre Penguins took a 1–0 lead deep into the third period before referee Dave Newell called a rare (in those days) third-period penalty. Flyers defenseman Behn Wilson either got his stick on a puck he had kicked before it crossed the line or he did not, but Newell allowed the goal, and the record was tied.

The pressure seemed to be flattening the Flyers, who to break the mark would have to do it at Boston Garden, where they had been routed from the playoffs in two of the last three springs. But I will never forget how eerily composed they were that afternoon. Fourteen years I covered the Flyers to four Stanley Cup Finals, and never did I see them play a better game under more pressure.

They were breezing, startlingly, 3–0 in the second period when defenseman Bob Dailey accidentally deflected a centering pass into his own net. On the next shift, goalie Phil Myre got caught flat-footed on Mike Milbury's goal through traffic, and suddenly it was 3–2. On the next faceoff, the Flyers took the puck into the Boston zone, where Jimmy Watson scored from the point, and they continued smothering the Bruins the rest of the way.

Boston fans, who had been gleeful at the Bruins' 1977 and 1978 semifinal finishings of the expansion franchise that had humiliated them in the 1974 finals, gave Quinn's team a standing ovation in the final seconds of a 5–2 win that was the culmination of the most magnificent feat in NHL history. "My God, it's almost halfway though the season, and they have one loss," said Boston coach Fred Creighton. "It's hard to comprehend."

It still is. The Flyers, with three defensemen and a goalie (Myre alternated through the streak with rookie Pete Peeters) who would be out of the league within two years, stretched the streak to 35 before losing. An amalgamation of Cup-team holdovers and high drafts of what would turn out to be a failed, new nucleus, they were relentless through four lines, rallying from one three-goal deficit and eight two-goal deficits during the 25–0–10 streak (regular-season overtime was still four seasons away).

But they weren't good enough to win the Cup, losing in the finals to the Islanders. "I pull the picture of that team and look at it and say 'How did we do that?'" Quinn recalled for a history of the Flyers I wrote years later. Since I can't explain it, either, I rate it the most amazing thing I have seen in thirty-four years of covering sports. Watching it beginning to end was my greatest privilege.

1992 AFC Wild Card Game, Houston Oilers at Buffalo Bills, Rich Stadium, Orchard Park, New York, January 3, 1993

The most astounding turnaround I've ever seen came on January 3, 1993, when I saw the Buffalo Bills, down 35–3 in the third quarter, beat the Houston Oilers, 41–38, in a playoff game. Unless I was hallucinating.

The Oilers' Warren Moon had conducted touchdown drives of 80, 80, 67, and 67 yards in a first-half performance so perfect the Bills had the ball for only 8:48. And when Bubba McDowell intercepted a tipped Frank Reich pass and ran it back 58 yards for a touchdown early in the third quarter, it would be this 40-degree January day in Buffalo, when the Bills, even coming off consecutive Super Bowl appearances, would come back.

The greatest comeback in NFL history took place in a playoff game, hard to believe, and I was covering it with proper disbelief for the *Toronto Sun*. After McDowell's return, the Oilers tried an onside kick, which the Bills fell upon with great insult and scored in ten plays.

Reich, playing for an injured Jim Kelly, threw a 38-yard touchdown pass to Don Beebe before an Oiler punt was knocked down by the wind and Andre Reed caught a 26-yard touchdown pass. When a Moon pass went through the arms of Webster Slaughter into the hands of defensive back Henry Jones, the Oilers were reeling. Reed caught another one in the end zone to make it 35–31, and after the Oilers botched a drive with a bad field goal snap, Reich hit Reed again to put Buffalo ahead.

Despite it all, Moon gathered the Oilers and conducted a last-minute drive to a tying field goal, but Nate Odomes intercepted a pass on the first Houston possession of the overtime and set up Steve Christie's winning goal, which I always will remember him saying was the only thing he remembered about the most memorable game he ever played. "Other than that it was all a blur," Christie said. If it was like that for the winners, imagine how it was for the stunned losers. As for the *Toronto Sun* columnist, he fortunately had Bills defensive coordinator Walt Corey to sum it all up. "We have all kinds of miracles here in Buffalo," Corey said. "Senior citizens should migrate up here."

1994 Stanley Cup Finals, Game 7, Vancouver Canucks at New York Rangers, Madison Square Garden, New York, New York, June 14, 1994

Certainly there was nothing anticlimactic about the 1994 Stanley Cup final. The Rangers, who had not won a Stanley Cup in fifty-four seasons, survived one of the most memorable semifinals ever, rallying from a 2–0 late-second-period deficit to survive Game 6, just as captain Mark Messier had promised, then outlasted the Devils upstarts, 2–1, in a Game 7 double overtime, after being tied in that game with only seven seconds left.

Still, those thrillers had only earned for the Rangers New York's sense that if they didn't finally win it all this time they would never get a better chance. And when the Vancouver Canucks stopped the Garden celebration by surviving a furious three-goal, game-tying Rangers third-period rally to win a strange Game 5, 6–3, then won Game 6 in Vancouver convincingly, 4–1, the sense of anticipation turned to fear.

That it had been reported that Coach Mike Keenan, not getting along with GM Neil Smith, was about to jump to Detroit added even an element of sabotage to Game 7, the most dreaded/anticipated hockey contest ever played in the city of New York.

On that night, June 14, 1994, the Rangers were ready, though, dominating the first ten minutes before Brian Leetch cut in from the point, took a pass from Sergei Zubov, spun, and scored the tension-cutting first goal. Adam Graves made it 2–0 less than four minutes later, but even after Trevor Linden scored, Messier poked in a power-play rebound, and the Rangers were in control 3–1 headed to the third period.

But Linden scored again, and the final sixteen minutes lasted fifty-four years, the fear palpable as Kevin Lowe's shot bounced off the crossbar like a clank of doom and the Canucks' Nathan Lafayette hit the post with five minutes left.

Four faceoffs took place in the Ranger end, one off an ominously bad icing call, in the final 1:31. The Canucks, winning a draw with twenty-eight seconds left, pushed the puck to the side of the goal, where it was frozen with 1.6 seconds to go, still enough time for the ultimate cruelty. But with the crowd trying to roar away its anxiety, Craig MacTavish pushed the puck to the corner, and the Rangers had won. Really. Finally.

NOW I CAN DIE IN PEACE was the best sign of all. Before the Cup ceremony, I had to run to the press room to file my middle-edition column for the *New York Post*. On the way, I made a point to look into the eyes of the people watching the Rangers celebrate. At least half of them were red.

Tom Hammond
Broadcaster, NBC Sports

St. Louis Cardinals at Cincinnati Reds, Crosley Field, Cincinnati, Ohio, 1950s

It was in the 1950s, and my dad took me to see the Reds play at home against the Cardinals. Stan Musial was playing for the Cardinals, but my hero was Ted Kluszewski, the Reds' first baseman. I was always big, and he was big, so I identified with him. We took the train, and the station was about two blocks from Crosley Field. I was so excited to make the walk, and when I finally came through the tunnel in the stadium and saw the field for the first time and how green it was and how brown the infield was and how brilliant everything was, after listening to games on the radio, it just exceeded everything I ever hoped or thought it would be. I was just blown away by that first look at everything. I don't remember any details from the game, but we had really good seats on the first base side, and I just remember feeling like I could reach out and touch everything. It has stayed with me forever.

110th Belmont Stakes, Belmont Park, Elmont, New York, June 10, 1978

I grew up with horse racing, and before I became a broadcaster, growing up in Lexington, Kentucky, I thought I was going to end up in the horse-racing business. I spent a lot of time as the announcer at the Keeneland Sales, where all the million-dollar yearlings are sold, and I would tell everyone about the horses before the auctioneer would sell them.

This background in horse racing, plus working for the NBC affiliate in Lexington, got me hired by NBC Sports for the first Breeders Cup. My friend, Chic Anderson, who had been the announcer at Churchill Downs, was then the track announcer at the New York tracks. Affirmed and Alydar ran two great races at the Kentucky Derby and the Preakness to open the Triple Crown, with Affirmed winning both times. Secretariat and Seattle Slew had both recently won Triple Crowns, but Secretariat's win snapped a twenty-five-year drought, so it was still a rare feat. I really wanted to see the third race between the horses, and Chic invited me to come up to the announcer's booth, and I stood behind him as he made the call of the race.

It was the greatest race I've ever seen, and people with a lot more experience than I have also say that. The two horses, these great rivals, hooked up with about a mile to go in the race and were never more than a head apart the rest of the way. Alydar got a brief lead, but somehow Affirmed willed himself to victory with Steve Cauthen aboard. They just found a way to win the race.

1995 Orange Bowl, Nebraska vs. Miami, Orange Bowl, Miami, Florida, January 1, 1995

Tom Osborne had tried and failed to win a National Championship with heavily favored Nebraska teams before, and here they were matched up with Miami again, who had been their nemesis. Miami took the lead, and in the third quarter they were dancing around, trash-talking, and I remember saying, "They oughta save some of that energy for the fourth quarter." Sure enough, Nebraska, with their huge offensive line, wore them down and was able to get the victory and give Tom Osborne his first National Championship, 24–17, after he had failed so many times before. And for it to come against Miami was sweet redemption.

1996 Summer Olympics, Men's 200 Meters Final, Centennial Olympic Stadium, Atlanta, Georgia, August 1, 1996

Michael Johnson came into the 1996 Olympics in Atlanta favored to do what no man had ever done in Olympic history—win the 400 and the 200. Leading up to the Games, he had dominated the 400, which was the first of the two events, and it was pretty much a foregone conclusion that, unless something drastic happened, he was going to win. And sure enough, he won it in impressive style. But then came the 200, which was not his specialty, and there were several talented runners in the race. It was so hyped and so anticipated that I remember being told that they stopped the games at the basketball venue so everyone could watch the race on the big screen. That ended up being the case at all of the Olympic venues; everything was paused so people could see if history could be made.

They start the 200 on the curve, so as they approach the straightaway, it is tough to see who exactly is winning the race (which makes it a nightmare to call). He didn't appear to be ahead as they made the turn and had some work to do. It was an interesting phenomenon to see the flashbulbs follow him through the stadium as people took his picture when he passed; it was like a wave of light following him. He also had golden shoes on, which were flashing as well. By our estimation, there were two or three runners ahead of him as he hit the turn for home, and then he just exploded with that unusual upright running style he had and managed to win the race, setting the world record in the process. It was so exciting that, as I was calling the race, I noticed that somewhere along the way, I stood up without even realizing it. With all of the buildup and with the manner in which he accomplished the feat, this was one of the most exciting things I've ever seen.

2000 Summer Olympics, Women's 400 Meters Final, Stadium Australia, Sydney, Australia, September 25, 2000

After running well but not winning the 400 in Atlanta, Cathy Freeman was expected to win the race in her home country. The pressure was just immense. She was selected to light the Olympic Flame during the Opening Ceremonies, which only added to the pressure. You could actually see her starting to bend as she carried the weight of the whole country on her shoulders. In addition, she was trying to become the first Aboriginal runner to ever win Olympic gold. An Australian woman won the first Olympic women's 400 in 1964, and as they got into the blocks to start the race, I said, "Cathy Freeman has waited four years for this moment. Australia has waited almost forty years. Aboriginal people have waited forever."

The race started, and it didn't look possible that she could win it, as she was way behind as they came to the home straightaway. She was wearing a unitard, and it looked like she started to stride out so far, farther than humanly possible, which is usually not a good recipe for running, and she started to inch ahead. With 105,000 people in the Olympic Stadium, she won the race. You can imagine the reaction by the Australian people. A few yards past the finish line, she just collapsed, not from fatigue but from the weight of the world being lifted off her shoulders. Later that evening, they held the medal ceremony, and for everyone in the stadium, whether you were Australian or not, it was incredibly emotional. The tears were flowing, not just on the medal stand but also in the stands themselves.

Kevin Harlan
Broadcaster, CBS Sports/Turner Sports

Kentucky at Kansas, Allen Fieldhouse, Lawrence, Kansas, December 10, 1983

I was the play-by-play man for Kansas basketball in 1983–84, when Larry Brown came to Lawrence from the New Jersey Nets to coach the Jayhawks. When he took the job, people were just in shock. Kansas is a great program but had some lean years, so this was a huge hire for the school. He had taken UCLA to the Final Four in his previous college coaching stint, so to lure him back from the NBA was a big deal. Kansas had been averaging eight to ten thousand fans a game before his arrival, but Allen Fieldhouse really started jumping again with Brown there.

One night, Kentucky came into the building, with Sam Bowie and Mel Turpin, Joe B. Hall coaching, and Cawood Ledford broadcasting, and beat Kansas handily, 72–50. The anticipation on campus for this game was amazing, and at tip-off the excitement level was something I had never experienced before. It was truly thrilling.

Kansas City Chiefs at Green Bay Packers, Lambeau Field, Green Bay, Wisconsin, December 10, 1989

My father, Bob, was the president and CEO and is now chairman of the Green Bay Packers, and when I was in high school, I was a ball boy for the team during training camp and on game days. During my lunch breaks, I would sneak up into the press box and go into the broadcast booth, close the door, and invent and broadcast an imaginary game. I made believe it was an actual game—there were players, scores, everything that would come up during a broadcast.

As time went on, I got into broadcasting as my career and was doing radio for the Kansas City Chiefs. The Chiefs made the trip up to Green Bay one season, and doing that broadcast was a dream come true. Ironically enough, when I went to FOX in 1994, my first assignment was also in Green Bay.

Kansas City Chiefs at Tampa Bay Buccaneers, Tampa Stadium, Tampa, Florida, September 5, 1993

Joe Montana was just a larger-than-life figure. When he came to Kansas City in 1993, the expectations were enormous. But the whole season was just terrific, with the Chiefs going all the way to the AFC Championship Game, before losing to Buffalo. Following and chronicling Montana throughout the season was such a treat and a pleasure. Marcus Allen was in the backfield with Joe, so there were actually two Hall-of-Famers there. The season opened at Tampa with a 27–3 win, and that really got things off to a memorable start. I worked with Len Dawson on the games, and during the flights home, Joe would wander over and spend some time with us, so I would have a chance to chat with two Hall of Fame quarterbacks during those trips.

Super Bowl XXXV, New York Giants vs. Baltimore Ravens, Raymond James Stadium, Tampa, Florida, January 28, 2001

I've worked the last four Final Fours for CBS Radio and Westwood One with Bill Raftery and John Thompson, and working that event is such a great honor. The enormity of what is involved is incredible. But doing the Super Bowl is a highlight for any broadcaster's career. CBS had the rights to the Super Bowl that year, but this was before there was one truck and broadcast crew for the regular and HD broadcasts, so I got to call the HD broadcast with Moose Johnston.

Green Bay Packers Hall of Fame Induction, Lambeau Field, Green Bay, Wisconsin, July 17, 2004

My father Bob's induction into the Packers Hall of Fame was a very personal moment and something that was great for my entire family. We got a chance to realize how impeccable his career has been and how much he loved the Packers. With all the ups and downs the team went through while he worked there, eventually winning a Super Bowl, and watching all of those games with him . . . his career culminating in being elected to the Packer Hall of Fame was a wonderful moment.

Merle Harmon
Broadcaster

Army vs. Air Force, Yankee Stadium, Bronx, New York, October 31, 1959

When college football games used to be played in Yankee Stadium, they were major events in New York, and since this was the first time that Army and Air Force ever played in football (Air Force was only a few years old at that point), every seat was filled. I think the Air Force Academy brought everyone to the game, including the walking wounded. General Nathan Twining was the chief of staff for the armed services, and the brass was sitting next to us on the balcony of the old Yankee Stadium. It was raining that day, but when Air Force did their parade on the field, the crowd gave them a tremendous ovation. Then Army came out and made for an incredible sight on the field as well.

All of a sudden, when they finished and turned to the brass to salute, an Army cadet started running between the columns in rightfield. Everyone thought he was crazy, but then he ripped off his Army coat and cap, and what happened? It was an Air Force cadet in disguise who had snuck into West Point and come in with the Army contingent. It was just one of those pranks that the service academies would pull on each other. The game ended in a 13–13 tie, and Air Force, as young as the football team was at the time, went on to play TCU in the Cotton Bowl that season.

Denver Broncos at New York Jets, Shea Stadium, Queens, New York, September 12, 1964

Nobody knew what to expect that night in Queens, since it was an AFL game being played in a new stadium and the World's Fair was being held right across the street. There was an immense amount of traffic, and no one really knew how many people would come to the game that evening—when the games were in the Polo Grounds, there might be five thousand people there.

Around half an hour before the game, though, there was a nice-size crowd on hand, and it kept growing and growing. The Jets decided to delay the start of the game because of all the traffic outside the building, although no one really knew if the traffic was for the game or the World's Fair. Otto Graham was my partner for the game; we were starting to get close to kickoff, and he wasn't there yet. All I thought to myself was, "Where's Otto?" I started kidding about it on the air and said, "If anyone sees Otto Graham, can you please let him know there is a game at Shea Stadium and he is supposed to be here?" As it turns out, he was trapped in the traffic jam outside! The game ended up drawing around forty-five thousand people, which just astonished everybody.

Minnesota Twins at Oakland Athletics, Oakland–Alameda County Coliseum, Oakland, California, May 8, 1968

The Twins had a powerhouse batting order, and Catfish Hunter mowed through it. He got down to the ninth inning, and rookie Rich Reese, who was a first baseman with a really good bat but was playing behind Harmon Killebrew, was up as a pinch hitter. The count went to 3–2, and Hunter just threw fastball after fastball after fastball, and Reese just kept fouling them off. There has been a lot of debate on the number of pitches that he fouled off, but I believe it was six before he swung and missed for strike three and the last out of the perfect game. That last at bat was just so dramatic.

Super Bowl III, New York Jets vs. Baltimore Colts, Orange Bowl, Miami, Florida, January 12, 1969

Everyone knows the story of this game, of course. When I got to Florida early that week, it was a very warm, balmy evening. I got out of the cab, and the first person I saw was Jets' defensive back Earl Christy, who ran up to me and started shaking me by the shoulders. He was all excited, yelling to me, "Merle, Merle, did you hear what Joe said? He said we are going to win the Super Bowl. Do you hear what I'm telling you? We are going to beat the Baltimore Colts! We are going to win the Super Bowl!" I said, "Earl, calm down. The game is four days away."

That team was so confident; that was my first actual exposure to what Namath had done by making the guarantee that they would win. That team really believed that they were going to win. The Jets felt that they could run the ball against the Colts, even though no one, including the Cleveland

Browns in the NFL Championship game, was able to do that. But after watching film, the Jets thought otherwise and all day long they pounded Matt Snell into the right side of the defense. When we left for the stadium, everyone said not to bring any baggage, since we were all going back to the hotel for the party. And we did just that.

Oakland Athletics at Texas Rangers, Arlington Stadium, Arlington, Texas, August 22, 1989

Rickey Henderson struck out swinging for the five thousandth strikeout by Nolan Ryan. This is a feat that no one will ever accomplish again. Someone might break the home-run record, but this one isn't going to be touched. It was pretty much a cinch that Ryan was going to reach the milestone that night, since he only needed six Ks to hit 5,000, and after Henderson became victim 4,998 and Ron Hassey struck out for number 4,999, the anticipation really started to build. Ryan had the count at 2–2 on Henderson to lead off the fifth inning and just barely missed strike three, which of course caused the entire stadium to moan and groan before Rickey became the historic strikeout on the 3–2 pitch, Ryan's seventy-first pitch of the game.

After the game, I took my score sheet to the clubhouse and got every person who participated in that game to sign it. When I went into the Oakland clubhouse, Mark McGwire saw what I was doing and said, "I know there is no amount of money that you would take for that score sheet, but I'm going to try anyway. How much do you want for it?" I told him he was right, though, and it wasn't going to happen! Even George W. Bush, who was the managing partner of the Rangers at the time, signed it. I had circled the historic strikeout and when I asked Henderson to sign it, he saw the circle and wrote across it, "I'm not ashamed to sign my name to becoming the five thousandth strikeout by Nolan Ryan."

Ernie Harwell

Broadcaster

Recipient of Baseball Hall of Fame's Ford C. Frick Award, 1981

The 1941 Masters, Augusta National Golf Club, Augusta, Georgia, April 3–6, 1941; the 1942 Masters, Augusta National Golf Club, April 9–13, 1942; and the 1946 Masters, Augusta National Golf Club, April 4–7, 1946

There wasn't one specific moment from the tournaments that really stands out, except that I was able to watch the great Bobby Jones play. After his retirement in 1930, the Masters was the only tournament Jones would play in. In 1941 I was working for WSB in Atlanta as the sports director (I was actually the only person in the department), and I made it part of my evening sports show. In 1942 I did the tournament for NBC, which was the first time a national network did the Masters. There were only three of us on the broadcast—Bob Stanton, a veteran NBC announcer from New York; Bill Stern; and me. Stern was in the tower, Stanton worked one nine, and I worked the other, covering the tournament with an engineer on a bicycle that had a console in a basket, plus an antenna. Byron Nelson topped Ben Hogan by one shot on Monday to win the tournament in an eighteen-hole playoff between two of the legends of the game. I worked for NBC again in 1946.

Brooklyn Dodgers at New York Giants, Polo Grounds, New York, New York, October 3, 1951

Everyone has heard the call by the great Russ Hodges, but I was working the game on TV for NBC, and no one ever recorded anything from that broadcast. Only my wife, Lulu, and I remember my being on that afternoon for Bobby Thomson's famous home run off Ralph Branca, sending the Giants into the World Series. There were a bunch of different radio broadcasts for the game, though. I thought I had the choice assignment that day, but the Lord works wonders and proved that incorrect. That homer was a great thrill, since I was one of the Giants' announcers, along with Russ, and we alternated between radio and TV, with it being my turn for TV that day.

1963 World Series, Los Angeles Dodgers vs. New York Yankees, Dodger Stadium, Los Angeles, California, and Yankee Stadium, Bronx, New York, October 2–6, 1963

Sandy Koufax and Don Drysdale were just outstanding in this Series, and Johnny Podres chipped in a win as well, as the Dodgers allowed just four runs in four games to the Yankees. Koufax set the World Series strikeout record at Yankee Stadium in Game 1 with 15 (including the first five), which was broken by Bob Gibson in 1968.

1968 World Series, Detroit Tigers vs. St. Louis Cardinals, Tiger Stadium, Detroit, Michigan, and Busch Stadium, St. Louis, Missouri, October 2–10, 1968

Game 1 will always be remembered for Bob Gibson's 17-strikeout performance, with the Cardinals winning the game in St. Louis. Then, Game 7 was back in St. Louis, after the Tigers came back from a three-games-to-one deficit. Mickey Lolich and Gibson tied up in a scoreless pitchers' duel until Norm Cash and Willie Horton singled in the seventh and Jim Northrup tripled over Curt Flood's head in centerfield, leading the Tigers to the title.

New York Yankees at Boston Red Sox, Fenway Park, Boston, Massachusetts, October 2, 1978

I did this game for CBS Radio with Win Elliot. It was "The Game," as they called it in New England at the time, and featured Bucky Dent's unlikely home run, which the Yankees rode to victory. I gave Bucky a tape of the game, and when I did, I apologized for saying his homer was just a fly ball to left, to which he replied, "Well, that's what it was."

Dan Hicks
Broadcaster, NBC Sports

1996 U.S. Amateur Championship, Pumpkin Ridge Golf Club, North Plains, Oregon, August 25, 1996

This would be Tiger Woods's final event as an amateur, and he would go out making history at Pumpkin Ridge GC. Nike founder Phil Knight was walking in the gallery, so it wasn't like there was much doubt as to his turning pro. It was the first U.S. Amateur on our network, and we knew Tiger was special, but we all left just blown away by what we saw. He was five down heading into the afternoon eighteen of the thirty-six-hole championship match with Steve Scott. But as he warmed up for the final eighteen, he suddenly had a smile on his face as if to say he had figured something out on the practice tee and was ready to go.

Was he ever. After he made a long curling putt for a birdie at 17 to square the match, I remember saying there are two guys who have the ability to actually "will" the ball into the hole: Jack Nicklaus and Tiger Woods. Pretty high praise for a twenty-year-old kid, but I had never seen such a young athlete handle pressure and rise to the occasion like that. It was an unprecedented third straight title, which launched the career of the greatest golfer in the world, and maybe ever, into the professional ranks. It was pure storybook and only the beginning.

1999 U.S. Open, No. 2 Course at Pinehurst Resort and Country Club, Pinehurst, North Carolina, June 17–20, 1999

I'd known Payne Stewart for several years, not as a close friend but as a broadcaster just trying to do my job. Early on he was very unpredictable—surly one moment, somewhat playful and cooperative at other times. But in the year or so leading up to the '99 Open, I noticed he was much more consistent and friendly, actually cordial. So after he had come agonizingly close to winning the '98 U.S. Open at Olympic Club, he came to Pinehurst No. 2 determined and focused, almost business-like. After watching him duel Phil Mickelson and dodge others like Tiger Woods, it came down to him and Phil at 18.

I was standing alongside the 18th green, waiting to do the presentation. He missed the fairway, then punched out to lay up and take his chances with a one-shot lead. When he hit his approach 15 feet short, I was thinking, "Here we go with an eighteen-hole playoff." But when he made that putt for par to win, it was the most emotion-packed single moment I've ever seen. He hugged his caddy, then grabbed Mickelson by the cheeks and said, "You're going to love being a father" (Mickelson's wife Amy had a baby the next day), then, all teary-eyed, embraced his wife with a hug that brought tears to *my* eyes.

I had the privilege of asking him the first question. That was tough. I simply said, "Most golfers grow up as little kids hoping and wishing their entire careers to make a putt like that to win the U.S. Open, and you just did. Can you possibly put it into words?" He just let out a whoop and holler as if to say, "I can't." It's still my most memorable U.S. Open, not because of his tragic death in a plane crash a few months later, but because I saw a guy so totally at peace and happy with who he was and what he had accomplished.

1999 Ryder Cup, The Country Club, Brookline, Massachusetts, September 24–26, 1999

I remember U.S. captain Ben Crenshaw's last words to the media assembled Saturday night after the Americans had gotten thrashed for the second straight day. "I'm gonna leave you all with one final thing. I have a feeling. I'm a big believer in fate. That's all I'm gonna say." We used the sound bite early in our Sunday telecast, and, even though we all thought very highly of Crenshaw, I can't say there was one member of our crew who believed the Americans weren't finished.

Then, the magic happened. As the Americans charged out and started winning their matches, it was like a tiny snowball that just kept rolling into a giant avalanche. Momentum is one of the most often-used and overused terms in sport. But this was the truest and most completely powerful form of it I've ever witnessed. As the U.S. roars echoed through the Country Club, I honestly had to take some deep breaths myself while sitting next to our European analyst Bernard Gallacher. The electricity was that apparent. It's the most charged atmosphere I've ever seen at a sporting event, and when Justin Leonard's putt dropped on 17, which eventually finished off the biggest final-day comeback in Ryder Cup history, it was like, "You've got to be kidding." It was the only exclamation point that could've been added to that story.

2000 U.S. Open, Pebble Beach Golf Links, Pebble Beach, California, June 15–18, 2000

It was my first U.S. Open as host of NBC's 18th tower, and it was even more daunting because it was the 100th U.S. Open at one of the greatest venues in the game. Just to add to the aura, Jack Nicklaus was playing his final U.S. Open. Needless to say, I was feeling a little pressure to not screw it up. What unfolded was the single best individual sporting achievement I've ever witnessed and one of the greatest ever, period.

Tiger was in the zone from the start, never once three-putting. I remember scrambling in the booth with my stat guys trying to put it all in perspective; in all, we dug up nine records, including the fifteen-shot win in a major. The bottom line is that it was the greatest performance in major-championship history. Even though it was a blowout, you couldn't take your eyes off him. Not one three-putt on not the truest of surfaces . . . poa annua greens. This was the first of four straight majors Woods would win and part of the greatest stretch of golf ever put together. I still believe now what I thought as I left Pebble that week. I've never seen a better display of golf, and I never, ever will . . . not even from Tiger.

2000 Summer Olympics, Men's 4x100 Meters Free Relay Finals, Sydney International Aquatic Centre, Sydney, Australia, September 16, 2000

The national pastime of Australia is swimming, so on Night One of the Olympics, the Americans, who had never lost the event at an Olympic Games, put their unbeaten streak on the line against a formidable Aussie quartet. In the buildup before the Games, American Gary Hall Jr. had half-jokingly said, "We're going to smash them like guitars." In the end, he couldn't catch Aussie star Ian Thorpe, who earlier in the night had won individual gold in the 400 free. After Thorpe touched the wall, Australian Michael Klim started playing air guitar to mock Hall and the Americans. To this day, that is the loudest roar of a crowd I have ever heard at any sporting event.

Steve Hirdt
Executive Vice President, Elias Sports Bureau

New York Yankees at Boston Red Sox, Fenway Park, Boston, Massachusetts, October 2, 1978

I was working for ABC, and we had all flown to Boston late Sunday night (after the Yankees lost to Cleveland's Rick Waits that day, necessitating the one-game tie-breaker playoff), except that Howard Cosell, one of our announcers, declined to attend in favor of staying in Washington to call that night's Cowboys-Redskins game. I remember that due to a technical malfunction we did not get on the air the batter-vs.-pitcher statistics for Carl Yastrzemski vs. Goose Gossage—a feature that I had brought to ABC's coverage of baseball—before Gossage got him to pop out to end the game. For the record, Yaz had been 10-for-23 before that out.

1986 American League Championship Series, Game 5, Boston Red Sox at California Angels, Anaheim Stadium, Anaheim, California, October 12, 1986

Maybe the greatest baseball game I've ever seen. The Angels needed one win to clinch a trip to their first World Series—and the first Series for their manager, Gene Mauch, after a lifetime of trying—and they held a three-run lead going to the top of the ninth. But Don Baylor cut the lead to one run with a two-run homer, and after a couple of pitching changes, Dave Henderson (playing for an injured Tony Armas) hit a two-out, two-strike homer to give Boston the lead.

But the game was just beginning: the Angels tied it in their time at bat and looked poised to win with the bases full and one out. But a back-of-the-bullpen guy named Steve Crawford got Doug DeCinces and Bobby Grich to end the inning, Jim Rice made a great catch at the fence off Gary Pettis's long drive in the tenth, and Henderson's sacrifice fly sent across what proved to be the game winner in the eleventh. Prior to that weekend, there had never been a postseason game in major league history won by a team that had been trailing by three or more runs going into the ninth inning. In Game 4, the Angels had won such a game, and in the classic Game 5, the Red Sox returned the favor.

Super Bowl XXV, Buffalo Bills vs. New York Giants, Tampa Stadium, Tampa, Florida, January 27, 1991

It was a fantastic game throughout: An early highlight was a great play by Giants quarterback Jeff Hostetler in the second quarter, when he tripped on a teammate's foot and was falling into his own end zone for a safety—but somehow warded off Bruce Smith, of all people, who was grabbing his arm trying to cause a fumble that would likely have resulted in a Buffalo touchdown. On the final drive, I remember using a graphic that showed that Scott Norwood had not had previous success on field-goal attempts of 40 or more yards on grass fields. A few minutes later: wide right.

1992 National League Championship Series, Game 7, Pittsburgh Pirates at Atlanta Braves, Fulton County Stadium, Atlanta, Georgia, October 14, 1992

I was in the CBS booth. Sean McDonough was our play-by-play announcer; Tim McCarver was the analyst. I remember that Sid Bream, one of the slowest Braves players, was the potential winning run at second base, and I urged Tim to say that the Braves should pinch run for him with a young Tom Glavine. Tim disagreed—Glavine's a pitcher, after all—and Bream scored the winning run, barely beating Barry Bonds's throw home (when Tim and I see each other, we still debate that play). Earlier in the series, I had seen Francisco Cabrera—the twenty-fifth man on the roster and someone whom even die-hard Braves fans would be hard-pressed to identify—approach President Carter's box seat prior to a game and ask for a photograph. After Cabrera was called off the bench in the ninth inning of Game 7 and got the winning hit with two out, I remember thinking that it would be Carter who would be trying to get a print of that photograph!

2004 NBA Western Conference Semifinals, Game 5, Los Angeles Lakers at San Antonio Spurs, SBC Center, San Antonio, Texas, May 13, 2004

With their 2004 Western Conference Semifinals series tied at two wins each, the Spurs and the Lakers battled in the closing moments of Game 5. Tim Duncan hit an impossible shot over Shaquille O'Neal with 0.4 seconds remaining in the fourth quarter to give the Spurs a one-point lead. But after a pair of timeouts (and after I encouraged our analyst, Doc Rivers, to explain the NBA rule that 0.4 seconds was enough time for a "catch-and-shoot" play), Fisher took the in-bounds pass and hit a turn-around game-winning shot, after which the Lakers ran off the court and huddled around a TV monitor in the hallway, while the on-court officials verified that the shot was good, confirming the 74–73 win.

Keith Jackson
Broadcaster, ABC Sports

The Rose Bowl, Pasadena, California

This is on my list not so much for the game as it is for the setting!

The stadium is settled in what an ole cowboy might call a "wash," which is an arroyo . . . Arroyo Seco, to be exact. Controls are in place to prevent the floods that once swept through, thus the reference to a wash. It is the history, the legend, the people, the city.

The first game was 1902, with Michigan and Stanford the first invitees. Fielding Yost's "point-a-minute" Wolverines hammered Stanford 49–0, and the Tournament of Roses folks decided to look elsewhere for a closing act. They tried chariot racing, but it was dusty and messy, and the second year the drivers and horse owners wanted more money and threatened a union. Then came ostrich racing—different, to be sure, but all that was done in when one of the cranky old birds kicked the chairman's wife in the stomach (that may well be a prime reason ostrich became an entree in Pasadena).

My first real interest in the Rose Bowl was probably the 1943 game between the Georgia Bulldogs and the UCLA Bruins. I was still a kid on the farm in West Georgia and listened to the broadcast on an old battery radio. Frankie Sinkwich, the Georgia tailback, won the Heisman Trophy that year, while Bob Waterfield was the quarterback and leader of the Bruins. Sinkwich came down with a pair of sprained ankles prior to the game, and a sophomore tailback named Charlie Trippi wound up the MVP, totaling 216 yards running and passing, as the Dawgs beat the Bruins, 9–0.

I wonder if that hundred feet of copper radio antenna is still hanging in that big old pecan tree. . . .

Washington vs. Leningrad Trud, Moscow, Russia, July 18, 1958

I was sports and special events director for KOMO-TV in Seattle, Washington. The University of Washington football program got caught in a slush-fund scandal, and the entire Husky athletic program was sanctioned. The rowing stewards who had sustained the crew program at Washington were incensed and, since they had their own property and wherewithal, sent their crew to Henley-on-Thames. It's a historic race of better than two hundred years and one of the most colorful events anywhere. I asked to go with them with a film cameraman to cover the races both on radio and film for delayed TV.

They met the Soviets in the Grand Challenge Final for eight-oared crews, and in a roaring thunderstorm the Soviets kicked 'em. But the broadcast went well with the BBC, and I had the chance to work with the BBC for some two months. It was really special since the legendary John Snagge was still there. Three days later a young man in a blue suit interrupted the Huskies' packing and offered them a chance to meet the Soviets again . . . in Moscow on July 18, 1958.

I set about exploring our going along, and after long and laborious negotiations, the Soviets surprisingly let us go along. During the week, while demonstrations were held outside the U.S. Embassy in Moscow, the Brits were sinking ships in the Suez, and U.S. Marines were flying into Lebanon, the Huskies hammered the same Soviet crew that had beaten them at Henley.

It was the first live sports broadcast from the Soviet Union to air in the United States. A bit of daring, a lot of help and luck, and some gritty oarsmen made it all very special in my life.

UCLA at USC, Los Angeles Coliseum, Los Angeles, California, November 18, 1967

The Pac-8 Conference Championship, National Championship, a Rose Bowl bid, and the Heisman Trophy were all on the table in this one game. USC won the game, 21–20, on two great runs by O.J. Simpson, but UCLA quarterback Gary Beban won the Heisman. It was a truly great college football game; I believe sixteen of the players from that game played on Sunday at one time or another.

1972 Summer Olympics, Men's Swimming, Dante Swimming Pool, Munich, Germany, August 28–September 4, 1972

Mark Spitz won four individual and three relay-race gold medals in swimming at the Munich Olympics. It was by far the most dominant performance ever in swimming and made him a household name, probably forever. Fortunately, all the water competition had been completed before the terrorists broke into the Olympic Village and killed the members of the Israeli team. Spitz was sent out of the country almost within hours of the attack and has done quite well in business in California.

1980 Winter Olympics, Men's Speed Skating, Lake Placid Speed-Skating Oval, Lake Placid, New York, February 15–23, 1980

Eric Heiden won five individual gold medals, setting an Olympic record and winning every race. It was and remains the most completely dominant performance in Olympic Speed Skating history. He almost missed the final race, the grueling 10,000 meters, but while racing to the outdoor skating stadium, he ate half a loaf of bread and drank a quart of milk. He got to the Oval, laced up his skates, warmed up, and set another Olympic record. Eric is one of the most remarkable athletes and people I have ever known. He graduated from Stanford Medical School, interned with Dr. James Andrews in Birmingham, Alabama, and is now at the top of the orthopedics staff at UC Davis hospital near Sacramento.

Gus Johnson
Broadcaster, CBS Sports/MSG Network

1996 NCAA Men's Basketball Tournament, First Round, Princeton vs. UCLA, RCA Dome, Indianapolis, Indiana, March 14, 1996

No one gave Princeton a chance to win this game. The UCLA team were the defending national champs and still had a lot of great talent. Princeton, though, came out in this game and, from the very beginning, had no fear. They ran their offense and had the feeling their system was going to cause the talented athletes of UCLA a lot of problems because they had more discipline than the Bruins. They ran their backdoor cuts and got lots of easy baskets, and, more importantly, were hitting three-pointers. And I mean *everyone* was hitting three-pointers that day. It was almost as if every player who stepped onto the floor that day for the Tigers played his best game ever.

All of a sudden, we get down to the end of the game, and Princeton is still in it. The Tigers came out of a time-out with a chance to win the game, and you could see, as they came off the bench, they had this look on their faces that said, "We aren't losing this game." And they didn't. Steve Goodrich threw a backdoor cut to a freshman named Gabe Lewullis. It was low, and Lewullis scooped it up like Derek Jeter and laid it in with 3.9 seconds left.

The whole building was on its feet. There was a giant vibration throughout the building, with everyone not from UCLA rooting for Princeton. UCLA wasn't able to score before time ran out, and it was over, 43–41. It was the most unbelievable thing I had ever seen. It was my first year working the NCAA Tournament, and I'll never forget thinking to myself, "I'll tell you what, Gus. If the games are all like this, you are really going to like this job!"

Andrew Golota vs. Riddick Bowe, Madison Square Garden, New York, New York, July 11, 1996

The fight was at Madison Square Garden, and there was a huge Polish representation in the arena rooting for Golota. Bowe was from the Brownsville section of Brooklyn, and if the entire Polish community of New York seemed to be there, it also felt like anyone who had ever touched down in Brownsville was there, too. I was there as a fan, just to sit and enjoy the fight. Golota was just a bull, a massive man with a massive head and body, sort of like Ivan Drago—everything on him was huge. He had lots of skill, though, and lots of experience.

Golota was just destroying Bowe until he hit Bowe low. Golota was winning by so much; he didn't even need to go to the body. The Polish fans in the arena were getting excited, with their guy winning big. Bowe was just about ready to go down, and Golota hit him low. BAM! Bowe went down. Rock Newman, Bowe's manager, jumped in the ring, and from where I was sitting, I could see Newman whisper in Bowe's ear, "Don't get up." Bowe stayed down, and Golota got DQ'd. Then, out of nowhere, one of the members of Bowe's entourage jumped in the ring with his walkie-talkie and started hitting Golota in the head with it. A riot basically broke out in the ring at this point.

I looked around, and the Brownsville fans and the Polish fans were getting it on. They were scrapping on all three sides of the ring except the one I was on. Chairs were flying, dudes were getting sucker punched. I looked up in the stands, and the same thing was happening in the upper levels over the Garden. It was a brawl. I was sitting behind the HBO broadcasting crew, and those guys were ducking under their table . . . except for George Foreman, who did not budge. He stood up, turned around, and, rumor has it, some guy in a wild fit was fighting and turned around and was ready to throw a punch, saw it was George Foreman, and Foreman said to him, "Son, don't even think about it," and the guy went and hit someone else. With all of this going on, here comes New York City mayor Rudy Giuliani and the NYPD riot squad into the Garden, and they calmed the whole building down in a New York minute, Giuliani leading the charge. The whole night was just a freak show. Sports have a way of bringing out the best in people—or the worst. That particular night, it brought out the worst in everybody except the police. I gained a lot of respect for Mayor Giuliani that night.

1999 NBA Eastern Conference, First Round, Game 5, New York Knicks at Miami Heat, Miami Arena, Miami, Florida, May 16, 1999

The Heat came out to James Brown's song "Payback" before the game:

I can do wheelin', I can do dealin', but I don't do no damn squealin'.
I can dig rappin', I can dig scrappin', but I can't dig that backstabbin'.

And here comes Tim Hardaway and Alonzo Mourning out on the floor. They wanted to beat the Knicks so bad it was crazy. Bruce Bowen had been talking trash to Allan Houston, because he had been guarding him so well all series. Patrick Ewing was a hero that night. Whatever ill feeling I had about Patrick Ewing over the years, that one particular game proved to me he was a great champion and a great winner. His Achilles tendon was shot. He was limping up and down the floor like Willis Reed and finished with 22 points and 11 rebounds.

The fans were on the Knicks the whole game, but they kept battling, and the game just kept going back and forth. Houston was having an awful day, but the game came down to the end, and he popped out at the top of the key, a little fake to the left, right-hand dribble down the lane, and just floated up a little teardrop. That sucker stayed up on the rim for an eternity. And then it just went off the front rim and in, and that's it. Knicks win by one, 78–77. That's the game.

Jacksonville Jaguars at Cleveland Browns, Cleveland Browns Stadium, Cleveland, Ohio, December 16, 2001

This started out as a normal football game. The Jags had lots of stars, and the Browns weren't very good, but it was a competitive game. The Browns had fallen behind and were mounting a comeback, when there was a questionable call with forty-eight seconds left in the game.

All of a sudden, the crowd turned on the officials on the field, to the point where I thought I was watching hooligans at a soccer game. The fans got angry and had been drinking beer out of plastic bottles. One fan took his bottle and threw it on the field. That was all it took for all hell to break loose. The bottles all of a sudden became projectiles. These bottles just started flying onto the field to the point where the officials couldn't stop it; they couldn't do a thing about it. The Jags were huddled close to one of the end zones and were just getting pummeled. It got to the point where both teams had to move toward the center of the field because the officials were trying to establish some kind of order. There was nothing doing, though.

It got so bad, and so many bottles were on the field, that the officials had to call the game. I had never seen an NFL game called because of rowdiness. As the Jaguars headed off the field, they just got hammered, and I mean hammered. Thankfully, they were wearing helmets and shoulder pads. It was the most bizarre thing I've ever seen in pro football. It is always going to be known, especially in Cleveland, as The Bottle-Throwing Game. It is just a good thing no one got seriously hurt, most importantly, all the kids in the stands.

2006 NCAA Men's Basketball Tournament Sweet Sixteen, Gonzaga vs. UCLA, Oakland Arena, Oakland, California, March 23, 2006

This game was over. Adam Morrison and Gonzaga were just killing UCLA. The Bruins had no offense and were losing by as much as 17 at one point. This game was over.

But all of a sudden, the Bruins started hitting shots, D-ing up, hitting shots, D-ing up, hitting shots, D-ing up, and the next thing my partner Len Elmore and I know, we looked up and they were down by one. Gonzaga got ready to inbound with 19.7 seconds left, and you figure they will get fouled, make their free throws since they are a good free-throw-shooting team, and win, right? Wrong. They inbounded to Morrison, but he didn't get fouled and instead threw a cross-court pass to J. P. Batista, and Jordan Farmar came over and stole it from him. He passed it inside to freshman Luc Richard Mbah a Moute (I couldn't even pronounce his name—I just called him "the freshman" because I didn't want mess it up; I knew this was going to be one of those historic calls), and he laid it up to go ahead, 73–71, with eight seconds on the clock.

Morrison just melted down on the court, breaking down in tears before the game was even technically over because he knew the game had just ended. Gonzaga got caught sleeping, and UCLA took advantage to come back and win the game. I love the kid for crying, because it showed just how much that game meant to him.

Daryl Johnston
Broadcaster, FOX Sports

The 1992 Masters, Augusta National Golf Club, Augusta, Georgia, April 9–12, 1992; the 1993 Masters, Augusta National Golf Club, April 8–11, 1993; and the 1994 Masters, Augusta National Golf Club, April 7–10, 1994

Anybody who is a golf fan has to go to Augusta. Nothing on TV does it justice, not even Hi Def, although that is getting closer. As a child, I used to sit and watch guys miss two-foot putts and wonder how that could happen, but after seeing the greens at Augusta up close, with the undulations and the pin placements, you wonder how the golfers *make* the putts. In the three years I went to the Masters and walked the course, I never saw one weed, one piece of trash or one pine needle out of its bed. The grounds are absolutely pristine. It is pure golf.

But the coolest thing I saw there was on a Sunday morning at the 18th green. All these chairs were set up around the green with no one in them. I asked my friend what that was all about, and he told me that people get up really early Sunday morning, put their chairs down, then go to church and brunch and come back to the golf course afterwards. When they get back in the afternoon, the chairs are still there, and no one is sitting in them.

1994 Indianapolis 500, Indianapolis Motor Speedway, Indianapolis, Indiana, May 29, 1994

This is another event that TV doesn't do justice. You really need to be there in person to appreciate the speed these cars are going. The year I went, they made an adjustment to the track in preparation for a new NASCAR race to be held there, and cars couldn't go into the turn three-wide any more, forcing the cars into lines as they hit the turns (which angered a lot of race fans, who thought this made the Indy 500 more like NASCAR). It took me ten to fifteen laps to be able to pick a car coming into Turn 3 and see who it was before it headed down the straightaway and into Turn 1. We went down near the track a couple of times just as the cars were coming by, and it was amazing how fast they were going. I used to watch the race as a kid, and they would have that one camera on the straightaway, so you could see and hear the cars go whizzing by. But TV never really captures just how long that straightaway is, and you need to see it in person to believe it.

1998 Australian Open, Second Round, Venus Williams vs. Serena Williams, Rod Laver Arena, Melbourne, Australia, January 21, 1998

My wife and I were staying at the same hotel as the Williams sisters in Melbourne and were having breakfast the morning of the match at the table right next to them. The amazing part is how big they really are—as we were walking out past their table, they were starting to stand up, and I still think to this day that I was looking at Venus eye-to-eye. There was so much media attention surrounding the match, since it was the first time they were going to be playing against each other, that it was easy to forget that they are also sisters. They actually moved the match to center court, and there were some people that weren't happy it was moved, but Rod Laver Arena was full to watch them play. It was neat to watch Serena start to follow in her big sister's footsteps.

Seattle Seahawks at Dallas Cowboys, Texas Stadium, Irving, Texas, October 27, 2002

I actually wasn't supposed to work this game for FOX that weekend, but with Emmitt Smith closing in on the NFL's all-time rushing record, I requested a switch so I could be there. The Cowboys were going to be on the road the next two games, and I knew Emmitt really wanted to break the record at home so that the Dallas fans could be there to witness it. Everybody always asks me why I came back from my first neck surgery, and it was to be on the field the day Emmitt broke the record. When I got hurt the second time and knew I wasn't going to be on the field with him, working this game provided me with the next best thing.

When Emmitt started to get close to the record during the game, I left the broadcast booth and went down to the sideline. Without being on the field, this was as close as I could have gotten. After he broke the record, there were so many people around him to celebrate that it seemed as though it would be impossible to get near him, and I knew he wanted to see his wife, Pat, and share the moment with his family. But all of a sudden, the mass of people standing between the two of us separated, and we had a direct line of sight to each other. That is when he came over and we embraced. This was a very special moment for me, on a historic day in NFL history.

2005 Gaelic Football Championships Quarterfinal, Tyrone vs. Dublin, Croke Park, Dublin, Ireland, August 13, 2005

Seeing this was just awesome. My wife and I were in Ireland on a tour, and our driver was a huge Gaelic football fan. He started telling us about it, and we decided to go check it out. The best part about the sport is that it is all amateur. The players are firemen, policemen, or doctors, and this is just a hobby for them, and they all play on club teams. Seventy-two thousand people were there that day for the game, which is amazing when you remember that it is an amateur sport.

The field is the size of three football fields, and the game is part soccer, part football. The athleticism and stamina of the players is unbelievable. And, as it is with most European sporting events, the fans are up all game, singing and chanting . . . all with no alcohol being served in the stands. At halftime, everyone gets a good meal, not American stadium fare like hot dogs and nachos. You go outside and eat your meal and drink your beers, then go back in. The game ended in a tie, and since there is no overtime, that is how it ended. Two weeks later, the teams got together and did it all over again.

Steve Jones
Broadcaster, ESPN

1984 NBA Finals, Game 4, Boston Celtics at Los Angeles Lakers, The Forum, Inglewood, California, June 6, 1984

The Kevin McHale foul on Kurt Rambis in this game changed the entire tone of the series, and Boston came back to win the Finals. The Lakers were clearly the superior team that year and were playing that way until that one physical moment altered the entire attitude of the Celtics. They became more aggressive and more hostile, and the Lakers began to sag, then ultimately lost. This one play turned the whole thing around.

1984 Summer Olympics, Men's Athletics, Los Angeles Coliseum, Los Angeles, California, August 4–11, 1984

No one since Jesse Owens had ever attempted to do what Carl Lewis was trying—the 100, the 200, the long jump, and 4x100 relay. Lewis was easily the best in the world, and it was exciting to see if he would be able to duplicate this feat. His entire approach to doing this was memorable. He was so focused in the 100 that it felt like there was no one else running that day, and he ended up winning by a record margin. Both of the sprints he won were done with such ease and authority that it was just a special time to be in the LA Coliseum.

1992 Summer Olympics, Men's Basketball, Palau d'Esports de Badalona, Badalona, Spain, July 26–August 8, 1992

This was more about the world's reaction to the Dream Team in Barcelona in 1992. Not the games, but the crowds. When you got to the arena, it was all flashbulbs. Everyone in the arena was taking pictures. People just couldn't get enough of this team. The opponents were more concerned with getting pictures taken with Michael Jordan, Magic Johnson, and everyone else. No one was there for the competitive effort. They were there to see these twelve individuals. It was an awesome event that will never be seen again, but there was never any doubt about the outcome. Everyone knew what was going to happen, including the teams playing against the U.S. On the train to Barcelona, all I heard was people who wanted to see the Dream Team. There were police escorts all the time, and they always played the featured game of the day to make sure as many people could see them as possible. It was a defining moment in international sports competition and a defining moment for spectators. The fans were in the company of royalty.

1995 NBA Western Conference Semifinals, Game 7, Houston Rockets at Phoenix Suns, America West Arena, Phoenix, Arizona, May 20, 1995

The Rockets were the defending NBA champs but had qualified with a low seed for the playoffs and had to play Game 7 of this series on the road in Phoenix. They fell behind three games to one in the series but fought back to force the deciding game. Charles Barkley got hurt, and Phoenix's little man, Kevin Johnson, put the team on his back and carried them as far as he could carry them, until Houston won, 115–114, on improbable hero Mario Elie's famous three-pointer from the corner and kiss.

I did this game for NBC, and before the game, we sat down with Johnson, and he polled the room. There wasn't a person in there, with the exception of myself, that said Houston was going to win. Everyone else told him Phoenix would win until he got to me, when I told him, "Kevin, you are done." He had an incredible game, scoring 46 points, and if Barkley had played, they might have won.

1999 NBA Eastern Conference Finals, Game 3, Indiana Pacers at New York Knicks, Madison Square Garden, New York, New York, June 5, 1999

What strikes me about the famous Larry Johnson four-point play wasn't that Indiana shouldn't have fouled or that Johnson made the shot. It was the reaction of all of the New York fans. In unison, they were all on their feet at the same time when that ball left Johnson's hand. Rarely do you get a crowd up and united in one big moment. When the ball went in, it was as if the fans knew it was going to go in. It was such an improbable moment.

Harry Kalas

Broadcaster, Philadelphia Phillies

Recipient of Baseball Hall of Fame's Ford C. Frick Award, 2002

Houston Astros at Cincinnati Reds, Crosley Field, Cincinnati, Ohio, April 30 and May 1, 1969

One night, Jim Maloney pitched a no-hitter for Cincinnati against the Houston Astros, and the very next night, Don Wilson of the Astros returned the favor by no-hitting the Reds. Wilson was an angry young man but was a very tough pitcher who pitched two no-hitters for Houston that I was able to call. Naturally, the fans in Cincinnati were really into the Maloney no-hitter but were stunned the next night at Wilson's performance.

Working with Rich Ashburn, 1971–1997

I think about His Whiteness every single day. He was just a great partner to work with and my best friend in life. We had a tremendous rapport. Besides a great knowledge of the game, he brought humor into the broadcast and was quite a character and a lot of fun to be around. Whenever a game would go late or into extra innings, Rich would get hungry. So he would say something like, "I wonder if the people at Celebre's Pizza are listening." Within twenty minutes, we would have pizzas delivered to the booth. This went on for several months, and eventually Phillies management called him in and told him that he had to stop doing that, since Celebre's wasn't a team sponsor.

Around a week later, it was another late game, and Whitey decided to do a birthday announcement, which we often did. This one was, "We have special birthday wishes tonight to the Celebre's twins, Plain and Pepperoni." Sure enough, that is what got delivered not much later.

1980 National League Championship Series, Game 5, Philadelphia Phillies at Houston Astros, Houston Astrodome, Houston, Texas, October 12, 1980

It was a gut-wrenching series between Houston and Philadelphia. In those days, the championship series was only five games, and four of the five games went into extra innings. In Game 5, with the series tied at two games each, it was Nolan Ryan pitching for the Astros against the Phillies' Marty Bystrom. Things didn't look good for Philadelphia, but they were able to pull it out. Once they won the League Championship Series, there was no doubt in my mind the Phillies were going to beat Kansas City in the World Series. One of the reasons I love the Philadelphia fans is that, in those years, the World Series was a network exclusive, and Richie Ashburn and I were unable to call the games. Phillies fans let themselves be heard, though, and went to the commissioner's office and the networks and told them how much they wanted to hear us call the games. The next year the rule was changed, and in 1983 Whitey and I were able to call the Series against Baltimore.

Philadelphia Phillies at Pittsburgh Pirates, Three Rivers Stadium, Pittsburgh, Pennsylvania, April 18, 1987

To have the opportunity to call the entire Hall-of-Fame career of Mike Schmidt was an honor. Michael Jack (I used his middle name a lot when I called games) was not only special offensively, but for a big man, he was very agile and was a great defensive third baseman. I was lucky enough to call all but a few of his 548 home runs. For homer number 500, you knew it was going to be coming, but you can't really prepare for something like that. It was just a thrill to call it, but it was also a meaningful home run, because it gave the Phillies the lead in the game against Pittsburgh. When his teammates came out to meet him at the plate, it was a touching moment.

1993 Philadelphia Phillies

The 1993 Phillies were a real cast of characters—Lenny Dykstra, John Kruk, my current partner Larry Andersen, Mitch Williams, Darren Daulton. This was a fun-loving group of guys that played hard and enjoyed themselves, but Daulton was the real leader of the bunch and made sure to keep them focused once game time came. He would let guys know just what to do and was an excellent team leader.

Peter King

Senior Writer, Sports Illustrated

Super Bowl XXI, New York Giants vs. Denver Broncos, Rose Bowl, Pasadena, California, January 25, 1987

"Tell me something, Charlie," Bill Parcells said from the back of the car the day after the Giants' 39–20 win over the Broncos. "Was Ditka as happy as I am right now? Was Ditka this happy a year ago?" NFL security chief Charlie Jackson, driving the car to the morning-after press conference, chuckled and said, "No, Coach, he wasn't."

I remember this game for a lot of reasons. My father, a fervent Giants fan, died a few months before the game, and I remember crying in the press box on a pristinely beautiful southern California day. I remember Phil Simms playing the best clutch game of a player that I'd ever seen: 22 of 25, with one drop and one flubbed catchable ball. I remember the glee of the fans who'd traveled three thousand miles to see this game, many of them crying in the stands after the game. Sports can lift jaded people to surprising heights, and this was one of those days that a sports event did just that.

Super Bowl XXXI, Green Bay Packers vs. New England Patriots, Louisiana Superdome, New Orleans, Louisiana, January 26, 1997

This I remember mostly because of the postgame scene. I needed time with Brett Favre, the quarterback of the 35–21 Green Bay victory, for *Sports Illustrated*, and he was as mobbed as any athlete I ever remember after a game. I followed him to his hotel. At the Fairmont downtown, I spotted him among the three thousand people at the Packer postgame party in the ballroom upstairs, and I said, "Give me five minutes. I have to have it." He said okay.

We looked around, and we saw a fire escape, and I opened the door to a back staircase. There was a luggage cart on the landing of the stairwell, and we sat there for forty-five minutes, him loving every minute of dissecting the game. "I remember lying in bed this morning, feeling sort of sick because I've been under the weather," he said. "And I'm watching the NFL Films channel on TV. There's Steve Sabol talking about one of the 49er Super Bowl wins. And I'm thinking, 'I hope one day in about forty years when Steve Sabol's 106 he talks about the game Brett Favre played in New Orleans.'" I told him: "He'll remember it. A lot of people will."

1999 American League Championship Series, Game 3, New York Yankees at Boston Red Sox, Fenway Park, Boston, Massachusetts, October 16, 1999

I've never been in a more bloodthirsty environment. From waking up in the morning and seeing the back page of the *Boston Herald* treating Clemens–Pedro Martinez in Fenway like Ali-Frazier in Manila to arriving at the park and hearing everyone in full throat when Clemens left the Yankee dugout to warm up, this was the most unforgettable sports events I've ever attended. And because I attended the game as a fan—a Red Sox fan—and not as a writer, I could revel in the slaughter. The chants, the passion, the sheer joy. . . . As a Red Sox follower, I've never had a day like it, and that includes the day they won the World Series in 2004.

2003 Essex County Softball Quarterfinals, Cedar Grove at Montclair, Montclair High School, Montclair, New Jersey, May 3, 2003

I'm big into high school sports. Always have been, particularly when it came to my two daughters, Laura and Mary Beth. On this early-May Saturday afternoon, before about four hundred people at our home Montclair diamond, Mary Beth, a junior southpaw, faced off against one of her good friends and softball-lesson partner, all-county senior righty Kaitlyn Sweeney. It was 2–2 after the regulation seven innings, 2–2 after eight, nine, ten, eleven, and twelve.

Mary Beth got out of two bases-loaded jams in extras and now was due to lead off in the bottom of the thirteenth. "I was finished," she said. "I couldn't have gone out there again. My arm was dead." Understandable after 167 pitches. Mary Beth never swings at the first pitch, a maddening tendency to her coach/father, but the thing was, Kaitlyn knew that too. She grooved a 59-mph fastball. Mary Beth ripped it to deep rightfield. Triple. She scored on a bloop single. Ball game. Mob scene on the Montclair side. Tears and thrown gloves on the Cedar Grove side. Thrill of victory. Agony of defeat. It happens thousands of times every day in America.

2004 New Jersey High School Field Hockey, North Sectional Final, Morristown vs. Montclair, Millburn High School, Millburn, New Jersey, November 10, 2004

Okay, enough of the high school stuff. Sorry. It's my list. These are my thrills. I'd watched two daughters play seven years of high school field hockey, and on a bitterly cold November afternoon in Millburn, New Jersey, as the clock wound down and only five minutes remained with Morristown up 1–0, I kept thinking, "This is it. This is the King family's last field hockey game." With 4:45 left in regulation, Montclair got a corner, which means its players line up in a semicircle in front of the goal, with the ball rolled from the goal line to one player, who takes a shot on goal as the defense charges from the goal line. It's got to be done quickly, obviously. Mary Beth, a midfielder, was at the top of the circle. Her best friend on the team, fellow senior Courtney DeBlis, walked up to her and said, just before the play began: "We can't go out this way! We can't lose! It's not our time!"

The ball was shot to Mary Beth, who settled it and shifted the ball slightly right to avoid the rushing defenders. She wound up, and BANG! The ball thudded against the back of the cage. Delirium. It went to overtime, and Montclair won 2–1. Hard to imagine any pro team could ever be more gleeful than the Montclair eleven on this day.

Tim Kurkjian

Broadcaster, ESPN

1986 NBA All-Star Saturday, Reunion Arena, Dallas, Texas, February 9, 1986

This was before the Slam Dunk Contest had gotten old, and it was the first year of the 3-Point Shot Contest. I was the baseball writer at the *Dallas Morning News*, but I was, and always will be, a lover of basketball. What made this day so great was that 5-foot-7 Spud Webb, who is 2 inches taller than I am, won the Slam Dunk Contest over, among others, Dominique Wilkins, whose violent dunks had to be seen to be believed. Webb didn't win because he was so short; he won because he deserved it: I've never seen anyone jump like that in my life.

What was equally inspiring was that Larry Bird, who is nearly 6-foot-10, won the 3-Point Shot Contest. As he let go of the final ball, he raised his right index finger in the air, signaling that it was going in, and he was going to win. He won ten thousand dollars making a bunch of shots, and nothing made Larry Bird happier than making that kind of money for shooting a basketball. In the postcontest press conference, Bird looked at the *Boston Globe*'s Dan Shaughnessy, whom he hadn't talked to in months in a mini-dispute, and yelled, "I just won the 3-Point Shot Contest, Shaughnessy—put *that* in your newspaper."

1986 American League Championship Series, Game 5, Boston Red Sox at California Angels, Anaheim Stadium, Anaheim, California, October 12, 1986

It was, and still is, the greatest game I've seen in twenty-five years of covering baseball. The Angels were three outs away from going to the World Series for the first time in franchise history, and three outs away from haunted manager Gene Mauch's first trip. The Red Sox, no strangers to horrifying losses, took the lead in the ninth on a stunning home run by David Henderson off Donnie Moore, who years later would take his own life. After the Angels tied it in the bottom of the ninth, the Red Sox won in extra innings, completing a game that was filled with sensational feats and extraordinary stories of triumph and heartbreak. The game was attended by my wife, Kathy, who is no great baseball fan. She went by herself. She sat in the top row of the stadium. When it was over, she asked me, naively, "That was a pretty good game, wasn't it?"

1986 World Series, Game 6, Boston Red Sox at New York Mets, Shea Stadium, Queens, New York, October 25, 1986

My story was in. All they had to do was press the button at the *Baltimore Sun* and my account of the Red Sox winning the World Series for the first time since 1918 would officially go to print. Then the Mets mounted one of the most amazing rallies of all time, scoring three times with two out to force a Game 7. When the ball rolled through Bill Buckner's legs, it was approximately 12:30 A.M. on a Sunday, about fifteen minutes from the final edition. Shea Stadium erupted around me as I sat in the auxiliary press box down the leftfield line. Shea was old and leaky even back then, and as I began to tear up one story and begin writing what would be the most important game story I had ever written, I was doused with what seemed like a keg of beer from the fans in the stands above me. With beer literally dripping from my hair, I wrote my story and got it in on time. I can't remember much about it; all I can remember is the first paragraph: Amazin'.

1992 National League Championship Series, Game 7, Pittsburgh Pirates at Atlanta Braves, Fulton County Stadium, Atlanta, Georgia, October 14, 1992

This would be the Pirates' last chance to get to the World Series for a long, long time. Everyone knew it. Soon, Bobby Bonilla would be leaving, and Barry Bonds would follow. The Pirates led the Braves entering the ninth inning, but with the bases loaded and two out, down by one run, up came pinch hitter Francisco Cabrera, the last player on the Atlanta bench, the man whose only duty that night was supposed to be catching the ceremonial first pitch. Instead, Cabrera hit a two-run single between third base and shortstop, scoring Sid Bream just ahead of Bonds's throw from left. It was, and still is, the only postseason Game 7 series that ended on a hit that turned a loss into a victory. As Atlanta Fulton County Stadium exploded around me, I looked at my writing colleague from *Sports Illustrated*, Steve Rushin, the only genius that I've met in my life. He said two words: "Abra Cabrera."

California Angels at Baltimore Orioles, Camden Yards, Baltimore, Maryland, September 6, 1995

It was the most emotional night I've ever spent at a major league ballpark. It wasn't just a night about baseball; it was about family, roots in a city, discipline, commitment, and all things good. An hour before Cal Ripken would break Lou Gehrig's record for consecutive games played, Bob Elliott, a writer friend from Toronto who had just arrived in Baltimore, and hadn't been a part of the week that led to 2,131, came to me and said, "I don't get it. I don't see it. I don't feel it." I told him, "Check back with me in the bottom of the fifth." After Ripken broke the record when the game became official after the top of the fifth inning, he made an unforgettable circling of the ballpark, during which he shook the hands of fans, teammates, and opponents, patted his heart several times, and hugged his wife and children. Much of the crowd was weeping. When play was resumed almost thirty minutes later, Bob Elliott came to me, with tears in his eyes, and said, "Okay, I get it."

Wayne Larrivee
Broadcaster, Green Bay Packers

Chicago Bears at Kansas City Chiefs, Arrowhead Stadium, Kansas City, Missouri, November 8, 1981

I was broadcasting for the Chiefs at the time, and Walter Payton had a run in this game that you see in all of his highlight films. It was overcast and rainy, and he just spun and pinballed his way through Marv Levy's Chiefs. It was one of those type runs that he became famous for during his playing days. The

Bears won in overtime, 16–13, but Payton singlehandedly took the game away from a Chiefs team that was contending for the first time in many years.

Chicago Bears at Miami Dolphins, Orange Bowl, Miami, Florida, December 2, 1985

I was with the Bears, and this was the only game they lost that season. It was a Monday night at the Orange Bowl in Miami. Dan Marino and the Dolphins played one of those phenomenal games that night. At one point in the second half, as the Bears were trying to come back, the Dolphins had the ball and Marino threw a pass that glanced off Dan Hampton but was caught by Mark Clayton and turned into a touchdown. This was when the Dolphins started bringing the players from their 1972 unbeaten team to the sidelines whenever someone got close to going undefeated. Little did we know in the broadcast booth that at halftime Mike Ditka and Buddy Ryan almost came to blows.

Another adjunct to this game was that the next day, after we got back to Chicago really late that night after the game, they shot the "Super Bowl Shuffle," which was ironic, since they were coming off their first loss of the season.

Super Bowl XX, Chicago Bears vs. New England Patriots, Louisiana Superdome, New Orleans, Louisiana, January 26, 1986

The game began with a Walter Payton fumble, which New England turned into a field goal. For weeks, everyone in Chicago was holding their breath, waiting for the Bears to blow this, because that was the mentality in Chicago since the 1969 Cubs. Everyone just assumed the Chicago teams were going to get close and lose. So the Bears got off to this kind of start, and everyone was thinking, "Well, here it comes." Of course, what happened after that is the stuff that legend is made of.

1997 NBA Finals, Game 5, Chicago Bulls at Utah Jazz, Delta Center, Salt Lake City, Utah, June 11, 1997

The Bulls were staying in Park City, Utah, during the Finals, and Michael Jordan had acute food poisoning. No one thought he was going to be able to play in this game, but not only did he play, he led the Bulls to a crucial series-turning victory. This was the most incredible performance I've ever seen, given the circumstances. Here's a guy who is seemingly close to death, and he comes out and puts forth this kind of performance. Jordan did this kind of thing a lot in his career, but I don't think he ever did it in a situation like this, where so much was at stake. Of all the games I saw him play, this was the one that stood out the most.

Green Bay Packers at Minnesota Vikings, Metrodome, Minneapolis, Minnesota, December 24, 2004

It was Christmas Eve in the Metrodome, and this was a winner-take-all game. The winner would take the NFC North and earn a home game in the playoffs two weeks later. The Metrodome was always a house of horrors for the Packers—even their Super Bowl teams lost there. The Packers had won earlier in the season in Green Bay, 34–31. This time, it was an incredible performance by both teams offensively, but in the end, we saw the worst and the best of Brett Favre. He threw an interception to Chris Claiborne that gave Minnesota a 31–24 lead with around eight minutes to go. Favre then marshaled the Pack downfield and hit Donald Driver in the end zone to tie the game. The Packers got the ball back again, and Favre drove them again to the doorstep of victory. Ryan Longwell hit a field goal as time expired to win it, 34–31, and give the Packers their third straight division title.

What is interesting about that game is that no one talks about it in Packers' lore. It was totally and completely nullified by a loss to the Vikings in the playoffs in Lambeau Field two weeks later, but it was an incredible moment. A week after the game, Mike Sherman told me it was a "program game" for both teams—it was a wonderful boost for the Packers and a setback for the Vikings. Of course, a lot of Packers fans never saw the game . . . they were in church for Christmas Eve.

Dan LeBatard

Columnist, Miami Herald

1993 World Series, Game 6, Philadelphia Phillies at Toronto Blue Jays, Skydome, Toronto, Canada, October 23, 1993

I've covered a number of great World Series moments. I could make this entire list about just moments and games in that Minnesota-Atlanta World Series of 1991. I could write a chapter about seeing Barry Bonds get within a couple of innings of his only championship in Anaheim. In the playoffs, I've gotten to witness the silence and fear in Chicago after Steve Bartman and the joy in Atlanta after Sid Bream hobbled home on Francisco Cabrera's single to left. But nothing matches the feeling and finality of a World Series and a season ending on a home run, as this did on Joe Carter's homer. You don't get to see many of those. The weight and size of the moment makes it hard to digest as it happens. Stakes make everything bigger. And you don't get much bigger than one pitch, one swing, one moment ending a season.

1997 National League Championship Series, Game 5, Atlanta Braves at Florida Marlins, Joe Robbie Stadium, Miami, Florida, October 12, 1997

This story transcended sports for anyone Cuban growing up in Miami. Livan Hernandez defected from Cuba after he had to steal detergent from hotels in international cities because his own national team was so poor, and he carried around the shame of that. When he defected so young, his mother almost had a nervous breakdown, imagining her son wandering the streets of America with his suitcases, lost. A lot of Cubans recognized his story. So to see him strike out fifteen and beat one of the best pitchers ever in a playoff game and throw a complete game and stagger off the mound exhausted on the final strikeout was a triumph for a lot of us. It was the only time I've ever cried on my keyboard on deadline.

1999 NBA Eastern Conference First Round, Game 5, New York Knicks at Miami Heat, Miami Arena, Miami, Florida, May 16, 1999

Heartbreak is every bit as interesting to me as triumph. To hear the silence and the pain in Miami's arena when Allan Houston's shot bounced on that rim and everyone in the place realized what it meant—that Pat Riley would have to blow up this team and that the enemy could be heard celebrating on the home floor of another wrecked Miami season. Afterward, Alonzo Mourning, in uniform, found Riley weeping at his desk in his office and demanded that Riley "do his damn job" by going to speak to the broken team in the locker room. The view from there made watching Riley, Mourning, and the Heat win the championship in 2006 behind infant Dwyane Wade all the more interesting.

2001 World Series, Games 4 and 5, Arizona Diamondbacks at New York Yankees, Yankee Stadium, Bronx, New York, October 31–November 1, 2001

I don't remember ever being so afraid that a stadium was going to fall on top of me. The home runs by Tino Martinez to tie Game 4 in the bottom of the ninth and by Scott Brosius to tie Game 5 in the bottom of the ninth, after 9/11, made Yankee Stadium shake in a way I've never felt a big building move before. I don't mean metaphorically. I mean actually. I was trying to write while the foundation around me seemed to be moving from all the noise and celebration. And in the middle of it, the reliever who gave up both homers, Byung-Hyun Kim, looked so clearly defeated, even though there were more pitches to be thrown, that Mark Grace came to the mound from first base and didn't so much have to console him as he had to physically hold him up.

1997 World Series, Game 7, Cleveland Indians at Florida Marlins, Pro Player Stadium, Miami, Florida, October 26, 1997; and 2003 World Series, Game 6, Florida Marlins at New York Yankees, Yankee Stadium, Bronx, New York, October 25, 2003

I'm stuck here. There are a bunch of moments I want to cram in, so I'll narrow it down to two, since I can't seem to choose between the 1997 and 2003 Marlins championships. One involved Game 7 and extra innings and Edgar Renteria ending everything with a swing in the loudest South Florida I've ever heard. The other involved Josh Beckett and Game 6 in the quietest Yankee Stadium I've ever heard. It was tough to leave out the Ohio State–Miami national championship football game, George Foreman becoming the oldest heavyweight champ ever, any Tyson fight in his prime, or the Rams-Patriots and Rams-Titans Super Bowl, though.

Will Leitch
Editor, Deadspin

Penn State at Illinois, Memorial Stadium, Champaign, Illinois, November 12, 1994

I've never had the good fortune to rush the field after my team won. In this age of confiscated airplane liquids, I doubt security will allow me to do so again (trying it at Yankee Stadium will certainly get me shot by a rooftop sniper). I was very close once.

It seems like decades ago—okay, it was decades ago—but University of Illinois football was once worth watching. I know. I was there. As a student in 1994, we had suffered through an extremely frustrating season from an extremely talented team. The Illini, headed by inconsistent but thrilling quarterback Johnny Johnson and a rocking defense with Simeon Rice, Kevin Hardy, and Dana Howard, was 6–3 as it played host to a late-afternoon game against No. 2–ranked Penn State. This was considered a dominant offensive Penn State team, with Kerry Collins, Ki-Jana Carter, Bobby Engram, and Kyle Brady, a quartet that is less imposing in retrospect than it was at the time. They were awesome; we were gonna get killed.

And Illinois jumped out to a 21–0 lead. And the Illini led 31–28 with less than two minutes left and rain starting to fall on a now-dark night. The Illini never played at night. It was beautiful. All we needed was one stop. The student section, I-Block, all crammed into each other while sneaking down to the field. All we needed was one stop; then we would sprint on that field and tear down those goalposts.

Another first down . . . another first down . . . another first down. Then a touchdown. Penn State went on to "tie" with Nebraska for the "mythical" national championship. Everyone went back to their dorms and got drunk. Illinois beat East Carolina 30–0 in the Liberty Bowl that December. I don't know a single person who watched.

Illinois vs. Missouri, Kiel Center, St. Louis, Missouri, December 20, 1995

I was covering this game, part of the yearly Busch Braggin' Rights game, for the *Daily Illini* and the *Chicago Daily Southtown*. I had an extra press pass and gave it to my father, because he'd never had courtside seats before. He said that he could see the outline of the referee's underwear and that being that close to Dick Vitale made him want to kill himself. The game went into overtime, and because of the tight deadline, I didn't have time to go to both Lou Henson and Norm Stewart's press conference. So I sent my dad to write down Stewart's quotes. My father came back, sweating. "He didn't say anything interesting, but I think his wife is too young for him." Being a sports reporter sucks, by the way. You know this, right?

Arizona Cardinals at St. Louis Rams, TWA Dome, St. Louis, Missouri, September 27, 1998

I am a lifelong St. Louis/Phoenix/Arizona Cardinals fan, as much as anyone can be a fan of a team that might be the worst franchise in sports and has about six fans, including myself. That said, I was living in St. Louis in 1998 and couldn't wait to watch them take on the then-boring and frivolous interloping Rams. The thing about this game was that, as is typically the case in St. Louis, more people were paying attention to Busch Stadium about a quarter mile away than they were to the events inside the TWA Dome. Mark McGwire, a superstar of such quality that his reputation could obviously never be impeached in any possible fashion, came into that Sunday with sixty-eight homers. This was a far more noteworthy local occurrence than whether or not June Henley would lead the team in rushing yards that year. (He would, edging out the immortal Greg Hill.)

Anyway, here's the circumstance, and why it's my favorite sports moment that I saw in person. The Rams, up by three and somehow favored, were driving late in the third quarter for what could be a decisive touchdown. It was fourth down and 1, inside the Cardinals' 10-yard line, and the Rams were going for it. A touchdown on this drive would cinch it. Quarterback Tony Banks called the signals . . . and then, out of nowhere, came a deafening cheer from the crowd. Banks, never the calmest signal caller, became confused, looking around, wondering if he'd missed something, if maybe his running back had suddenly broken into a pantless jig. He pulled away from center, spun around and . . . then the whistle. Delay of game.

What had happened? McGwire had hit his sixty-ninth homer, off Expos rookie Mike Thurman. The TWA Dome fans, watching their televisions and listening to their Bartman pocket radios more closely than they were keeping tabs on Banks, went crazy after McGwire's shot. The chatter caused Banks to lose his bearings and end up with the delay-of-game penalty. The Rams were forced to kick a field goal, and the Cardinals ended up reaching the end zone on their next possession. They won the game en route to their first playoff appearance in sixteen years. As a fan of both the football and baseball Cardinals, I couldn't have scripted it any better.

St. Louis Cardinals at Chicago Cubs, Wrigley Field, Chicago, Illinois, September 2, 2003

In college, my best friend was named Mike. He was a Cubs fan, and I understand all that is right and good in the world and like the Cardinals. Our friendship survived that, barely. By 2003 I had moved to New York, and he, like most University of Illinois graduates, was living in Chicago. And he was engaged to a mutual friend of ours from the college newspaper. The Cardinals and Cubs were in the midst of a tight pennant race that year, and the Cubs were proving surprisingly resilient. This made for a stressful day of friendship at the park. When the seventh-inning stretch came along, Mike said, "Hey, would you mind being the best man at our wedding?" I was deeply honored and said yes and shook his hand. And then the game went fifteen innings. By the *second* seventh-inning stretch, I turned to Mike. "If the Cardinals lose this, I'm changing my mind."

Jeff Fassero gave up a two-run fifteenth-inning home run to Sammy Sosa, and the Cardinals indeed lost. Considering what would happen to the Cubs that postseason, however, I didn't have the heart to refuse the best-man request. Mike had certainly suffered enough.

2006 World Series, Game 5, Detroit Tigers at St. Louis Cardinals, Busch Stadium, St. Louis, Missouri, October 27, 2006

Through happy circumstance, I stumbled across face-value tickets for Game 4 of the World Series. Going into the Tigers-Cardinals Series, the general consensus was that this game would be the Tigers' coronation. I just hoped it wouldn't be an elimination game, a hope that was realized when Anthony Reyes was oddly dominant in Game 1. With Kenny Rogers's palm happiness in Game 2, it was assured I wouldn't see a Cardinals clincher, but Game 4 promised to be a pivotal one. I showed up with my parents, all of us decked out in loud red (of course), and we prepared to watch our first-ever World Series game.

And it rained. Not only did it rain, but a frigid wind made the night miserable for anyone who braved it all the way to the end. We learned afterwards that our tickets were good for the ultimate Game 5. When the Cardinals won an amazing Game 4, it almost seemed like destiny. We would be there to see the Cardinals play to win the World Series. There was only one problem: I'd seen the Cardinals play seven games all season, and they were 0–7. I had a personal curse to overcome; I had only Jeff Weaver to overcome it.

And he did. When Adam Wainwright struck out Brandon Inge to win the Cardinals' first World Series in twenty-four years, my family screamed and jumped and howled and laughed and soaked it all in. We did this all evening and reminisced about Cardinals past, remembering the bad times just as fondly as the good ones. The Cardinals were a fabric of our family, and it was . . . it was beautiful.

Steve Levy
Broadcaster, ESPN

1981 AFC Wild Card Game, Buffalo Bills at New York Jets, Shea Stadium, Queens, New York, December 27, 1981

Up in the mezzanine in the enclosed end zone at Shea, the wind really whips and hits you right smack in the face. Shea was rocking that day. I always thought it was a great football stadium. It was the Jets, and I thought they always had a great homefield advantage. It was never a nice day for a Jets game weatherwise, and this was no exception . . . gray, cold, and ugly. The place was a dump then, but it was my dump, and there was no place on earth I'd rather have been.

Prior to the opening kickoff, the place was literally shaking. The Jets won the toss and received. Little, exciting Bruce Harper received the kick and took off, only to fumble the football. With that, all the air was sucked out of the stadium. Of course, the Bills went on to score and score and score. My Jets were down 24–0 in the second quarter and 31–13 with ten minutes left in the game. And then, all of a sudden, Richard Todd got the team back in the game. Two touchdowns later, down four, at the Buffalo 11 with fourteen seconds left. Once again, the stadium is literally shaking. We were on the verge of witnessing a great comeback when Buffalo's Bill Simpson stepped in front of a Todd pass and picked it off at the 2-yard line. Ball game.

To this day, that's the best football game I ever attended. I remember thinking I must really be a sports fan. Even though my team lost in heartbreaking fashion, I was still able to appreciate what's great about sports . . . the drama that's often involved, even when the wrong team wins.

1986 World Series, Game 6, Boston Red Sox at New York Mets, Shea Stadium, Queens, New York, October 25, 1986

Thanks to some good parenting, my folks let me come home from college. I had tickets to Games 1 and 7 at Shea Stadium and wrangled a press credential for Game 6, which I got from Steve Malzberg of WABC Radio. I had interned for him the previous summer, and he wasn't going to the game, so he let me take his pass. My seat was in the auxiliary press box. We are talking really auxiliary, since, while I was on the press level, I was also out by the rightfield foul pole.

The Mets were obviously in big trouble, so I called to commiserate with my buddy, Jeff Levick, who was so annoyed he turned the TV off. Anyway, the game appeared to be over, and all the other members of the press seated in my area had already gone downstairs to be near the clubhouse to get quotes. Their stories were already written, because this game was over. Or not. Mookie Wilson chops one through Bill Buckner's legs, and I am screaming my head off. I learned a few years later about "no cheering in the press box," but not yet. The kicker to the story is, I am jumping up and down yelling all by myself. There is not another person within a hundred feet of me. I call my pal back to tell him the news, since he really had kept the TV off. By this time all the other members of the media were scrambling back to their seats in my section. They had to rewrite their leads.

1994 Stanley Cup Finals, Game 7, Vancouver Canucks at New York Rangers, Madison Square Garden, New York, New York, June 14, 1994

It was my first NHL postseason working at ESPN, and I served mostly as a reporter during the Stanley Cup Finals. It was Game 7 at the Garden. Now, this building always has a buzz—I think it has something to do with the ceiling. But it has a different buzz during the playoffs for both the Knicks and Rangers. It has always been a special place for me, and you can imagine the electricity buzzing through the building for a Game 7 of the Stanley Cup Finals. What I remember most is that, after waiting my entire life (twenty-nine years at that point), even though I was in the joint, I never really got to see the Rangers carry the Cup.

Let me explain . . . ESPN was a rights-holder, meaning we had first crack at the best location in the winning dressing room. But because that positioning is such a big deal, you have to be all set up and ready to go really early. So, with five minutes left on the clock in the third period, I'm already all hooked up with microphone in hand on the podium in the Rangers room and have to watch those final five minutes on a little TV monitor. My mind is in the stands, but my body isn't. So the Rangers win, the celebration is underway and there is craziness 100 feet from me, yet I might as well have been in Vancouver. After what seemed like an eternity, the Rangers start to trickle in from the on-ice celebration.

I got Adam Graves to stand next to me, and we're ready to go. By this time, we've already finished the game broadcast and thrown to *SportsCenter*, and they're going to throw it back to me for locker-room reaction. So Graves, a super guy, was being unbelievably patient. It seemed like we waited fifteen minutes, although in reality it probably was much shorter than that. Graves and I are watching in disbelief as *SportsCenter* is showing Cleveland Indians highlights, even though I've got the Rangers' fifty-goal scorer standing by, idling his celebration engine. I've already apologized numerous times, he's already messed up my hair with the champagne shower, and, with ESPN producer Tom McNeeley trying to keep me calm, Graves bends over and says to me, "I know how important this was to you, too."

To this day, that blows me away, that in the middle of the best night of his life he remembered that I was a native New Yorker and that it was the best night of my life, too. They finally came to us, we did the interview, and I thanked him and let him go. Hours later, after the final few people had finished lingering, someone offered me the chance of a lifetime. Professional? Probably not. But you know what? I drank from the Stanley Cup that night.

1996 NHL Eastern Conference Quarterfinals, Game 4, Pittsburgh Penguins at Washington Capitals, USAir Arena, Landover, Maryland, April 26, 1996 and 2000 NHL Eastern Conference Semifinals, Game 4, Philadelphia Flyers at Pittsburgh Penguins, Mellon Arena, Pittsburgh, Pennsylvania, May 4, 2000

I've been privileged to broadcast the three longest Stanley Cup Playoff games on television (there have been longer games, but they took place before hockey was televised). In April of 1996, we were at the old Cap Centre, which was a dark and dingy building, for the Penguins and Capitals. By the time the fourth overtime rolled around, we had already witnessed Mario Lemieux getting kicked out of the game and a penalty shot in the second overtime. At some point in the third overtime, I was running out of words. I was just using the last names of players (Pivonka, Miller, Johnson, etc.), and at some point in the fourth OT, I just stopped speaking as play was going on. Fortunately, the game was on TV, not radio. My partner, Darryl Reaugh, looked over at me, and on the air I just said, "What?" and we started to giggle. It was late, my mind was fried, and my chest was tight after broadcasting so long at such a high excitement level.

Petr Nedved finally ended it at around 2:30 A.M., and you know what? He came on live with us and did an interview. I remember walking out to the parking lot and seeing Washington coach Jim Schoenfeld going to his car. He was always so positive about everything, but even he was having a tough time swallowing this loss.

I also remember the awful Holiday Inn right near the arena. They lost my laundry that night, so I was prepared to handle a five-overtime game like the one in Pittsburgh in May 2000, against the Flyers. The Igloo ran out of coffee in the second overtime, there was food in the truck during the third overtime, but there was no way to get it to us upstairs in the broadcast booth because it was so late that our runner's mother had come to pick him up and take him home. It was a school night! It seemed like every thirty seconds, I was being passed a note that said we just passed another game on the list of the longest games of all time. Keith Primeau was the hero on this night/morning. Afterwards, since we hadn't had anything to eat since the awful press meal at 6:00 P.M., my faithful sidekick Darren Pang and I made our way to Pittsburgh's legendary late-night sandwich place, Primanti Brothers. It was after 3:00 A.M. now, and we walked in and were met with a standing ovation, which was good because with everyone standing, we were finally able to sit down.

2001 GMAC Bowl, Marshall vs. East Carolina, Ladd-Peebles Stadium, Mobile, Alabama, December 19, 2001

The amount of preparation that goes into broadcasting a college football game is mind-boggling, and as is the case in prepping for any sporting event, only about 25 percent of what you have ready ever actually makes it on the air. Well, on this night I used 100 percent and could've used more. East Carolina led 38–8 at halftime, and this baby was over. We were in garbage time from the start of the third quarter and started using the A, B, C, D, E, and F material, trying to keep it somewhat interesting for whoever was still watching this blowout. Thousands of fans that were at the game left the building . . . and missed a pretty good second half.

Marshall came all the way back to tie it at 51 on a touchdown in the final seconds of the fourth quarter on this crazy night and just needed to hit the extra point to win. Of course, they missed it. The game had four defensive touch-downs. Byron Leftwich had his fifth 400-yard passing game of the season and finished with 576 yards passing and a 64–61 Marshall win in double overtime. It was the highest scoring bowl game in history and at the time the second biggest comeback in college football history behind only Frank Reich at Maryland in 1984 against Miami. Lesson learned? Never leave a sporting event early.

Josh Lewin
Broadcaster, FOX Sports/Texas Rangers/
San Diego Chargers

California Angels at Baltimore Orioles, Camden Yards, Baltimore, Maryland, September 6, 1995

Working pre- and postgame radio for the Orioles, the sheer drama of Cal Ripken Jr.'s homering on both the streak-tying and streak-breaking games was emotional enough . . . but when he took that impromptu "victory lap" around Camden Yards, it was pretty tough to keep one's journalistic integrity intact. When the Ripken kids hugged Cal wearing shirts that read "2,130+ hugs and kisses for Daddy," I broke down and wept. It was such a tender, beautiful moment.

1996 American League Championship Series, Game 1, Baltimore Orioles at New York Yankees, Yankee Stadium, Bronx, New York, October 9, 1996

I was in the Orioles' cozy broadcast booth at Yankee Stadium when twelve-year-old Yankee fan Jeffrey Maier helped the Yankees win Game 1 of the ALCS. Tony Tarasco was all set to bring in Derek Jeter's fly ball at the base of the wall, but obviously, it didn't work out as expected. People sometimes forget that L'Affair Maier only tied that game. . . . Bernie Williams won it with a bomb of a home run in extra innings, off Randy Myers. Also of note—Jon Miller's play-by-play call was perfect. Not whiny, just factual, and born of fourteen years' worth of accumulated credibility. Because Jon wasn't an abject "homer" crying about every "missed call" in random ball games, when the Orioles really were robbed, Jon was able to hammer the point home effectively.

San Francisco Giants at Houston Astros, Enron Field, Houston, Texas, October 4, 2001

Barry Bonds's 70th home run in 2001 was a spectacular upper-deck moon shot against a bewildered kid named Wilfredo Rodriguez, tying Mark McGwire . . . well before either man would be linked to anything rancid. Looking back now, how appropriate that in light of the Enron escapades and the recent steroid disclosures that Bonds hit #70 at Enron Field! We interviewed Barry live after that national broadcast on FSN, and he was a pussycat.

Boston Red Sox at Baltimore Orioles, Camden Yards, Baltimore, Maryland, October 6, 2001

I always thought it was highly appropriate that Cal Ripken Jr. finished his Hall-of-Fame career with 3,001 games played. That extra "one" symbolizes the fact he always gave just a little bit more than was necessary, whether it was on-field effort or an off-field autograph.

For the record, number 8 flied out in his final at bat, to the centerfielder (position #8) in the eighth inning. The Orioles almost got him up again in the ninth, but his good friend Brady Anderson struck out after a draining at bat, and the Great Cal Ripken ended his career on deck.

2003 National League Championship Series, Game 6, Florida Marlins at Chicago Cubs, Wrigley Field, Chicago, Illinois, October 14, 2003

I was the "dugout reporter" for FOX that fateful night, camped mere yards from the offending area where Steve Bartman was seated. When the poor kid with the circa-1977 earphones reached in front of Moises Alou, who knew at the time where that all would lead? For the record, I did indeed ask our production crew if they wanted me to go talk to or interview the now-reclusive Bartman, but it was decided—probably very correctly—that putting a camera in the guy's grill may have incited a riot. I remember walking out of Wrigley after it was all over, amid the thunderstruck Cubs fans, and chatting with Thom Brennaman and Steve Lyons about whether or not our coverage of the incident had been fair. We didn't find out Bartman's name until the next afternoon and never fully appreciated the magnitude of what had happened until after Game 7 had ended the following night.

Jim Litke
Columnist, Associated Press

1988 Summer Olympics, Men's 100 Meters Final, Jamsil Olympic Stadium, Seoul, South Korea, September 24, 1988

Ben Johnson and Carl Lewis had been taking turns winning smackdowns all around the globe for nearly a year by the time they settled into the blocks. I had walked down to the basement of the stadium to the AP photo lab, then followed some photographers onto the track and sat about 25 yards from the inside lane, at the midpoint of the straightaway. Johnson was a powerful starter. Lewis, whose strength was closing speed, had a habit of glancing across at his rivals right around the 50-meter mark to gauge where he stood. This time, when he looked to his left and didn't see Johnson anywhere in the frame, he knew he was in trouble. The whites of his eyes flared to the size of saucers, or so it seemed. A moment later, "9.79" and "WR (World Record)" flashed on the scoreboard, and the entire stadium exhaled at once. I remember looking over at Lewis; his eyes were not quite as wide as they'd been at 50 meters, but like the rest of us, he'd clearly seen something he was having a hard time believing.

Mike Tyson vs. Evander Holyfield, MGM Grand Garden Arena, Las Vegas, Nevada, June 28, 1997

A heavyweight fight in Vegas is like a Fellini movie, layered with weirdness, and I had the best seat in the house for this one, about a dozen rows from the ring. It was apparent from the start that Holyfield wouldn't be bullied, and that made Tyson more desperate by the minute. The first time he bit Holyfield, I saw a flash of light reflecting off his teeth, then jumped out of my seat, screaming, "He bit him! He bit him!" Most of the writers around me thought I was crazy and kept telling me to sit down. Soon enough, Tyson bit Holyfield again, and everybody else was up on their feet.

Food, half-filled cups, and even the occasional chair began flying toward the ring from every direction. Chaos reigned, and something that sounded like gunshots ratcheted up the frenzy. Sitting down to write in the middle of that would have been impossible—except that this was a story that practically wrote itself.

1998 NBA Finals, Game 6, Chicago Bulls at Utah Jazz, Delta Center, Salt Lake City, Utah, June 14, 1998

Everyone on press row was certain we were going to spend at least one more night in Salt Lake City. A few of us had gone into the press room with about five minutes left to start writing. Inside, on a TV monitor, I saw Michael Jordan strip the ball and started walking toward the court like I'd been hypnotized. What everybody remembers is Jordan holding his pose as the ball falls through the net. What I'll never forget is the moment that preceded the shot. Jordan suckered Bryon Russell into reaching for the ball with a crossover dribble. The moment he sensed Russell was losing his balance, Jordan reached down and gave him a little shove, just to make sure Russell wouldn't recover in time to get back in his way. Then he launched it. I'd covered Jordan all around the world for nearly fifteen years by that point. It remains the perfect tableau for the most competitive SOB I've ever seen.

1999 British Open, Carnoustie Golf Links, Carnoustie, Scotland, July 15–18, 1999

No championship course had ever been set up more diabolically, which may explain how, in the span of a few minutes and few hundred yards, this turned into the most wayward adventure I've ever seen. And it didn't seem things could get much funnier when Jean van de Velde stood in the burn fronting the 18th green at Carnoustie—his socks and shoes on the bank, trousers rolled up to mid-calf, hands on his hips—and considered whether to hit his next shot from shallow water. That's when playing partner Craig Parry, an Aussie, walked over to the edge of the green and with perfect timing and pitch said, "Stay there another minute or two. By then, the tide will be going back out."

1999 Tour de France Final Stage, Paris, France, July 25, 1999

Lance Armstrong won the opening stage of the 1999 race, and everybody in France loved him. The Tour was still reeling from a drug scandal the year before, and as a cancer survivor with no performance-enhancing allegations clouding his past, he became its poster boy. Then, just before the midpoint, he locked up the Tour with a withering ride into the Alps, and because Armstrong wasn't known as a strong mountain rider before, the tone in the French newspapers turned on a dime.

Yet for all the ugly, hurtful things they said about him, their real sin was believing they could rattle him. Someone who has outraced cancer, after all, is hardly going to be stopped by bad reviews. I was one of a handful of American writers on the Champs-Élysées that afternoon, and because security at events wasn't what it is now, I talked my way into the grandstand where the award presentation took place and sat between Armstrong's mother, his then-wife, Kristin, and his oncologist. For all the twists and turns his story has taken since, for a while it felt exactly like it should have—one of the best, most joyous comeback stories ever.

Verne Lundquist
Broadcaster, CBS Sports

1967 NFL Championship Game, Dallas Cowboys at Green Bay Packers, Lambeau Field, Green Bay, Wisconsin, December 31, 1967

I was new to Dallas at the time and had moved there in September of that year after previously working in Austin and San Antonio. The very first week I was in town, September 27, 1967, to be exact, I got a call from Al Ward, who was the vice president of the Cowboys under Tex Schramm. He welcomed me to town and asked me if I wanted to go with the team on the charter to Washington, D.C., for that weekend's game. I was thrilled, of course, and knew I was now on the periphery of the big leagues. On the way to Washington, Al sat down beside me and asked me if I wanted to do the postgame show with play-by-play announcer Bill Weber (who is still a close friend of mine) and the great writer Blackie Sherrod, who was the color guy. I didn't have permission to do it but was thrilled and figured no one I knew would listen to it, so I said yes.

Of course, I was wrong about no one listening and was called in the next morning at work and asked why I did it. I was glad I did, though, and the Cowboys liked it and asked me to do the last game of the year in San Francisco and any playoff games the team played. This was the start of my relationship with the Cowboys, who played a huge role in my broadcasting career.

The team made the playoffs and traveled to Green Bay. We got there the day before the game and flew up on a Braniff 27, which is one of those planes that had the steps in the back that you could use to get on and off the plane. I was sitting in front of George Andrie and Bob Lilly, and when the players starting filing out, they told me to hide behind them because it was going to be really cold out. When we went down the steps, though, it wasn't really that bad—around 20 degrees, not much wind. My cameraman and I headed to Lambeau Field and were able to get an interview on the field with Vince

Lombardi to air before the game. The main subject of the conversation became about an electronic grid that had been installed under the turf to ensure that the field wouldn't freeze. The next morning, the wakeup call came, and I was told the temperature outside was 13 degrees below zero.

The game itself went back and forth, and, given my duties, I just stood in the back of the radio booth. Ray Scott, Pat Summerall, Frank Gifford, and Jack Buck were doing the game for CBS. In those days, CBS assigned an announcer per team; Scott was the voice of the Packers, Buck was with the Cowboys, Gifford and Summerall were the analysts. I knew them a little, and they invited me to stay in the TV booth if I wanted, since it was a little larger, and I ended up alternating between booths. The other thing I have a vivid memory of was going down one level to where the writers sat. In the press box, the more prestigious writers were assigned to the front row. Of course, on this day, each of those guys sitting in the front was given an ice scraper, so they would sit there and constantly have to scrape the ice so everyone could see, while the lesser lights in the back row were the beneficiaries.

In the game Dallas had things under control and was up 17–14 late in the game, when the Packers went on the famous drive. Bob Lilly to this day talks about how impossible it was to stand up on the ice, and the Packers just kept running draw plays on the last drive before the gutsy call by Lombardi and Bart Starr for the quarterback sneak with no timeouts left. I went downstairs for the postgame show and had Don Meredith on, and he was just heartbroken; he ended up playing just one more season. On the flight home, guys were talking about frostbite, and some of them still have it—George Andrie, in particular, is still affected by it. After we landed, there was a party at Tex Schramm's house, which was about as sad a New Year's Eve party as you could imagine.

The 1986 Masters, Augusta National Golf Club, Augusta, Georgia, April 10–13, 1986

Of all of the events I have been lucky enough to be a part of, this one is still the top thrill I have witnessed. I think that has a lot to do with the unexpected nature of it, which is really the reason why doing live sporting events is so much fun. Jack Nicklaus had essentially been dismissed as a golfer. He was forty-six years old, trailed Greg Norman by four shots, and sat behind eight golfers when the fourth round started on Sunday. On the 8th hole, he made a really nice save for par, and Lance Barrow, who is now the coordinating producer for golf but was an AD at the time, told Frank Chirkinian, the executive producer, that he had the save on tape, to which Frank said, "Don't bother me with Nicklaus. He's not a part of this story." But then Jack birdied 9, which we got on tape, and when he birdied 10, he was very much a part of the story.

The old cliché at Augusta that the Masters doesn't start until the back nine on Sunday was never truer. I think the drama built from the time he hit 10, and it became obvious that he might challenge. And it just built and built from there. He birdied 11 and bogeyed 12, which took the wind out of everyone's sails for a few minutes. Then he birdied 13 and parred 14, and when he eagled 15, it started to get really dramatic. He almost had a hole in one on 16. On that back nine, there was drama on every swing he took. He was standing on 17 when Seve Ballesteros found the water on 15; he had a clean approach from about 120 yards to the hole after a nice tee shot, which he put 12 or 13 feet from the pin with a nine iron.

At that point we knew, and all of America knew, that if he made the birdie putt, he was going to take the lead at the age of forty-six. To this day, I've never heard a golf gallery make that much noise. When he did something, the noise just reverberated through the back nine. It became an absolutely special Nicklaus roar; the people who were standing around us on 17, for example, when he eagled 15, didn't have to ask who it was. They could tell from the sound. He made the putt, which wasn't an easy one and had a tiny little double break to it, and took the lead, and to be able to call that was about as big a thrill as I've had in my career. As loud as the roar for Tiger was at 16 in 2005, it was more sustained for Jack in 1986.

I've given this moment such a special spot in my memory box that maybe it is going to take something Herculean (which is what Tiger pulled off) to surpass it. But I still believe the noise was louder for Jack. I lost my brother in 2004 and lost my best friend on Thursday the week of the 2006 Masters, and this was the only time either of them were able to make the trip to Augusta for the tournament, which also makes this whole event special for me. But I'll also never forget, when we went to commercial as Jack walked to 18, I took off my headset in the tower and turned to CBS Sports president Neil Pilson, who was in the tower with me, and neither one of us could say a word. We both knew we had seen something special.

1992 NCAA Men's Basketball Tournament, East Regional Finals, Kentucky vs. Duke, The Spectrum, Philadelphia, Pennsylvania, March 28, 1992

When I saw Grant Hill come out of the timeout with 2.1 seconds to play, I thought back to when he was born. His father, Calvin, was playing for the Cowboys, and I was doing their radio broadcasts in 1972. He was born on a Friday night, and Calvin called me to give me the news. So as they broke out of their huddle, I couldn't help but think about how neat that was but was also concentrating more on him getting ready to throw the ball in than on Christian Laettner at the other end of the floor.

My partner that day was Len Elmore, and we began to talk about how Rick Pitino had decided not to contest the inbounds pass, putting all five players at the defensive end, giving Hill an unimpeded pass, albeit one that had to travel around 70 feet. That paid huge dividends for Duke, because the pass was just about perfect, and Laettner caught it, turned, and made the shot. You try to lay out in moments like this, and I did for thirty or forty seconds while trying to come up with the appropriate thing to say. I did allude at that point to the fact that his father played football and he had thrown a perfect football pass to Laettner. We knew throughout the game that we were watching something special and that it was going to go down to the wire. But when you take something special, then factor in the programs that are playing in Duke and Kentucky, plus that it was for a spot in the Final Four, the only thing that would have elevated the status of the game as it is now remembered would have been if it was for a national championship.

When the game was over, we took off our headsets, but neither one of us said a word for a good fifteen seconds. We just watched the scene play out in front of us. Bob Ryan of the *Boston Globe* came over to us and looked at Len and said, "Until tonight, I thought Maryland–North Carolina State in 1974 was the greatest basketball game I had ever seen. I thought this one was better; what do you think?" Len had played for Maryland in that game, and to his credit, he didn't reply flippantly. He thought about it and said, "You know what? The stakes were higher here. This was a better game." That conversation made me sit back and realize just how special this game was.

After the game, I'll always remember Coach Krzyzewski making a beeline for legendary Kentucky announcer Cawood Ledford, who had announced that he was retiring at the end of the Wildcats' season. I thought that was so classy, especially considering the circumstances. A few minutes later, we were leaving, and the Duke players were still celebrating on the floor. I saw Coach and went over to congratulate him, and he said to me, "I knew if we could get it in the son of a bitch's hands, he'd score."

1994 Winter Olympics, Ladies' Figure Skating, Hamar OL-Amfi, Hamar, Norway, February 23–25, 1994

This was the most hyped event I've ever been a part of and hyped for all the wrong reasons. This story was more suited to *People* magazine or the *National Enquirer*. The most vivid memory I have from the entire experience isn't the night they skated, but is Scott Hamilton's insistence that those of us who were there to cover the sport of figure skating pay attention to covering the sport. He was offended by everything that was going on, especially since he didn't believe Tonya Harding belonged on the team by virtue of her skating ability. She was on the team in 1992 and finished fourth in Albertville but had lost conditioning and wasn't skating well, so he believed, even before the whacking incident in Detroit, that Harding wasn't going to make the team and had no place on it, making him really indignant about things leading up to the event. At one point, he said on the air that Tonya Harding "has hijacked the Olympics," which summed up his feelings fairly well. Having said all that, it was an amazing experience.

I always tell people these stories, which I find extraordinary. Nancy Kerrigan had gone over to the Olympics early to get acclimated and train and to do the whole Olympic experience. Tonya, on the other hand, didn't arrive until just a couple of days before her first skate, after the Olympics had already started. When she came over to Lillehammer, she was accompanied by Connie Chung of CBS News, which some of us thought was a little inappropriate. Connie made the entire trip with Harding, from Portland through all the connections to Norway, and the day Harding arrived and the two skaters were scheduled for their first practice together was one of the weirdest days I've ever seen.

They practiced in the local hockey team's practice arena, which was connected by a walkway to the Olympic Ice Arena, but there were only three hundred seats in it, all on ice level, and a bunch of balconies. The Lillehammer Olympic Committee allowed only rights-holding broadcasters to be on the ground floor. Every other accredited journalist had to be upstairs, a group that numbered around four hundred and included many of the top American journalists that happened to be covering the event. They all stood there from around 7 in the morning until about 11, when the skaters took the ice. It was like the terraces at an English soccer match, with everyone elbowing and pushing each other and jostling for position.

Scott and I were the lucky ones, and since we were the rights-holders and were covering the practice, we got to sit down by the ice and watch this zoo as it unfolded before us. That was the morning practice, which lasted around an hour and a half. Late that afternoon, they moved over to the main Olympic Ice Arena. The media rules were the same, and the print contingent was four hundred strong again. They sat in the stands near the two coaches, and when the coaches moved, the media followed. It was like watching a school of fish.

Meanwhile, and here's where I don't let CBS off the hook, Scott, Tracy Wilson, and I were sitting at our announce position, which was kitty-corner from where the print journalists were, and were 10 to 12 feet above the ice. I looked around and saw the following people: Susan Spencer of CBS News and a camera crew, Mark Phillips of CBS News and a camera crew, Martha Teichner of CBS News and a camera crew, John Blackstone of CBS News and a camera crew, Bill Geist of CBS News and a camera crew, and, coanchoring the *CBS Evening News* just 20 feet from where we were, Connie Chung and her crew. That made six CBS News crews in the building. At one point, I said something to Susan Spencer about why she was there, and she said she was interviewing the Polish ice dancers as her angle on the story. The whole scene was just unbelievable.

In the aftermath of all of this hype, on Wednesday night, when Harding and Kerrigan and eventual winner Oksana Baiul skated the short program, we had 126 million viewers and a 48.5 rating, making it still the sixth highest rated show of all time. Tonya skated the way we all thought she would skate, which was not well. Kerrigan skated great and was first after the short program, with Baiul second and Harding tenth. Two days later was the long program, and that night it was our intention, with more than half of the primetime show allotted to our event, to come on the air early on, show a young skater who was going early, then throw it back to the studio and say there is more to come. When we came back, we planned on starting with Tonya, who was going to skate in the middle of the second-to-last group, as determined by a random draw. The intent was to show Harding in totality, bid her farewell for good, and come back later in the evening and do the last six skaters in a block, since that was where the story was.

At least, that was the intent. We had a robotic lipstick camera perched above the arch on the door, and around six minutes before Harding was supposed to come out and skate, our producer, David Winner, got Scott and me on the headset and said, "You won't believe what is going on backstage." Because we had that camera there, though, we watched the whole thing. Her bootlace had broken, and this frantic scene unfolded, and that became the incident that caused Scott to say she had hijacked the Olympics.

It was a mad scene as they tried to get her lace fixed; then she ran out after she was introduced (she has two minutes from when she is introduced to take the ice or be disqualified, and the clock was running). It was a surreal moment. She finally started skating and missed her first jump, then missed her second, and famously skated over and put her right leg up on the judge's stand and pleaded for time. Scott said something to the effect of, "This never, ever, ever happens in skating, but it is the fourth time it has happened to Tonya Harding." He just let the implication sit there for everyone.

The 2005 Masters, Augusta National Golf Club, Augusta, Georgia, April 7–10, 2005

In terms of one specific moment, this was the greatest shot I've ever seen. I think as the years evolve and his accomplishments grow, the remembrance of the chip shot on 16 in 2005 will probably be more recognizable to the general public than Jack's putt in 1986. Obviously, it was a much more difficult shot. It took a lot of creativity and imagination to just get the ball close. A lot of it has to do with the fact that it was Tiger making the shot, of course; if it were another player, we probably wouldn't be talking about it in these terms. But it was, and it will grow in proportion with his continued accomplishments.

As the ball was hanging on the lip of the cup, I think years of reminding myself to not overreact played into things. I just waited for things to unfold but was in disbelief as the ball just sat there. Afterwards, somebody put a clock on it and said it sat there for two seconds, which sounds about right. When it finally went in, all I could say was, "Oh, wow!!!" You just react, and that is all I did. People have asked me if I thought about what I was going to say, but you really can't plan for moments like these. I do remember a passing thought I had, though, that Nike was going to love this. That was definitely in my thought process. I let things play out for a moment and then asked, "In your life, have you ever seen anything like this?" That was all I could think of, because what we all had witnessed was so unimaginable.

Bill Macatee
Broadcaster, CBS Sports

Texas–El Paso Invitational, Kidd Stadium, El Paso, Texas, May 23, 1972

I was a pole vaulter in high school and grew up in a track-and-field town, El Paso, Texas. One of the guys I loved to watch was a pole vaulter named Bob Seagren, who was the top American pole vaulter (and who actually won the very first Superstars competition). I've always thought pole vaulters were the best all-around athletes because you have to be fast to build up speed, strong to bend the pole enough, agile so you can turn your body . . . it is a very, very complex pursuit. The University of Texas–El Paso had a really good track program and has won multiple NCAA titles, and they hosted a couple of professional track and field competitions there.

One day they hosted a meet that was sanctioned by all of the governing bodies, and it was just one of those weeks where the conditions were perfect for what happened. The world record at the time was 18' ½", and no American had ever vaulted 18 feet. But this week there had been guys clearing 19 feet in practice. So what they did, and I'm not sure how they arranged this, was set up a pole-vault-only meet the next day. There were no other events, just a sanctioned pole-vault competition. There were probably fifty people there, and I had my home-movie camera, just so I could record and take a look at their technique.

The number-one vaulter in the world at the time was a Swedish former gymnast named Kjell Isaksson, who I thought was great, and he broke his own world record this day with a vault of 18' ¾". Then, on Seagren's last vault, he made it and tied Isaksson's record. There were so few people there, it was like we were just doing something in the backyard. I was just trying to stay out of the way, but I remember Seagren sitting there, looking into my camera and smiling as he was getting ready for his last jump. I put the camera down so he could get ready, but he said it was okay and that I could just go ahead and shoot him like that. It was so odd to me that he was getting ready to go for the world record, but it was all right for a sixteen-year-old kid to stand there with a movie camera in his face. I just thought to myself, "Now that's a big-time athlete." And he made the jump.

Texas Rangers at Kansas City Royals, Royals Stadium, Kansas City, Missouri, May 18, 1984

It was Willie Wilson's first game back after being suspended for drug-related issues. Before the gates opened to let the fans in, Wilson was alone, jogging in the outfield. Watching him from the empty seats was a young boy. Given the circumstances, there's no question Willie was nervous about how the fans would react to him. As he turned to jog back in the direction of the boy, their eyes met. After a moment, the child yelled out, "Welcome back, Willie." Wilson flashed a big grin and waved at the boy. In that one moment, all of Wilson's dread about coming back seemed to disappear. He knew the fans would forgive him and everything would be okay.

1991 U.S. Open, First Round, Jimmy Connors vs. Patrick McEnroe, National Tennis Center, Flushing, New York, August 28, 1991

This is a tough one for me, because Patrick McEnroe has become a good friend. Jimmy Connors came from two sets down in the first big-time tennis match that I ever called. It was a remarkable night but one that had to be one of the toughest of Patrick's life. The match was amazing for two reasons, though. It will surely go down as one of the greatest comebacks in tennis history, and it kicked off Jimmy's incredible year at the age of thirty-nine, which saw him get to the semifinals.

However, what was equally impressive was the way Patrick handled it that night. The match basically turned into a slugfest that ended at 1:35 A.M. Because there were so many people who thought the match was over, there were a ton of empty seats down near the court. As the match went on, they allowed the fans to move down and fill in those seats. The atmosphere was electric. The people who were left that night were either hard-core tennis fans or just loved being there at the Open. The match went on and on and on, and for Patrick it had to be like watching an accident unfold in slow motion. You just couldn't believe what was happening. It occurred to me over and over again that everyone in Louis Armstrong Stadium and whoever was still watching on television had to be cheering for Connors.

But between points I was watching Patrick and couldn't stop thinking about how hard it had to be for him. He was playing a guy who was on fire, plus knowing that almost everyone in the stands was waiting to erupt every time something went against you. To me, that was the epitome of sportsmanship and what being an athlete is all about. He gave the best he had but ran into magic from a legend. It was too much to overcome. Patrick McEnroe gave everything he had and held his head up high and was a man about it every step of the way. It was as courageous and admirable a performance as I've ever seen.

1996 U.S. Open Quarterfinals, Pete Sampras vs. Alex Corretja, National Tennis Center, Flushing, New York, September 5, 1996

Pete Sampras was on the ropes but battling the whole way against Alex Corretja, who was about as brave and fearless as anyone can be on a tennis court. People don't always consider tennis players to be warriors, but these guys were warriors that night. It was a warm, late-summer New York evening, and these two just battled into the night, to the point where Pete gagged a couple times and vomited on the court during the fifth-set tiebreaker. It was 7-all in the tiebreaker when he served a second-serve ace. Corretja then double-faulted to give Sampras the match.

I was calling the match with John McEnroe, and there are times, and they happen more frequently than announcers allow them to, where words are not necessary. This was one of those times. John looked at me and started to say something, and I just put my fingers to my lips to indicate that we should be quiet. So he just sat there, as we all did, along with everyone at home, and just watched. This was so dramatic. I think the only thing I said for about five minutes was, "We are watching right along with you." Sampras went on to win the Open that year. Both players needed IVs and fluids afterwards but got a standing ovation as they walked off the court that seemed to last forever.

The 2004 Masters, Augusta National Golf Club, Augusta, Georgia, April 8–11, 2004

Like many from my generation, I grew up idolizing Arnold Palmer. He was a very special person in my life. My dad loved Arnold Palmer, my grandfather loved Arnold Palmer, we all loved him and rooted against anyone competing head-to-head with him. Arnold Palmer defined greatness in the game of golf for half a century. He always managed to find a way to win or go down fighting if he didn't and had that swashbuckling attitude about it.

Starting in 1990, I've been lucky enough to be in Butler Cabin for the first two days of the Masters broadcasts. In sports, there are certain athletes whose mere presence is special. That would be Arnold Palmer. Every time he was in a tournament I was covering, I would go out and watch him play. It didn't matter to me how he played, I just wanted to be there to see him.

Arnold's final Masters was in 2004, and as I sat in Butler Cabin, the control truck rolled a highlight package of his day, which I had not seen. All my producer, Lance Barrow, told me in my ear was, "Here's the great man's day," and I just started talking. I knew a lot of people were watching. It was the Masters, and it was the final competitive round at Augusta National for one of the sport's legends. As I was speaking and watching the video on the monitor in front of me, I had the most unique experience of my career. Sitting there, I felt almost detached; as if I was watching this unfold from across the room. I don't think my senses as a broadcaster have ever been more alive than they were at that moment. It was a spot I had never been in before, and in retrospect, it was so interesting.

I heard myself saying something that I thought about a lot but had never verbalized: "The great thing about Arnold Palmer is that he never acted like Arnold Palmer. He was always one of us." Then, out of the corner of my eye, I noticed that someone had taken a seat beside me. I took a quick glance over and realized that it was Arnold. He was sitting there, listening to me narrate his final day of competition at the Masters. I looked at his eyes, and they were welling with tears. For me, that may have been the most amazing moment of my career. I can't think of anything else that could even come close. I was able to represent all of us from my generation who grew up adoring this man. And I got to say "thank you" for everything he gave us.

Jack McCallum
Senior Writer, Sports Illustrated

Recipient of Basketball Hall of Fame's Curt Gowdy Award, 2005

1987 NBA Finals, Game 4, Los Angeles Lakers at Boston Celtics, Boston Garden, Boston, Massachusetts, June 9, 1987

I have long thought that the significance of Magic Johnson's famous "junior sky-hook," as he called it, has been blown slightly out of proportion. It did give the Lakers a 107–106 win, but they were pounded in Game 5 two nights later and didn't win the title until five days later, back in LA. But, clearly, this was a memorable moment, and it took place right in front of my baseline seat. Magic caught the ball on the left side of the basket, did a little hitch dribble, and came gliding across the lane. Both Robert Parish and Kevin McHale came out to guard him, and so did Larry Bird, doing the right thing with a little feint at him, then a retreat to his own man. But Magic never hesitated, never even thought about passing, and hit the runner that completed LA's rally from a 16-point halftime deficit.

1988 NBA Eastern Conference Semifinals, Game 7, Atlanta Hawks at Boston Celtics, Boston Garden, Boston, Massachusetts, May 22, 1988

What I remember was the pure joy of this game, watching players on both teams get such a kick out of the shooting show put on by the Celtics' Larry Bird and the Hawks' Dominique Wilkins. 'Nique was always criticized for being a gunner, but I liked his game and liked him personally, and this Sunday afternoon in Boston stamped his greatness as a scorer, albeit in a loss. 'Nique finished with 47 points, but Bird got 20 of his 34 in the fourth quarter as the Celtics won, 118–116.

1988 NBA Finals, Game 6, Detroit Pistons at Los Angeles Lakers, The Forum, Inglewood, California, June 19, 1988

Pistons' guard Isiah Thomas was never one of the media favorites. The press found him distrustful and devious. But no one ever argued that the man couldn't play. A year after his disastrous public-relations faux pas, when he said that Larry Bird would be "just another guy" if Bird weren't Caucasian, Thomas scored a Finals' record 25 points in the third quarter, despite playing on an ankle so severely sprained he could barely walk. I still remember him taking a jumper from the left corner, near where I was sitting at the press table, and watching him wince in pain when he came down. It went in, too. Nevertheless, the Pistons lost both that game, 103–102, and, without their leader, Game 7, 108–105.

1989 NBA Playoffs Opening Round, Game 5, Chicago Bulls at Cleveland Cavaliers, Richfield Coliseum, Richfield, Ohio, May 7, 1989

I was having my breakfast in a Cleveland hotel on this morning, with Michael Jordan and a few of his teammates sitting nearby. When Jordan got up, a young lady dashed to his table and claimed his fork, clutching it as if it were a religious icon. I was still thinking about that—and in fact used it in the lead to my story—when Jordan hit his oft-replayed, buzzer-beating jumper over Craig Ehlo to give the Bulls a 101–100 victory. I also remember Jordan pumping his fists in triumph and, just as vividly, the look of agony on Ehlo's face, not the last time he would be tortured by His Airness.

Liberty vs. Allen, Liberty High School Stadium, Liberty, Pennsylvania, May 14, 1998

Chris McCallum, a junior, had finished third or fourth in the mile run in a couple of other earlier meets but could never break through to win, mostly because he had a strong team and couldn't beat its two tough senior runners. But on this day, with one of the seniors not competing, Chris's strong kick with about 200 yards remaining pushed him past an Allen runner and into first place, his time (somewhere around 4:40) a personal best. What I remember most vividly is that Chris started to raise his arms in triumph but put them down and instead turned and congratulated the young man he had beaten.

Curt Menefee
Broadcaster, FOX Sports

Michigan at Iowa, Kinnick Stadium, Iowa City, Iowa, October 19, 1985

Iowa was ranked #1 in the country at the time; Michigan was #2. I was twenty years old and working for a local TV station in Cedar Rapids, Iowa. I grew up in Atlanta but went to Coe College in Iowa and got my initiation in how important the farm communities are there, as well as how important football is to these communities. The hype that week was amazing. At that time, it felt like the only thing the people in Iowa felt they had going for them was the Iowa football team, and after a down period, they were now #1 in the country. The players were wearing ANF (America Needs Farmers) stickers on their helmets, showing just how important this was to the whole state.

#1 vs. #2 games usually don't live up to the hype, but this one did. It was rainy, not a downpour, but just enough rain to make you know it. It was a raw, windy, college-football Saturday, but everyone was pumped anyway. I was on the field in the end zone, shooting from there, and it was one of those games where it seemed like no one in the stands moved the entire time, for fear of missing something. Iowa played really well on both sides of the ball, but when you looked at the scoreboard, they were down 10–9 in the fourth quarter. With time running out, Iowa's walk-on kicker, Rob Houghtlin, after missing an earlier fourth-quarter field goal, kicked the winner. I was standing right under the goalposts and following it through with the camera. I panned back down, and all I saw were the backs of people running onto the field. The crowd just engulfed me. You try not to get trampled or knocked down, but I was still shooting.

Eventually, I had to stop and head to the locker room but couldn't move. The students were starting to tear down the goalposts, security was trying to stop everything, but it was safe. A walk that should have taken a minute was now ten minutes old, and I still wasn't there. All of a sudden, the band started playing the

"Star-Spangled Banner," the rioting stopped, and I was finally able to cut through the crowd and go to the locker room (it turns out security asked the band to play the song because it was the only way they could think of to get everyone to stop).

California Angels at Texas Rangers, The Ballpark in Arlington, Arlington, Texas, July 28, 1994

It was the summer of 1994, right before the baseball lockout, with the game on the verge of this impending work stoppage. At the same time, though, Dallas was into baseball because it was the first season of the new ballpark there and the Rangers were in first place. I was working for the station that did the Rangers games at the time, although this night's game wasn't on our air. We had a suite where we would do our live reports for the news, and that is where I was that night. This was Kenny Rogers's first full season as a starting pitcher after being converted from being a reliever, and he was having a great season.

People were still skeptical of his success, though, and were waiting for the wheels to come off eventually. Around the fifth inning, everyone started to realize he had a perfect game going, but the attitude was still, "It's Kenny Rogers; he'll blow up." Well, innings go by and all of a sudden, we were in the seventh, and he was still perfect. In the seventh, he went to a three-ball count on all three hitters but got them out anyway. Somehow, there were now more people in the stadium than there were at the start of the game. I don't know if they just opened up the gates and let anyone in, but it went from a sellout crowd to every seat actually being taken and people standing wherever they could. I have no idea where all these people came from.

When the Rangers were up, the fans wanted them to make outs so Rogers could pitch. Every pitch had every emotion riding on it. And Rogers never blew up. Rusty Greer made a diving catch in centerfield to start the ninth, the place went nuts, and at that point, everyone realized this was meant to be. The last two outs were almost anticlimactic. We went on to do a live report at the end of the game, and it might have been the most enraptured crowd I've ever been around, pitch by pitch.

1994 NFC Championship Game, Dallas Cowboys at San Francisco 49ers, Candlestick Park, San Francisco, California, January 15, 1995

It was the third straight year the Cowboys and Niners played in the NFC Championship Game, with this one in San Francisco. I spent the week in

San Francisco covering the team for the station I was working for in Dallas, and being around that Niner team, I realized they had a confidence unlike either of the two previous years and even more than the Cowboy teams of that era, with all of those stars. There was just something about this Niner team, and they came out and jumped right on the Cowboys, leading 21–0 early. The Cowboys made it close, but the game was never really in doubt.

What amazed me was after the game, though. It was a sense of relief by the Cowboys that they had lost that game. It stunned me to see a team like this relieved that they had lost. They were a dominant team, but I got the feeling that the hype and expectations around the team to win their third straight Super Bowl were just overwhelming. After they lost, the attitude was one of "well, we had a good run," and there was a sense that these guys were under so much pressure to keep things going that once it was done, they were absolutely fine with it. It was absolutely stunning.

2003 American League Championship Series, Game 7, Boston Red Sox at New York Yankees, Yankee Stadium, Bronx, New York, October 16, 2003

I was working sidelines for FOX, and my job was to interview the losing manager. The game is in the seventh inning and the Sox are ahead, so I'm starting to get ready to interview Joe Torre. Pedro Martinez is pitching a gem, and I head down to the field to get ready. My producer, Mike Weisman, tells me that they might have me interview Pedro on the field first before going to talk to Torre. Even after Grady Little doesn't take Pedro out, I'm still saying there is no way the Sox are going to blow this game. Of course, the Yankees come back, and Aaron Boone hits the extra-inning home run to win the game.

The stadium is going crazy; I rush out on the field and am told to grab Boone, who is still running the bases. I find a spot and, as he touches home plate, I go over to grab him. MLB security stops me, though, and tells me I can't go there. I'm about 10 feet from home plate, the Yankees are celebrating, the stadium is wild, players are jumping up and down all around me, and finally, an MLB PR rep sees me and grabs Boone out of the crowd and brings him over to me. This is literally twenty seconds after he has rounded the bases. So I am doing this interview, and I look into his eyes to see the blankest stare I've ever seen anyone have. You could see in his face that he had no idea what was going on at that moment. I asked a question, and all he could say was, "I don't know what to say right now." It was just pure joy on his face.

Minnesota Vikings at Carolina Panthers, Bank of America Stadium, Charlotte, North Carolina, October 30, 2005

This was one of the greatest individual performances I've ever seen. The Vikings were going through a rough stretch but thought they had turned it around heading into Carolina. Steve Smith was having a good season, but cornerback Fred Smoot thought he was going to shut Smith down. Smith was at 120 yards by halftime, and it was clear the Vikings weren't going to stop him all day. He finished with 203 yards. I've never seen one player dominate a game like this, especially a wide receiver that everyone knew was getting the ball—the Vikings couldn't stop him from getting the ball or stop him once he had it. On one of his touchdowns, he celebrated by rowing a boat to mock the Vikings recent "Love Boat" scandal. I just don't know if I've even seen one individual dominate a team sport like Smith that day.

Gary Miller
Broadcaster, ESPN

Northern Illinois at Northwestern, Dyche Stadium, Evanston, Illinois, September 25, 1982

One of my all-time most memorable sporting events is one I wasn't even covering. I was actually looking for work for the two months between my initial job at WSAV-TV in Savannah and starting at CNN. Back in my hometown of Naperville, I hooked up with my good friend and colleague from SIU; we never had any better way to spend our time than to attend a sporting event . . . *any* sporting event. And so it was that I happened to be one of the chosen few in

Dyche Stadium in Evanston on Saturday, September 25, to see Northwestern play football—in person for the only time in my life.

The local Big Ten team had been a humiliating embarrassment during my youth, but the Wildcats had now outdone themselves, having lost thirty-four consecutive games, the longest losing streak in Division 1-A football history. I just wanted to be able to say I saw one of the games of this epic feat of futility, spend an afternoon with a good buddy, and take the odd chance that, just perhaps, we'd be there as the purple gang broke immortality. After all, they were playing Northern Illinois, and in those days even my alma mater could occasionally beat the Huskies.

Wouldn't you know . . . Dennis Green's gang got the better of NIU 31–6! Some of the same undergrads who the year before had torn the goalposts down shouting, "We're the worst!" after a particularly dehumanizing loss to Michigan State, were now carting the goalpost up the side of the stadium and tossing it down to the street below. I found out later that the mad chorus we watched carting it away had taken it all the way down to Lake Michigan and dumped it in. Now that's school spirit!

1986 American League Championship Series, Game 7, California Angels at Boston Red Sox, Fenway Park, Boston, Massachusetts, October 15, 1986

Everyone remembers Dave Henderson's home run off Donnie Moore in Game 5, but the Red Sox still had to go back to Boston and win two more. After they clinched the pennant in Game 7, there are four distinct images I will remember forever. The first was interviewing Jim Rice in the Fenway dugout before he went into the clubhouse. Like most media members, I had had a stormy, unpleasant relationship with the Red Sox leftfielder over the years, but that day he sat in the dugout, alone, and beamed. The white teeth in his mouth outsized his trademark moustache, and he couldn't stop smiling. I've never seen a player before or since, especially one with such a surly reputation, react with such pure, warm, satisfied, calm pleasure.

After that it was on to the Angels' clubhouse for reaction to one of the worst collapses in postseason history. As I interviewed Bobby Grich, Doug DeCinces, and others about the disappointment, I could hear someone behind me saying, "Man, that's a bitchin' coat! Where'd you get that coat? Man, that is a bitchin' coat." As I wrapped the interview, I turned around to discover it was Reggie Jackson, admiring a rainproof duster I had bought to combat the

Boston elements. In the midst of all that was happening to this club, Reggie was making fashion observations.

From there it was into the manager's office. Gene Mauch is one of the most respected and liked men in baseball. I happened to catch him alone. As I asked him to describe what he was going through, considering how close they'd come to a World Series, his eyes reddened and welled with tears. All Mauch could manage was, "It burns, it burns. You know, in your gut, it burns me inside." That image of the late leader is just as fresh twenty years later.

The fourth and final image from that fateful October afternoon in Boston is preserved on tape to this day. WCVB-TV in Boston was doing live interviews in their tiny locker room. Rice and Don Baylor were trying to put it in perspective while constantly turning around to see what all the chaos was behind them. Turns out reliever Rob Woodward was doing a striptease with a towel in the background of their *live* interview and didn't know the show was going on for all of greater New England. Teammate Al Nipper eventually spotted the scene on a monitor in the clubhouse and rushed to share it with the other Sox, and an oblivious Woodward, Rice, Baylor, and broadcaster Mike Dowling, as the X-rated show went on uninterrupted. That was my final lasting image of that postseason . . . before Bill Buckner.

1986 World Series, Game 6, Boston Red Sox at New York Mets, Shea Stadium, Queens, New York, October 25, 1986

Which brings us to Buckner. Once again, behind the curtain of coverage. For you see, even though I was in Shea Stadium that night, covering the event for CNN, I never actually saw the Bill Buckner gaffe from the press box. As usual, the media goes down in the eighth inning to be prepared for postgame interviews and reaction and, ostensibly, to get in line for your turn with the assembled mob. That night, with the game and the Series seemingly in hand, we media members gathered in what used to be the Jets locker room, where we saw the MVP trophy that was to be presented to Bruce Hurst of Boston. He had a shutout in Game 1, and beat Doc Gooden in Game 5 to earn the writers' MVP votes, in helping secure the Red Sox' first World Series title since 1918.

But while we were underneath the stands, we could hear a lot of ruckus overhead. The Mets were rallying and had tied it, as we heard from various reports that filtered in. We snuck back out to glimpse the great comeback and to watch Boston blow yet another lead, this time in the tenth inning. A lot more changed on the night of October 25, 1986, than you probably realize, including the mantle of Bruce Hurst.

1988 World Series, Game 1, Oakland Athletics at Los Angeles Dodgers, Dodger Stadium, Los Angeles, California, October 15, 1988

Working for CNN, I went down in the top of the ninth to be outside the A's locker room for reaction and to be ready to go live after the game from the field. Waiting through an uneventful top of the ninth, I took the opportunity to make a restroom stop, and who should be standing next to me in the men's room but Ryan O'Neal. Only in Hollywood.

In the layout at Dodger Stadium in 1988, there was a tunnel leading up to home plate between the opposing locker rooms. All I could see from where I stood were Kirk Gibson's feet in the batter's box, as I listened on a radio with intermittent reception. The ensuing roar said it all. All of our plans and ideas for Game 1 coverage were suddenly turned completely upside down. Out on the field after the game, we interviewed Alfredo Griffin and Mickey Hatcher, and even with the stadium mostly empty, fifteen minutes after the homer, there was an electricity still in the air that I've never felt anywhere else at anything approaching that level. It was eerie in a way, as if some outside source had completely changed the atmosphere.

Then the next day Kirk himself shattered all that karmic energy with his hostile attitude and literally throwing bats at NBC cameras as he battled through a batting practice that proved he wouldn't be able to play. I've never experienced anything like the tingle in the air or the reaction of the hero that October night in Chavez Ravine.

1989 World Series, Game 3, Oakland Athletics at San Francisco Giants, Candlestick Park, San Francisco, California, October 17, 1989

I was sitting at the top of Candlestick Park waiting for Game 3 of the World Series, with a meager box lunch between my legs. Watching the players go through pregame rituals, I heard a roar and thought there was a flyover. Almost instantaneously, the entire sixty-thousand-seat stadium shifted several feet toward first base . . . and then back the other way. My colleague from CNN, Michael Cowman, was based on the West Coast, and as I stared at him in gape-mouthed disbelief, he said, "We just had an earthquake!"

Having grown up in the Midwest, I was stunned and speechless. Having had concrete move that distinctly beneath me, I was convinced the entire structure was about to crack in half, and our top section would freefall down below, survival chances minimal. While my life passed before me, the crowd erupted in spontaneous applause, because they knew what had just happened. Initially, with all the power out and no PA system, security told us to stay seated and wait for instructions. That lasted about a minute, and then, still convinced there was no way Candlestick could hold together, Cowman and I decided to get out of there. From the top, it took a while to get out, and you had to descend down concrete ramps that spiraled with concrete right above you, not to mention fighting the crowds still pouring into the stadium.

I was never so relieved as when we finally cleared the superstructure. Only when we got to the satellite truck did we realize how disastrous the 7.1-magnitude earthquake had been. I could probably write a book on what happened from there, but suffice to say, with CNN unable to get anyone into the area, I became the lead reporter for the network. Reporter involvement taken to extremes—and obviously nothing that could ever happen in any game could compare with that.

Jay Mohr
Actor, Jerry Maguire

1994 NBA Finals, Game 5, Houston Rockets at New York Knicks, Madison Square Garden, New York, New York, June 17, 1994

Patrick Ewing draining a three pointer? That's what I saw. That's what around twenty thousand of us saw at Madison Square Garden that night. Time was running out at the half, and the Rockets' defense had broken up the first scoring options of the Knicks. As the game clock (the shot clock was off) clicked down to three, none of the slashing or cutting by John Starks and Anthony Mason was working. A kickout pass to the three-point line with two seconds left drew a gasp, as all in attendance realized it was being caught by Sir Patrick (*What the hell was he doing out there*??!!).

Patrick caught the ball and gave it a quick backspin in his hands and launched the ball toward the rim. It looked like the ball had been catapulted, but it went in. Straight in. No rim, nothing but hot nylon. The Garden erupted. In MSG there is a railing around the mezzanine level for people in wheelchairs to park at and watch the games. My hand to God, I saw no less than ten people get up from their wheelchairs and jump up and down cheering. We all left the Garden chanting, "Knicks in six!" What dopes.

Seattle Mariners at New York Yankees, Yankee Stadium, Bronx, New York, May 14, 1996

No-hitters are rare. Being at one is rare and terrifying. I think what separates seeing a no-hitter live from any other event is, at other big events, you bring your hype with you. This was just a Tuesday-night baseball game. After the first inning, when no hits have been surrendered, my friends and I always jokingly say, "He's got a no-hitter going!" At the time, we didn't realize we would say it again in the fifth, sixth, seventh, and eighth innings. too.

Between the eighth and ninth innings, I had trouble breathing. Doc Gooden already had thrown over a hundred pitches. *If*, and that was a big *if*, he came out for the ninth, he would have to face Alex Rodriguez, Ken Griffey Jr., and Edgar Martinez. Not only did he face them, but he did everything he could to walk each of them, and he did start off by walking A-Rod. The last out was recorded, and Doc was carried off the field, the first time anyone had been carried off the field at Yankee Stadium.

1998 World Series, Games 1 and 2, San Diego Padres at New York Yankees, Yankee Stadium, Bronx, New York, October 17–18, 1998

Did the Padres even know they were in the World Series? The entire team looked like tourists. Newsreel footage of Tony Gwynn touring Monument Park dominated the sports shows. The energy in Yankee Stadium felt like what it must have been when they fed Christians to the lions. Every Yankee chipped in. Every play was crisp, clean, and perfect as pinstripes.

For Game 2, I brought my mother. I forget who the Padres starter was, but he was getting shelled. Our seats were in leftfield near the railing of the San Diego bullpen. As Andy Ashby was warming up to come into the game, my demure mother leaned over the railing and screamed, *"Sit down, Andy! Your mother's calling you!!!"* She got a big ovation in our section for that one. It was amazing to watch a team that you knew at the moment was going down in history as one of the best ever.

Super Bowl XXXVI, New England Patriots vs. St. Louis Rams, Louisiana Superdome, New Orleans, Louisiana, February 3, 2002

Tom Brady walked away with the MVP award, but I don't think he should have. I am not even sure the MVP award should have gone to an actual person. If I had a vote, I would have given the MVP award to Adam Vinatieri's right foot. Maybe just his toes. Perhaps his right leg?

The Rams were *huge* favorites going into the game, and few could argue. It wasn't until Ty Law intercepted a Kurt Warner pass and took it to the bank that it seemed the impossible might actually happen. With five seconds left, Vinatieri lined up for what would be the Super Bowl winning field goal. You could have heard a mouse pissing on cotton. The kick was perfect and split the uprights. Confetti rained down from the Superdome ceiling, and the Pats took the field in celebration. On the drive home, we wondered why the Rams weren't allowed a kickoff, since there was still three seconds on the clock. After the game we had just watched, though, we didn't care.

Marc Antonio Barrera vs. Erik Morales, MGM Grand Garden Arena, Las Vegas, Nevada, June 22, 2002

Morales was as badly robbed in this rematch as Barrera was in the first one. The fight itself was less than stellar, but the trash-talking prior was epic. Morales said Barrera couldn't win because he came from Mexico City, and they were all rich snobs there. Barrera responded by saying that Morales came from a long line of drunken border people that don't have shoes. Morales came into the ring with *La Frontiera* on his trunks—a nod to his peeps back in the border town.

Barrera mostly danced in the first few rounds but eventually bobbed Morales with a right hand to the bottom that you could hear if you were in the casino gambling. Morales responded to the bomb by sticking out his mouth-piece, laughing and pointing to *La Frontiera* on the front of his trunks. The message was clear. You just hit me with the best punch of your career, and it did nothing. The entire place swung over to Morales's side after that, and I wish I spoke Spanish just so I could have understood the brutal heckling Barrera took for the rest of the fight. *La frontiera*, baby.

Chris Myers
Broadcaster, FOX Sports

1989 World Series, Game 3, Oakland Athletics at San Francisco Giants, Candlestick Park, San Francisco, California, October 17, 1989

I was with Joe Torre, who was between managing jobs at the time and was doing some work with Chris Berman, Bob Ley, and me at ESPN, and we were in the auxiliary press box at Candlestick Park, ready to file reports. Then we heard this noise, a loud rumbling. I live in California, so I've experienced minor earthquakes before. You could almost see the noise, and you thought that a plane had hit the stadium because of the shaking and the noise. Then, you could see the field almost ripple. The stadium was built on bedrock, so it didn't crumble, but you certainly could feel the vibrations. For people around us who had never been through something like this, you could see them turn pale and wonder exactly what was going on.

After things started settling down, you could see players come out on the field and start looking for their families and collecting them so they could make sure they were okay and get out of the stadium. I remember talking to Tony LaRussa after the Series ended and his A's swept the Giants, and realizing how bad we felt for guys who played their whole career to make it to a World Series and for this to happen, where the games were nothing more than an afterthought and so unimportant.

1990 West Coast Conference Semifinals, Portland at Loyola Marymount, Gersten Pavilion, Los Angeles, California, March 4, 1990

I was the West Coast ESPN reporter, and it was my night off. I was out watching the movie *Born on the Fourth of July*, when I checked my messages and found out that I had gotten a call from the assignment desk telling me to get to the gym at Loyola Marymount because something had happened to Hank

Gathers. I rushed over to the gym and found out that he had collapsed on the court and was being rushed to a medical center in Marina Del Rey, which was the first indication to me that this was a very serious situation.

When I got to the hospital, Gathers was being rushed inside. As I stood there, Coach Paul Westhead and all of Gathers's teammates began to arrive and go in, but my camera crew and I waited outside. ESPN went on the air with *SportsCenter* at this point, and given the fact that I was totally unprepared physically to go on the air (I was in such a rush to get to the gym, I hadn't shaved or gotten dressed for TV), I borrowed a coat from an AP reporter for my report.

A medical representative came out to tell us that the family and coaches were being informed that Hank Gathers had passed away and that it was believed to be from a heart attack. I confirmed the story with someone else who was inside and broke the story live on *SportsCenter* once I knew that the family was, in fact, informed of his death. All this happened literally within minutes of the doctors' telling the family, so it was almost as if we were passing the story along as it was happening. At that point, a medical center spokesman came outside, and I pulled him into the shot, where he confirmed everything and gave more details. Then Loyola Marymount's athletic director came out, and we did the same thing. I've always been proud of the way we handled the story, not just by breaking it accurately but with the sensitivity it warranted.

1996 Summer Olympics, Centennial Olympic Park, Atlanta, Georgia, July 27, 1996

I was on the rooftop of the Commerce Center in downtown Atlanta, right in the thick of all the Olympic activity that night and was taping a wrapup for *SportsCenter* when we heard a loud "boom." I paused for a second but then kept going on the report, thinking it was just fireworks or something like that coming from Centennial Park. Then, I turned around and saw the lights and people scrambling and realized that it was something serious. We had a pretty good view of the park but didn't know exactly what was going on.

As security told us to evacuate, and more information became available, I stayed with a camera crew and was able to get security to let me stay and finish the reports. I was able to move around with the security people and interview medical people and others about the situation as the National Guard came in to clear the area. We ended up being the only ones there to feed any information from inside that evacuated area. It looked like a vacated war zone, and we stayed on pretty much through the night giving reports.

2001 Daytona 500, Daytona International Speedway, Daytona, Florida, February 18, 2001

This was the first Daytona 500 broadcast for FOX. Dale Earnhardt was the face of his sport and was actually in a blocking position for his teammate Michael Waltrip at this point in the race. When he hit the wall in the wreck, at the time it didn't look pretty, but everyone assumed it was just another crash—Earnhardt had walked away many times from worse-looking accidents. But the way the car hit the wall, along with the way the seatbelts were adjusted, led to his unfortunate death. You could see in the way some of the track personnel and drivers ran over to his car that something was terribly wrong. When they all stepped away the way they did, you could see they knew by the look on their faces. On the broadcast, of course, you can't say anything of that nature until you have absolute medical clearance to do so, so people questioned our delay in reporting his death. Unfortunately, there was nothing we could do in the situation. Just like that, the face of racing was gone.

2004 American League Championship Series, Game 4, New York Yankees at Boston Red Sox, Fenway Park, Boston, Massachusetts, October 17, 2004

I was the field reporter for FOX starting with Game 4 of the ALCS, when the Sox were down three games to none. It was a rainy night in Boston for Game 4, and I remember Derek Lowe coming out of the dugout before the game, seeing the rain and gloom and commenting that it felt like everyone was coming to a funeral. That really was the feeling at Fenway that night, from the fans and from both teams. After the Red Sox pulled out the game that night, though, you really could feel the shift in momentum. The Sox just felt like a different team after that—usually a day off will stop any shift in momentum, but it didn't in this case. After they finished off the Yankees by winning Games 5, 6, and 7, beating the Cardinals was almost an afterthought.

Bob Neal
Broadcaster, Turner Sports

1986 Goodwill Games, Moscow, Russia, July 4–20, 1986

I was the host for the Games for Turner Sports and was on the air in the studio at the Russian National Television Center for 113 of the 129 hours the games were on over sixteen days. There is no one thing that really stands out from the Games. It was just an incredible event that had low ratings and very little notice to speak of but was literally the first time an American company and the Soviet Union went into business together to televise something, with a mix of American and Soviet technicians involved in the broadcast.

Ted Turner thought of the whole idea nine months before the Games, so that is all the notice we had to get everything ready. The USOC was not exactly happy that Ted was doing these Games, which he initially thought of in Los Angeles in 1984 when the Soviets boycotted the Olympics. I was in Bob Wussler's office when Ted came in and told him about the idea he had for these Games. He was talking about getting the United States and the USSR to both participate and create a lot of goodwill, and that is how he came up with the name of the Games, just like that.

When I got home from Russia, I was more exhausted than I've ever been after an event. And because of the minimal coverage in the States, people would come up to me and ask me what I've been doing lately, even though I was on the air almost the entire length of the Games.

1987 NBA Eastern Conference Finals, Game 5, Detroit Pistons at Boston Celtics, Boston Garden, Boston, Massachusetts, May 26, 1987

Over the years, I had become friends with the late Red Auerbach, going back to the mid-eighties, and before the game, he told me, "I want you to remember one thing about this game. We are going to win it, and Larry Bird is going to make a big play." That didn't strike me as much, of course, because the game was in Boston, so you had a feeling the Celtics were going to win, and Larry Bird made big plays all the time. But, the Celtics were down a point with 27 seconds remaining, and all the Pistons had to do was inbound the ball.

Isiah Thomas is getting ready to inbound the ball right in front of our table and is standing just in front and to the left of us. He is going to inbound it back to Bill Laimbeer, who is standing right around the free throw line. I see both Dennis Johnson and Larry Bird out of the corner of my eye at around half-court. I was calling the game for Turner with Doug Collins, and Doug is one of the best at anticipating things. Just before the ball is thrown in, he says, "Uh-oh, there's Bird." This was even before Isiah threw the ball in. Thomas, who was one of the smartest players ever to play, lobs the ball back to Laimbeer, Bird breaks in and steals the lazy pass, but Laimbeer steps in front of Bird. The key play was Johnson breaking down the court, so Bird can get the ball to him for the layup and the Celtics' victory, 108–107. All this after Red's prediction.

Chicago Bulls at Cleveland Cavaliers, Richfield Coliseum, Richfield, Ohio, March 28, 1990

There are two things about this game that really stand out. First is something that was in the paper that day. Cleveland coach Lenny Wilkens was talking about how to stop Jordan and the Bulls and said that he thought he knew how to do it. Basically, he said "I'll put a great defensive player in Craig Ehlo on Jordan and let him get his 25 or 30 points, and then we can hold everybody else down." Before the game, Jordan came over to us and said, "I'm going to have a big game tonight." And he did. He hit 23 of 37 field goals on the way to a career-high 69 points and added 6 assists and 18 rebounds. When the game ended, he came over to our table for a postgame interview, and on the air, I asked him to sign the final scoresheet from the game. He asked me what to write, and I had him sign it, "To Bob, Thanks for the help. Michael." To this day, that sheet is framed and hangs on my grandson's wall.

1990 World Cup, Italy, June 8–July 8, 1990

I was in Italy doing the English-language broadcast for TNT and other channels. I did seventeen games in thirty days, including the final between West Germany and Argentina that West Germany won, but my favorite memory is about a game I wasn't even at. Due to a quirk in the schedule, we did not televise the semifinal between Italy and Argentina. Argentina was having a down year and wasn't expected to do much, while Italy was the favorite to win it all.

I was driving by myself to Milan, and the night of that game, I stopped over in Santa Margherita, which is a beautiful tourist city. I had a hotel room there, and as I pulled into town, there was a drive right along the waterfront, where all the shops and restaurants look out on the bay. The streets were just overflowing when I pulled into town. It was like a party, people dancing and singing in the streets, all because of the World Cup game that night in Milan. People were sitting in the streets with TVs, just sitting and watching the game. I got to my hotel room to watch the end of the game, which Argentina won on a penalty kick.

I looked out my hotel window, and the streets were deserted, just minutes after the game ended. I hadn't eaten dinner, so I went outside and found a restaurant that was open, and no one was inside. They let me in, and the waiter cried the entire time he was serving me. There were a lot of great moments at that World Cup, including the United States' qualifying and Cameroon's pulling a huge upset in the round-robin part of the tournament, but the deserted streets in Santa Margherita and the waiter who cried are what I remember most from an incredible experience.

1991 PGA Championship, Crooked Stick Golf Club, Carmel, Indiana, August 8–11, 1991

I was anchoring the TBS coverage before CBS took over. No one knew who John Daly was. He was the ninth alternate in the tournament, and when they found him in Arkansas, he drove all night to Indiana to get there in time to play. On the first day he played with Billy Andrade, who is a friend of mine. Daly was a great story, given how he got into the tournament and how he drove all night, and he was playing really well as the day went on. Andrade was one of the few players under par for the day, so we were talking about him and his partner, this kid from Arkansas, who ended up shooting 69 and leading after the first day.

After we were done, I went into the clubhouse for a drink and saw Billy, who started telling me about this incredible day he had with Daly. A few minutes later, Daly joined us, and the first thing I asked him was how it felt that, after everything that happened, now he was leading the PGA. His reply was,

"I don't know, I may still be a little drunk. I know I'm still hungover. Let me get a beer." He then orders two boilermakers—he didn't get drunk, but we ended up having a great chat. But he said to me, "If I can just stay a little drunk, I can win this thing." He was kidding, of course, but, incredibly, went on to win the tournament. I still remember him hitting that shot into 18 to wrap up the win. He could hit the ball a long way and had about as much talent on the course as anyone I've ever seen play.

Dave O'Brien
Broadcaster, ESPN

1991 World Series, Game 7, Atlanta Braves at Minnesota Twins, Hubert H. Humphrey Metrodome, Minneapolis, Minnesota, October 27, 1991

I was a 27-year-old Braves radio play-by-play man at the time. This was truly an October Classic, as we know. Game 7 would end a spectacular Series. In the pregame, Jack Morris, who would stage one of the great pitching performances in MLB postseason history, was warming up inside the already deafening Metrodome. The sound had no place to escape. It hurt to hear. The old Detroit Tiger then came out to pitch the top of the first, to the music playing on the sound system. You could barely hear it, but I guess he had requested Marvin Gaye's Motown classic, "Let's Get It On." I said to my radio partner, Hall-of-Famer Don Sutton: "The Braves are screwed. It's his third start of the Series, and he can't wait to stick it to us." Jack Morris did, indeed, get it on.

Florida Marlins at San Francisco Giants, 3Com Park, San Francisco, California, June 10, 1997

I had called three no-hitters before, but never had I seen such a dominating performance in person. Kevin Brown was magical from the first pitch and would have thrown a perfect game had Marvin Benard—the little Giants' leadoff man who had a history with Kevin—not leaned into an eighth-inning pitch ever so slightly and gotten brushed. The no-hitter came amidst a rare slump for him on the hill. Some in the media had suggested Brown needed an off-speed pitch, which rankled him (about everything did). I was on the field at old Candlestick the next day, and Larry Rothschild, the terrific Marlins pitching coach, was walking by a gaggle of South Florida press near the dugout. He never even looked at the writers, but with eyes straight ahead said just loud enough for them to hear: "So much for the f–ing changeup, fellas."

1997 World Series, Game 7, Cleveland Indians at Florida Marlins, Pro Player Stadium, Miami, Florida, October 26, 1997

In five years of broadcasting the still-new Marlins franchise, I had never seen such a sight: the upper decks at Pro Player Stadium totally packed. Nearly seventy thousand. For the World Series, it was four times an absolute madhouse. But the *sound* is what I remember: When Edgar Renteria, who spoke only a bit of English, hit that single into the outfield to score Craig Counsell with the game-winning run in extra innings, the *sound*, from the Latin-based majority crammed in on that warm October night . . . it was unbridled passion. The hairs on the back of your neck stood up. And that sound—of cheers, laughter, and shouts, mingled with English and Spanish—carried deep into the night, all the way to Cuba.

2004 American League Championship Series, Game 4, New York Yankees at Boston Red Sox, Fenway Park, Boston, Massachusetts, October 17, 2004

During batting practice, Derek Jeter said, "I think we'd better win this thing tonight. If we don't, we could be in serious trouble." The Yankees led 3–0 and were about to sweep Boston in an embarrassingly quick series. They had, presumably, already broken New England's heart—again.

But the Yankees' heart and soul were sounding an alarm, on the field at Fenway, that this Red Sox team was different. Up three games to none, nine innings from clinching the pennant, Jeter was worried. Amazingly, not twenty minutes after Jeter's ominous words, Boston's Kevin Millar was saying the same thing, almost exactly: "They had better finish us off tonight," he said, "or we are gonna come back and shock everybody. Our pitching sets up perfect. Tonight is the whole Series—for both of us." Nobody could have believed what unfolded next—the greatest comeback in sports playoff history. Except the men who played in it. They knew.

2006 World Cup Finals, Italy vs. France, Olympiastadion, Berlin, Germany, July 9, 2006

The match was, of course, a showpiece for Zinedine Zidane—one of the grand soccer masters of his generation. He would retire at the end of the game, ending not only a brilliant career but a thrilling World Cup, one that saw his form return to a younger, glorious time. Shockingly, he never saw the end: Zidane's notorious headbutt of Marco Materazzi in overtime bought him a red card, and the stunned capacity crowd at the famous Olympiastadion would watch with mouths open as he was sent off to the locker room, his head low, his eyes welling with tears, while the whole planet wondered, "How could that *happen*?" The lingering picture of one of the world's greatest all-time talents walking within a few yards of the Cup itself, down the tunnel, disappearing into history in such humiliating fashion . . . it was among the most bizarre exits in sports history. That Italy would soon celebrate a world championship on that same pitch was nearly an afterthought.

Keith Olbermann
Host, Countdown with Keith Olbermann, *MSNBC*

New York Yankees at Boston Red Sox, Fenway Park, Boston, Massachusetts, October 2, 1978

Everybody knows about Bucky Dent's homer in that game, but few people realize that unlike a typical Yankees–Red Sox game, there was no "mixed crowd." The playoff tickets had only gone on sale forty-eight hours earlier, so when Dent homered, maybe a hundred of us Yankees fans stood and cheered—everybody else moaned. It was a death moan. Worst of all, it was my best friend, a Red Sox fan, who had gotten us in there, and when Jim Spencer struck out just before it all happened, he leaned back in his seat and said, "Thank goodness, Bucky Dent's no home-run threat." I asked him if he understood what he'd just done, what had to happen next, and he went all white. He still thinks he caused it.

I've seen a lot of great events—some of them recently, like the run of Yankees rallies in the '01 World Series—but the luster has only grown for me on this one because of what we now know about the only seasonal comebacks that rival the '78 Yankees. The 1951 Giants stole signs from their scoreboard, and the 1914 Braves had three pitchers who all learned how to scuff the ball with emery paper at mid-season. They bent the rules. The '78 Yankees simply bent the time-space continuum.

1979 ECAC Hockey Tournament, Opening Round, Providence at Cornell, Lynah Rink, Ithaca, New York, March 5, 1979

I did a list like this for the book Dan Patrick and I wrote a decade ago and got a lot of grief for including a college hockey game, but this is still the greatest single-game comeback I ever saw. Cornell was the top-ranked team in the East, still stinging from an opening-game loss the year before to Providence—and they were losing to Providence, again, early in the third period,

5–1. I was a Cornell senior and sports director of the radio station, and I was thinking how my staff and I were going to go in and interview our classmates about how they'd gacked again, and then Cornell scored. And scored again. And scored again.

And in the final minute, after Cornell pulled the goalie, a Providence player named Behn Wilson—I still remember the spelling—missed an empty net, and our captain Lance Nethery, who was a friend of mine, pretty much took the puck end-to-end and scored the tying goal. The 6–5 win in OT was almost a given. I screamed myself hoarse. Last year, somebody at the Cornell hockey office found a black-and-white tape of the game, with the radio play-by-play, and made a DVD out of it—and I screamed myself hoarse again!

1980 Winter Olympics, Ice Hockey Semifinals, United States vs. Soviet Union, Olympic Ice Center, Lake Placid, New York, February 22, 1980

I was about a month past my twenty-first birthday, still at my first job at UPI Radio, and my boss Sam Rosen had given me most of the peripheral stuff to cover—including this nondescript hockey team that just kept winning and winning and winning. By the time of the game against the Soviets, Sam had taken over the game coverage, but he wanted fan reaction, so he had me sit in the stands—center ice, maybe thirty rows back. All I had to do was watch the game and interview fans afterwards. Fantastic action, tension that never let up (to this day I still get a chill thinking of the Russian coach actually pulling the world's greatest goalie, Vladislav Tretiak, in favor of his backup), and this extraordinary sense of its being our little secret in Lake Placid. Everybody watched the game on television that night—but it was tape delayed! This was a Friday afternoon in February, and afterwards it was literally as if just a few thousand of us there knew the importance of what had happened. It really was the beginning of the end of the Soviet Union.

1988 World Series, Game 1, Oakland Athletics at Los Angeles Dodgers, Dodger Stadium, Los Angeles, California, October 15, 1988

This is, of course, the Kirk Gibson game, which I covered as sports director of KCBS in Los Angeles. I remember being in the tunnel downstairs as the bottom of the ninth began, with Alexis Denny, who was producing coverage for CBS News, and she said, "So what do we ask Dennis Eckersley?" And I said, "We ask him about that homer he's going to give up to Kirk Gibson," and she just looked at me. To this day I don't know where this came from, but I said it calmly and with no boasting or prophecy to it. "C'mon, isn't it obvious? Gibson can't actually sit the whole game out. He'll pinch-hit the game-winning homer, or the tying, whatever." Boy, was I surprised. That's ESP for you—never enough time to get down a bet.

2000 World Series, Game 2, New York Mets at New York Yankees, Yankee Stadium, Bronx, New York, October 22, 2000

This was far from the best game I've ever been to, far from the best World Series game, even. But it had something special: Roger Clemens throwing a bat handle at, near, or inadvertently in the general direction of . . . me. I was hosting the Series for Fox and reporting during the games from the Yankees' dugout. And from that perspective, when Clemens threw the piece of Mike Piazza's bat, everybody in that dugout had as much reason to think they were the target as Piazza did. I also had to be the first to interview Clemens afterwards, and having known him since he was a rookie and I was a Boston sportscaster, I knew if I just blurted it out there was every chance he'd end the interview right there on national television. So I let him bring it up (and got ripped in the *New York Times*, the next day).

The bat overshadowed two other facts about that game: Clemens was brilliant for eight innings, and the Mets scored five in the top of the ninth off Jeff Nelson and Mariano Rivera and with two out trailed just 6–5—but Bobby Valentine didn't pinch-hit for Kurt Abbott. Might've changed the whole Series.

Bob Papa

Broadcaster, NBC Sports/New York Giants

1978 American League Championship Series, Game 3, Kansas City Royals at New York Yankees, Yankee Stadium, Bronx, New York, October 6, 1978

I was a freshman in high school, and my birthday was in September, so, as a birthday gift, my dad got some Yankee playoff tickets through some friends of his. He couldn't go to the game that day, though, so I went with a cousin of mine who was ten years older. The seats were unbelievable, ten rows behind the Royals' dugout. The Yankees were having a difficult time getting George Brett out the entire series—whenever he came up, you just hoped it was with no one on base because you assumed he was going to get a hit, and he actually hit three solo homers in the game.

This was what October-afternoon baseball was all about, with the shadows creeping through the Stadium as the day progressed. The Yankees fell behind 5–4 in the top of the eighth, and I still remember hoping that Thurman Munson would get a chance to turn things around. When they first remodeled Yankee Stadium in 1976, the fence in left center was 430 feet from home plate (it has since been moved in to make room for Monument Park). Very few guys in those days hit homers over that 430 sign.

When Munson came up, though, you could just feel that this was the moment something was going to happen and that he was going to get something done and save the day. The moment he swung and the ball left his bat, there was no doubt he had crushed it. I can still hear the sound and see the trajectory. It looked like a golf ball and started on a line, then began to soar. All you could think, though, was that he just hit it to the worst part of the ballpark. But the ball just kept traveling and traveling, and the outfielders started to slow down. Guys like Reggie Jackson would hit homers like this back then, not guys like Thurman Munson. But when the outfielders started to let up, you realized that the ball was going to be gone. The place went absolutely nuts after the two-run homer, and the Yankees went on to win by that 6–5 score and clinched the pennant the next day. After the game, everyone just loitered outside the stadium for a couple of hours, waiting for the Yankees to come out, and you could just sense that this team was about to go on to win the World Series.

Super Bowl XXV, Buffalo Bills vs. New York Giants, Tampa Stadium, Tampa, Florida, January 27, 1991

The Super Bowl really seemed to start in San Francisco one week earlier at the NFC Championship Game, since the Niners were going for a three-peat. After the Giants won in California on a late Matt Bahr field goal, they flew immediately to Tampa, since there was no off-week before the Super Bowl that season. Everyone at the hotel and in the NFL was expecting the Niners to be there, though, not the Giants, so when the Giants arrived at the hotel, a lot of San Francisco 49er paraphernalia was still hanging in welcome—even the coaches' cars that were provided by the league had the San Francisco coaches' names on them.

As the team settled into Tampa, they adopted a very business-like approach to their preparation, because many of the players on the team had won four years earlier, while Buffalo was the brash, up-and-coming wild horses. That entire week in Tampa, you saw a lot of Bills out past curfew, whereas the Giants' veterans took it upon themselves to make sure the younger guys were out of the clubs and bars and in cabs to the hotel as their curfew approached.

We all know about the national anthem by Whitney Houston before the game, with the game occurring during the Gulf War. I'll never forget the military presence and how long it took to get into the stadium because of all the security measures in place. The game was like a heavyweight fight, with the Bills being the fast welterweight and the Giants the heavyweight trying to lean on the smaller guy. The big question in the press box, though, was whether the Giants could continue to keep the ball away from Buffalo, because their offense was so potent.

At the time, I was doing shows with Giants linebacker Carl Banks, and I remember him telling me that they had all these subtle ways in which they were going to slow the Bills down, such as "accidentally" tripping on the ball after the officials placed it on the field, so that Buffalo would have trouble going into their no-huddle offense. That was the type of stuff that Bill Belichick instilled in the defense that day to keep the Bills from finding their rhythm but also to help conserve energy. Even after the Giants went ahead 20–19, though, you just couldn't help but think there was nothing they could do to stop Buffalo. It was such a fierce-hitting game that, combined with the warm, thick air and maybe even some of the partying the Buffalo players did, the Bills' stamina really might have been affected as the game went on, especially their defense, which spent so much of the game on the field.

On the last drive, you couldn't tell if you were watching a slow death or not, because Buffalo started moving the football down the field, and it really felt like the clock wasn't moving fast enough. One of the biggest plays of the game was the open-field tackle Everson Walls made on Thurman Thomas, keeping him from gaining another 12 or 13 yards and moving Scott Norwood's field goal attempt that much closer. On grass, at night, with a little dew on the ground, a 47-yard attempt is a lot to ask of a kicker used to kicking on artificial turf. NFL Films did a tremendous job with their film of the field goal and how they edited the radio calls from the two announcers, but that is exactly how it felt in the stadium. It felt like the ball hung in the air for five minutes, and in your head, the only thing you could think was that the Giants might lose this game despite outplaying the Bills. Then the kick sailed wide right, and it was as if the stadium, which was predominantly Giants fans, blew out a breath of air. It was one of the most compelling games I've even seen.

1992 Summer Olympics, Barcelona, Spain, July 25–August 9, 1992

There is nothing like the Opening Ceremonies at the Olympics. Living in the United States, we are used to the World Series, the Super Bowl, and all the other high-profile events, but those are U.S. events. The Olympics are a world event, and to see all of the nations coming together in the Parade of Nations and the way the Olympic cauldron was lit was spectacular. The Bosnian war was going on at the time, and they actually stopped the war so that the ten athletes from Bosnia and Herzegovina could get out of the country and go to Barcelona without the plane being harmed. When those athletes entered the stadium during the Parade of Nations, it was just unbelievable. The U.S. contingent was enormous, the Spaniards were obviously the home team, the Berlin Wall had come down and the German team was united, the Soviet Republics had all splintered off but were competing under one flag, and there was really a feeling of change politically in the world.

But when these tattered Bosnian athletes came marching into the stadium, the ovation and feeling of humanity that swept through the eighty-thousand-seat building was a moment that transcended sport. It was one of the most moving experiences of my life, and because of that night, at every Olympics I have worked since, both Summer and Winter, I make it a point to go to the Opening Ceremonies. It is more than just sport. It is a feeling of world community unlike any other place.

The 1992 Olympics were where Oscar de la Hoya had his coming-out party. He wasn't the most highly touted of the American boxers, and a lot of people might have felt that he didn't deserve to be on the team. Here was this kid from East LA with a strong family structure who would point to the heavens after his fights to honor his mom, who had passed away a couple of years earlier from cancer, and he went through the tournament and won the gold medal.

This was also the Olympics that featured the original Dream Team. Their hotel was on the same block as the hotel I stayed in for NBC, and they actually had to close the block off. The hotels were on a side street off the Ramblas, which is the main community area in Barcelona, where there are street vendors and carnivals and musicians, and is the epicenter of culture in the city. So, to see Charles Barkley and Karl Malone and Michael Jordan and all of the others walking through the streets and along the Ramblas, mingling with the world community, it is the exact opposite of the way the Dream Teams since then have approached things. These guys really dove into the spirit of being ambassadors of the game of basketball. They showed up at other Olympics events, including many boxing matches.

I remember Barkley standing in the crowd, not far from our broadcast position, pumping his fists as Americans were fighting, Evander Holyfield high-fiving him while Vernon Forrest, who was a Holyfield protégé from Georgia, was in the ring. It felt like real sportsmanship; all of the big business of the Olympics didn't seem apparent. I happened to have a night off and was able to go watch the Dream Team win the gold medal. It was such a celebration in the building. Everyone knew what the outcome was going to be before the game even started, but to see the show these guys put on, and the passion they had and the sportsmanship they exhibited, made you proud to be an American, first of all, but it also made you proud to be a part of the sports community. It wasn't just about the winning, but the competing, the sportsmanship, and the mutual respect between the competing countries, too. All of these things made the 1992 Olympics one of the coolest experiences I've ever had.

1994 Stanley Cup Finals, Game 7, Vancouver Canucks at New York Rangers, Madison Square Garden, New York, New York, June 14, 1994

As a kid, pre-cable television, my Sunday nights were spent listening to Rangers games on the radio, through all of the close calls the Rangers had over the years. I was like every other Ranger fan. I was convinced the Rangers were never going to win a Stanley Cup in my lifetime. There are certain things you come to believe, and that was one. There was a big part of me that was nervous about going to Game 7 against Vancouver, but I had to go and be there for it.

As the game went on and the Rangers got closer and closer to winning, I found myself reflecting back to Ed Giacomin's return to the Garden with the Red Wings after being waived and to when J.P. Parise and the expansion Islanders knocked the Rangers out of the playoffs and to all the other Rangers failures over the years, almost preparing myself for something bad to happen and the Rangers losing the game. As time wound down, though, and you could feel the Rangers about to win, there was that one more faceoff—in typical Rangers fashion, that last minute just couldn't play out and end. There had to be one more faceoff, and all I could imagine at that point was some freak thing happening that would lead to Vancouver's tying the game and Rangers fans getting clubbed again.

But when the final seconds ticked off, I went nuts. Here I was, working in the business, having done some work for the NHL on TV, but now, I was just a fan, and I went out of my mind for a couple seconds. I just couldn't believe what had just happened, and I welled up with tears. Madison Square Garden has a very unique sound, part din, part roar, part rumble, and you can always tell on television when the game you are watching is taking place there, and that night, the sound was unmistakable. I was sitting across from the benches, and on the ice, gloves and sticks were flying in the air in pandemonium. I went from screaming to stunned. I had spent so much of my life going to games in the Garden, and there was always that empty feeling that the Rangers were never going to do it. Now, they finally had. The craziest thing was that, amidst all this celebration, I found myself bolting out of the Garden, because I wanted to get home and soak up the postgame show. Even though I was there for it, I needed to get home to see it on TV to make sure it really happened.

2000 Summer Olympics, Sydney, Australia, September 15–October 1, 2000

Sydney is the greatest place on the planet, and I'll never forget being in downtown Sydney the night Cathy Freeman ran for the gold in the 400 meters. The social implications, with Freeman being an Aborigine, were immeasurable. Freeman was running for her country in her prime event with literally the whole nation watching, but more importantly, she was carrying the banner for her people.

The city of Sydney did a great job with the Olympics, because they had giant TV screens set up all over the city, where people would congregate and watch various events. The night Freeman won, every person in the nation had his or her neck craned toward a television, and when she won, you could hear the eruption in the streets, in the buildings, and from the stadium. The whole city of Sydney rejoiced, whether you were Australian or not. Every single person was pulling for her to win the race. It was one of the most emotionally charged races ever, and it was spine-tingling from the introductions before the race until the moment she finished and won. I've never heard an entire city, or country, cheer at the same exact moment, and probably never will again.

Edwin Pope
Columnist, Miami Herald

Recipient of Football Hall of Fame's Dick McCann
Memorial Award, 2002

Muhammad Ali vs. Sonny Liston, St. Dominic's Arena, Lewiston, Maine, May 25, 1965

Bud Collins, George Plimpton, Mort Sharnik, and I rode with Ali and sparring partners on the bus ride to Massachusetts for the fight with Sonny Liston. Laugh a minute, Ali driving part of the way, then the bus breaking down, and us waiting beside a little pound outside Fayetteville, North Carolina, for a Southeastern Stages vehicle to replace Ali's beat-up old clunker. The funniest thing (though only in retrospect) was that we hadn't even cleared Miami city limits when Ali, at the wheel, turned around and said, "Hey, we ain't got no gas, and I ain't got no money. Somebody loan me a hundred dollars." As soon as he spotted me for the mark (why, I'll never know, because I certainly couldn't have looked that prosperous in 1965), I tried to melt into my seat. He got me anyway. "Pope, you got a hundred dollars?" I said, "When you going to pay me back?" And he said, "Soon as we get to Massachusetts." (The fight was scheduled for Boston before the boxing commission there banned it, and it was moved to Lewiston, Maine.) So I gave him the hundred dollars and said, "Don't worry about it. No use both of us worrying." He smiled, and three days later, when we arrived in Massachusetts, I asked him to pay me, and he said, "See Angelo [Dundee]." I had to wait two more days for Angelo to get there and pay me. A hundred dollars was money in those days.

Super Bowl III, New York Jets vs. Baltimore Colts, Orange Bowl, Miami, Florida, January 12, 1969

I have to admit; I didn't realize it was so big at the time. Only in retrospect did its importance penetrate my numbness. Like almost everybody else, I had picked the Colts, but I picked the first two Super Bowl losers, too, so what else was new?

My pick was 42–7 Colts, and I was at a pro-am golf tournament a few weeks later when Joe Namath was teeing off, and he looked over at me and said, "Forty-two to seven!" and spit on the grass. He didn't speak to me for the next thirty-five years, and even though he never said it, I always thought that was the reason.

1980 Winter Olympics, Ice Hockey Semifinals, United States vs. Soviet Union, Olympic Ice Center, Lake Placid, New York, February 22, 1980

I didn't know a hockey puck from a volleyball, except that when the round thing went into the nets it was a goal. A lot of media had already gone home from Lake Placid because they wouldn't allow anyone to drive in the town. About as soon as they left, it was permitted. Anyway, a lot of those who left missed one of the great sporting events ever. As I said, my ignorance about ice hockey was boundless, but I was sitting beside Tim Horgan, a great guy from the *Boston Herald*, and when he got excited, I knew we were on to something. When the game was over, I was so carried away I guess I threw an expensive pair of dark glasses into the air along with my cap. I went back the next day looking for both of them and never found either. An even sadder part: After I worked hours on a column and finally filed, I looked over at William Taaffe from Washington, who suddenly looked as though a member of his family had died. I asked him what was the matter, and he said, "I lost my whole column. It just vanished from the screen. It's gone . . . gone. . . ." He had written 50 or 60 inches and had to start from scratch. Isn't it funny what you remember the most?

Boston College at Miami, Orange Bowl, Miami, Florida, November 23, 1984

I was standing in the end zone nearby when it happened—Doug Flutie's pass to Gerard Phelan. Most amazing play I ever saw. Selwyn Brown, Tolbert Bain, and Darrell Fullington were all back about as far as they could get—they had been told not to let anyone behind them no matter what—and then the guy just slipped in and grabbed it. I have heard Fullington blamed totally for this play, but I am a lot more inclined to credit Doug Flutie and Gerard Phelan than to blame any of the DBs. To me, it seemed like God was watching out of one tiny corner of an eye and said, "Flutie, you're going to make this play even if all hell is lined up against you." It was one of those plays that had to happen, or else someone would have made it up—like John Tunis or Burt L. Standish did in those long-ago kids' sports-fiction novels.

1989 World Series, Game 3, Oakland Athletics at San Francisco Giants, Candlestick Park, San Francisco, California, October 17, 1989

Blackie Sherrod was sitting beside me, and the first thing he said was, "That's the last time we eat at that damn restaurant." Pretty spooky. I was scared. I had been in some smaller quakes in LA but nothing like that 7.1 in San Francisco. Big chunks of concrete were falling off the walls. I turned to Mike Littwin and said, "What do we do now?" and he said, "Get under one of those tables." I said, "Mike, those tables are plastic, and there's a million tons of concrete above every one of them." He said, "Don't argue with me . . . I'm from Los Angeles, and I know. But I guess the next best place is a doorway." So I tried to stand in a doorway, but it was too crowded. We sat down with our laptops on our laps out on the concourse, but then the cops ran us all off. It took an hour and a half just to get out of the parking lot. I decided that night I wasn't ever again going to complain about a game lasting too long. But of course I did.

Elliott Price

Cohost, Morning Show with Denis, Elliott and Shaun, *Team 990 Radio Montreal*

1970 Major League Baseball All-Star Game, Riverfront Stadium, Cincinnati, Ohio, July 14, 1970

Yes, I was there, wide-eyed and thirteen years old, when Pete Rose ran over Ray Fosse. And thank goodness I made it to that one, since I missed the '71 All-Star Game in Detroit, when Reggie hit the light tower, because I had to go to summer school for English of all things. We had traveled seven hours in a car from Montreal to Cincinnati. The Reds hadn't done much that night, including pitcher Wayne Simpson (do you remember he was 13–1 at the break before blowing out his arm?). I remember a crush of media and fans on the field before the game and only being able to see Frank Howard's head above everyone else. It all happened so fast after a long hot night: Jim Hickman's hit, Amos Otis's throw, and Ray Fosse's career. The Cleveland catcher was never the same, but maybe it helped him get traded to Oakland, where he won a pair of World Series rings.

1982 University Cup Finals, Moncton vs. Saskatchewan, Moncton Coliseum, Moncton, Canada, March 14, 1982

I have covered or been to more than a thousand NHL games. I have seen the Stanley Cup won on a number of occasions. Few, however, have stood out in my mind like this little-known Canadian college championship. The coaches are better known than any of the players. The fact that the game was played in Moncton and that the home team won their first-ever college championship of any kind had a lot to do with it. It didn't hurt that the game was decided in the final minute. When the winner ended an incredibly tense affair between Moncton and the University of Saskatchewan, the Moncton Coliseum shook like no other building I've ever been in except one. The coaches? Jean Perron and Dave King. Perron, of course, was also the winner when that Roy kid stood on his head in 1986. It didn't hurt, however, that Perron's team had two players on it named Jean Beliveau.

1983 Norris Division Semifinals, Game 1, St. Louis Blues at Chicago Blackhawks, Chicago Stadium, Chicago, Illinois, April 6, 1983

I grew up a Chicago Blackhawk fan in Montreal. I don't think I have to explain my childhood torture to you. I went every Saturday night to the Montreal Forum and cheered for whichever team was visiting. The Blackhawks usually lost, and Claude Provost almost always blanketed my hero, Bobby Hull. Somehow, Kenny Wharram would score the Chicago goals. Sunday nights meant the radio under the pillow to listen to Chicago home games when they played the Canadiens. The loudest venue in sports, Chicago Stadium, sounded like magic on radio. As a radio sports reporter in 1983, I was to go to Chicago to cover the Expos' season opener at Wrigley Field. Safe to say my first visit *there* was something special, but the day itself was one of the best ever.

The Hawks had gone through a few rough years, but they were back that season, finishing in first place and hosting a playoff opener against St. Louis. When they took the ice and the place erupted, the hair stood on my neck and arms, and my eyes welled with tears. I was ten years old again . . . and yes, they lost again. But I didn't have to go to school the next day and face the music.

1986 Wales Conference Finals, Game 3, Montreal Canadiens at New York Rangers, Madison Square Garden, New York, New York, May 5, 1986

Really, the Patrick Roy Show was a daily affair en route to his becoming the youngest player to ever win the Conn Smythe trophy as Stanley Cup MVP. It's hard to believe it was ever a question whom the Canadiens would go with down the stretch and into the playoffs: veterans Doug Soetaert or Steve Penney or the kid who played just twenty minutes in the NHL before that season? If the Canadiens lose that game in New York, they probably don't win the series, but he wouldn't let go. Wave after Rangers wave turned aside by the phenom. On and on, save after save. As much as that performance, where he stopped everything flung at him as the Canadiens held on for dear life, was impressive, it was his performance after the game that was extraordinary. Sitting on a bar stool outside the Canadiens' dressing room fielding questions from hundreds of assembled media members like he'd been around for a hundred years. You knew then he was going to be something special and that the Canadiens were about to win a Stanley Cup.

Montreal Expos at Los Angeles Dodgers, Dodger Stadium, Los Angeles, California, July 28, 1991

Two nights before, Expos right-hander Mark Gardner carried a no-hitter to the ninth inning. He got the three outs but not the no-hitter. His teammates forgot to score for him, and he lost it in the tenth on an infield chopper. Interestingly, Gardner would finish his career with 99 wins. I was the radio play-by-play announcer. So instead of yelling, *"Mark Gardner has pitched a no-hitter!!!!!"* I got to say meekly, "And now we go to the tenth." For two nights and a day, I wallowed in my bad fortune since I only called about forty games a year at the time. When would I ever come that close again?

Less than two days later, that's when. Sunday afternoon, Dennis Martinez pitched a perfect game. The Expos finally got some runs, as Mike Morgan entered the sixth inning of that one with a no-hitter as well. What more do you need to know about the history of the Montreal Expos? They pitched two no-hitters that weekend and still lost two out of three. Incidentally, I also got to call David Cone's perfecto against the Expos at Yankee Stadium. Not to mention, a perfect game in history lost in extra innings (Pedro Martinez). By the way, only Vin Scully has called more perfect games on radio. How's that for trivia?

Mel Proctor
Broadcaster

1979 NBA Finals, Seattle SuperSonics vs. Washington Bullets, King-dome, Seattle, Washington, and Capital Centre, Landover, Maryland, May 20–June 1, 1979

The Bullets had won the championship the season before against Seattle in 1977–78. I joined the broadcast team the following season. The Bullets had a great team then, with Wes Unseld and Elvin Hayes, Kevin Grevey and Bobby Dandridge, and a great coach in Dick Motta. And this was my first experience in the NBA. The team just rolled over everyone in the league until facing Seattle again in the Finals, where they lost because Grevey and another guard, Tom Henderson, got hurt. And they haven't been back to the Finals since.

1986 AFC Championship Game, Denver Broncos at Cleveland Browns, Municipal Stadium, Cleveland, Ohio, January 11, 1987

It was Denver at Cleveland at the old Municipal Stadium in the AFC Championship Game on January 11, 1987. Our broadcast location was up on the roof, and there were almost a hundred thousand people in the stadium just shaking the place. John Elway was leading this incredible march down the field, completing one pass after another, culminating in a pass to Mark Jackson to send the game into overtime, where the Broncos won on a field goal. The Browns had the Dawg Pound, and I went down on the field after the game; the end zone was just filled with dog bones and dog food. The poise Elway showed on that drive was just phenomenal. I'll never forget the stadium just shaking the whole time.

California Angels at Baltimore Orioles, Camden Yards, Baltimore, Maryland, September 6, 1995

The excitement was building as Cal Ripken Jr. was moving closer to the record, with a countdown being posted on the warehouse in rightfield. The Orioles arranged for me to do a one-on-one interview with Cal about two hours before game time. For some reason, I was terrified that something was going to happen to me on the way there, so I left a lot earlier than I normally do and got to the park really early and had to wait for Cal to get there to do the interview. I still get tears in my eyes when I think about the game. It was moving when Bobby Bonilla and Rafael Palmeiro had to push Cal out of the dugout to take his impromptu "victory lap" around the warning track. I remember looking at the box where Cal Sr. and the Ripken family were sitting, and there wasn't a dry eye in there. It was just an incredible moment.

San Diego Padres at Montreal Expos, Olympic Stadium, Montreal, Canada, August 6, 1999

We went into St. Louis, which is just a great baseball city. Mark McGwire was at 498 home runs, and Tony Gwynn needed just a couple of hits to get to 3,000, so it was possible that both milestones would be accomplished in the same game. Busch Stadium was packed, and the Cardinals fans are knowledgeable enough to know to cheer Tony as much as McGwire. They really wanted to see both things happen. McGwire got his two homers, both off Andy Ashby, but Gwynn fell one hit shy. He did get it the next day in Montreal, though, although there weren't quite as many people there to see it.

Arizona Diamondbacks at Washington Nationals, RFK Memorial Stadium, Washington, D.C., April 14, 2005

It was one of the most emotional, incredible moments I have ever experienced: 45,956 fans packed RFK Stadium as baseball returned to Washington for the first time in almost thirty-four years. President George W. Bush threw out the first pitch, and the Nationals beat Arizona, 5–3. It was amazing to see many fathers who had probably attended Washington Senators' games years ago, sitting with their sons or daughters sharing the joy of baseball's return. The fans actually shook the stadium, just as they did when the Redskins used to play at RFK. At first, I thought maybe it was an earthquake but realized it was the delirious Nationals fans shaking the old stadium. I will always be able to say that I broadcast the Nationals' first home game as baseball returned to our nation's capital.

Merrill Reese
Broadcaster, Philadelphia Eagles

1960 NFL Championship Game, Green Bay Packers at Philadelphia Eagles, Franklin Field, Philadelphia, Pennsylvania, December 26, 1960

I was a young teenager and had sent in an entry blank from the newspaper to enter a lottery to buy a ticket for the game and was selected as one of the people who could buy a ticket. It had snowed earlier in the week and was extremely cold. I sat in the far corner of the end zone in the horseshoe, where there were benches with seat numbers on them. There were snow piles in the back of the end zones, and I'll never forget Norm Van Brocklin throwing a touchdown pass to Tommy McDonald, who caught the pass and then slid into a snowbank. The game ended with the Eagles' Check Bednarik sitting on top of Green Bay's Jim Taylor as the clock wound down, giving the Eagles the 17–13 win; supposedly, Bednarik looked up at the clock (which wasn't digital and had one hand on it) and, as it ran out of time, said to Taylor, "Now you can get up."

I don't mean to take away from the Super Bowl, but when the title games were played at a home team's stadium, it was something really special. I am someone who truly believes that no matter how space age the stadium or how beautiful it is, there is no such thing as a nice dome, since it has such a large impact on the weather and the feel of the game. Football does not belong inside and battling the elements is a part of the game.

Philadelphia Eagles at New York Giants, Giants Stadium, East Rutherford, New Jersey, November 19, 1978

It was a very unspectacular, ordinary game. I was broadcasting with the late Jim Barniak, who was a newspaper columnist in Philadelphia. As the Giants were going into their victory series, I remember saying on the air, "Let's see what lies ahead for the Eagles. Next week, they'll be in St. Louis." As I said that, inexplicably, Joe Pisarcik tried to hand the ball off to Larry Csonka. I can still see it clanging off his hip, before Herman Edwards picked it up and ran it in for the touchdown.

My exact call from the game was, "Under thirty seconds left in the game, and Pisarcik fumbles the football. It's picked up by Herman Edwards. He's at the 15 . . . the 10 . . . 5. Touchdown, Eagles! I don't believe it. I don't believe it. I do not believe what has just occurred here, ladies and gentlemen. As Pisarcik came forward, he fumbled the football. Charlie Johnson hit him, and Herman Edwards picked it up and ran it in for the touchdown." That broadcast was picked up by Armed Forces Radio and was played all over the world, and in ensuing weeks I got letters from all over the globe.

1980 World Series, Game 6, Kansas City Royals at Philadelphia Phillies, Veterans Stadium, Philadelphia, Pennsylvania, October 21, 1980

I was doing morning sports at WIP, so my days started around 4:30. After my shift, I would go to Eagles practice, then would nap for an hour, and then go to the Phillies World Series game, which I would watch, then edit tape after. I think I went through that World Series on about three hours' sleep a night.

But even with the lack of sleep, I, like everyone else who was there, will never forget this game. All of us will always remember the final out, where Tug McGraw struck out Willie Wilson. There were policemen on horses rimming the field so that no one could run out. The Phillies had never won a World Series in their history, and here they were. There was a moment in the game where a foul ball bounced out of the glove of catcher Bob Boone that would have given the Royals life, but it bounced from Boone's glove into Pete Rose's. There are so many things that just stand out in my mind, but more than anything, it is Tug McGraw pounding his glove, rocking his arms. There was no question in his mind that he was going to strike Wilson out. It was absolutely electric.

1980 NFC Championship Game, Dallas Cowboys at Philadelphia Eagles, Veterans Stadium, Philadelphia, Pennsylvania, January 11, 1981

It was bitterly cold at Veterans Stadium. Just frigid. Few people gave the Eagles much of a chance to beat the Cowboys. Before each playoff game that season, Dick Vermeil would take the team to Tampa to work out at the Buccaneers' facility, where we would spend the week in the sun and come back the day before the game. Vermeil was very humble with the media all week, talking very complimentarily toward the Cowboys. But supposedly he told the team the night before the game, "Twenty-four hours from now, you guys are going to be the NFC champions. We have the Cowboys right where we want them. I've never been more confident that this team is ready to stand on the field and beat our biggest rival."

There were 70,696 people at the Vet that day. There was a hit by John Bunting on Tony Dorsett in the Dallas first offensive series that set the tone, but the play that is remembered more than any other is when Wilbert Montgomery exploded off the right side between Woody Peoples and Jerry Sisemore and ran 42 yards for a touchdown. Even though it was still the first quarter, at that point everyone in the Philadelphia area knew the Eagles were going to the Super Bowl. We just knew they weren't going to lose.

The game was 7–7 at the half, but the Eagles really dominated the second half. A Tony Franklin 26-yard field goal put them ahead, Leroy Harris had a 1-yard touchdown run, and Montgomery ran for 194 yards in the game, while the Eagles' defense held Dorsett to 41 yards, en route to a 20–7 victory. At that point, it was the biggest win in the history of the Eagles franchise.

Harvard at Penn, Franklin Field, Philadelphia, Pennsylvania, November 13, 1982

It was a back-and-forth game, and Harvard took a one-point lead late in the game. Penn drove the length of the field and, with three seconds to play, lined up for a 38-yard field goal, but their kicker, David Shulman, missed the kick.

After this big comeback, they were going to fall short, and you could see all the Penn players just lying there, motionless on the field; they were so exhausted and so drained. All of a sudden, I noticed a flag on the field that had been hidden under some players. The game was over; Harvard had just won this emotional contest, but now, it wasn't over after all. The official starts waving, and makes the call. It was roughing the kicker against Harvard, giving Penn another chance from 15 yards closer. This time, Shulman made the kick to win it for Penn. This game was over; no one saw the flag for the longest time, and players were starting to walk out of the stadium. But Shulman got another chance and gave the game an amazing ending.

Jimmy Roberts

Broadcaster, NBC Sports

1980 Winter Olympics, Men's Speed Skating, Lake Placid Speed-Skating Oval, Lake Placid, New York, February 15–23, 1980

I personally think this is the greatest individual athletic achievement ever. It is like someone winning the 100 meters and the marathon and every other distance in between. I had graduated from college the year before and was new to the business but was able to catch on with ABC Sports, and this was the first job I had; I was the production assistant and did the graphics for speed skating in Lake Placid. Everyone knew Eric Heiden was going to be good, but I don't think anyone really expected what happened. To Eric, it was all a game, and the idea of the game was to do the best you can; and he did. If the U.S. hockey team didn't beat the Soviets at the same Olympics, can you imagine how big a deal this would have been? He has unfortunately become a side-light in American sports history, and in my estimation, there has never been a greater individual accomplishment in sports. It certainly is the most under-rated achievement ever.

1992 NCAA Men's Basketball Tournament, East Regional Finals, Kentucky vs. Duke, The Spectrum, Philadelphia, Pennsylvania, March 28, 1992

Believe it or not, Christian Laettner's shot isn't what I remember most. For me, it was the shot that was next to last, when Sean Woods of Kentucky hit a runner across the lane. For me, it is all about the story, and for Kentucky to make it to the Final Four would have been impossible to imagine. They were like a landlocked country with a navy. They were limping along with a bunch of players who were only there because it was Kentucky. They were on probation, people had left the program, and there seemed to be no hope. But if there was ever an example of why Rick Pitino was and still is a great coach, this was the season. He took those kids—John Pelphrey, Richie Farmer, Sean Woods; added a great recruit in Jamal Mashburn; and turned them into as unlikely a contender team as there ever has been. So when Woods hit the shot while running across the lane, I remember thinking to myself, "Kentucky is going to the Final Four. You couldn't have made this up."

I remember being disappointed when Duke ended up winning, only because I root for good stories, and these guys were so worthy of being cheered for. They stayed when everybody else left and abandoned ship. Of course, Grant Hill is as worthy an athlete to root for as there ever has been, in my estimation, and is all that is good about sports. I remember going outside after the event was over and doing my stand-up in front of the Rocky statue that's in front of the Spectrum and saying, "Rocky almost won this time but didn't."

1994 Winter Olympics, Men's 1000 Meter Speed-Skating Final, Vikingskipet Olympic Arena, Hamar, Norway, February 18, 1994

I really love the Olympics and have been to eleven of them. But when Dan Jansen won this medal, there were so many things about it that made it special. This wasn't the gold medal he was supposed to win. He was supposed to win the 500. At that distance, Jansen was Tiger Woods; he was that dominant and close to unbeatable. This was the third Olympics, though, where something awful happened to him. In 1988 in Calgary, he was really good, but he wasn't the stone-cold lock. A lot was made that year of his sister's death on the day of the race and his subsequent fall in the race; all of that was terrible.

In 1992 it was warm, so the ice was slow and evened the field out, favoring the slower skaters. The circumstances around this race, though, you just couldn't imagine. After he slipped in the race he was supposed to win, the 500—and finished eighth, you just couldn't believe it could happen to him again. You couldn't help but pull for him, given the history and what a genuinely nice person he was. So when the 1000 came along, he wasn't nearly the force that he was in the 500, which made the win so surprising. Coming around the last turn in the 1000, he slipped again, and I just thought to myself, "Oh, no. This can't be. Why does this have to happen to him again?"

But he ended up not just winning but setting a world record in the process. I get goose bumps just thinking about it. All of the other competitors were applauding him; you never see that. Afterwards, they passed his baby daughter, Jane, over the crowd to him, and he skated around the rink with her. It was such a wonderful moment. This represented triumph to me. It was the only time I ever cried watching a sporting event.

The 1996 Masters, Augusta National Golf Club, Augusta, Georgia, April 11–14, 1996

I had developed a pretty good relationship with Greg Norman, so for those of us who have been around golf and seen him tortured over time, this was the day you thought, "Finally." Regardless of how you might feel about him, he was the Tiger Woods of his time. He was the most magnetic, arguably the most talented, certainly the most charismatic player. He was the guy who moved the needle on each telecast and the guy people wanted to watch. He wasn't smoke and mirrors; there are still people who think he was the greatest driver of the golf ball ever. He was just enormously talented. I had seen him tortured a bunch but had also seen him win, too.

I was there at Royal St. George's when he won his second British Open in 1993 and was at the Players Championship when he set the scoring record in '94, so I had seen what he was capable of. There are people who might not have liked him because of his style, but what was undeniable was his talent. When he was good, he was *really* good. For those of us who had seen him crash and burn, you just felt that this wasn't going to be one of those occasions. I did an essay for *SportsCenter* that Sunday morning, and I still remember a line from the essay, where I said, "He should win. It shouldn't even be close. But if he doesn't, you have to wonder if he'll win anything ever again."

Once the round started, though, he was a dead man walking. He claimed it was a problem with his shoulder that created a swing flaw. I claim it was his stubbornness on certain things. The single image I have of that day is his second shot into the 9th hole. The traditional Sunday hole location on 9, which is a par 4, dogleg left, down the hill, with a severely sloping green back to front with a false front, is in front. The fool's play is to try to go for the hole, when you need to play it above the hole. Birdies are rare there on Sunday, because it is too easy to spin the ball back off the hill if you go for the pin. That is exactly what he did, though. I think the thing that made him great was the thing that made him vulnerable. He was going to do it his way. I argued with him about it at the time, and he insisted it was because of his shoulder, but to me, that crystallized the entire day. I think he had problems with his swing, and not long after, he did have an operation on his shoulder, but that day was just one of the most uncomfortable feelings. You just wanted it to be over; it was so difficult to watch, and you couldn't help but feel badly for him. You don't want to see anyone suffer like that. But he handled it so gracefully.

The 1997 Masters, Augusta National Golf Club, Augusta, Georgia, April 10–13, 1997, and 2000 U.S. Open, Pebble Beach Golf Links, Pebble Beach, California, June 15–18, 2000

I was not one of those people who saw Tiger's performance at the 1997 Masters coming. I knew Tiger Woods fairly well at the time and was the only person he did a sit-down interview with afterwards. But he was ready. It was a moment in time that is indelible. I don't remember particular shots, aside from maybe his second shot on Sunday on 18, when he had to hit it from within the crowd. People don't understand how hard it is to win a major golf tournament. For someone to win at that age, by the margin he won by, was incredible.

To me, while the 1997 Masters was memorable, the 2000 U.S. Open was even more impressive. He won at 12 under par, while the next closest guy was at 3 over, a difference of 15 shots. I played that golf course the Saturday before the tournament, and it was the hardest golf course I had ever laid my eyes on. He was playing a different game than everyone else that week. At the

Masters he shot 40 on the front nine on Thursday, so it was a bit of a comeback for him. But at Pebble Beach, it was right from the start. It isn't the details that make these two tournaments so memorable for me. It was the historical significance of his win at the Masters and the biggest butt kicking I had ever seen and sense of awe I had ever experienced at Pebble Beach.

Ken Rosenthal
Broadcaster, FOX Sports

1987 Fiesta Bowl, Penn State vs. Miami, Sun Devil Stadium, Tempe, Arizona, January 2, 1987

First major event I covered; I was working then for the *Courier-Post* in southern New Jersey. I was supposed to watch the game on television in an arena across the street, but the organizers found a seat for me about half an hour before the game, smack in the middle of the press box, right at the 50-yard line. I couldn't believe it. It was the game in which Penn State beat Miami when Vinny Testaverde threw five interceptions. My game story, which I'm sure wasn't very good, focused on Testaverde's blowing it. Little did I know that my sports editor was a big Penn State fan. When I got back home, he told me, "You didn't give enough credit to Penn State." Oops!

1991 World Series, Game 7, Atlanta Braves at Minnesota Twins, Hubert H. Humphrey Metrodome, Minneapolis, Minnesota, October 27, 1991

The climax of the best World Series I have ever seen. The games were so close, so well played. I remember being very excited just leaving for the park each day. It was a feeling I hadn't experienced before or since. Game 7 was majestic: John Smoltz and Jack Morris, putting up zero after zero. After it was over, with Morris pitching all ten innings of the Twins' 1–0 victory, I asked Twins manager Tom Kelly in the news conference, "What would it have taken for Morris to have come out of that game?" Kelly's response is forever in my memory. "A shotgun."

1992 Summer Olympics, Opening Ceremonies, Estadi Olimpic de Montjuic, Barcelona, Spain, July 25, 1992

It was my first Olympics, I was not yet thirty, and I felt like I had really made it. Not every writer who covers the Olympics gets to attend the Opening Ceremonies—the number of tickets is limited—but somehow I was given one at the last minute. It was just a beautiful occasion. I remember my then-colleague, Bill Glauber, turning to me and saying, "You can feel the emotion of the crowd, can't you?" I don't know that I would have gone that far, but the event was something to behold. I do remember having tears in my eyes.

California Angels at Baltimore Orioles, Camden Yards, Baltimore, Maryland, September 6, 1995

Cal Ripken Jr. breaking Lou Gehrig's record was perhaps the all-time, feel-good sporting event and one in which I played a major role in covering as a columnist for the *Baltimore Sun*. I was very nervous beforehand; so many of my colleagues from around the country were in town, and I knew they would be reading me the next day. This was back in the pre-Internet age. Your peers didn't often see your work. I would have been even more nervous if I had known that my column would appear on the front page—and that the *Sun* would later sell thousands of posters and T-shirts of that front page. The event disproved the notion that sportswriters constantly look for negative stories to "sell papers." The *Sun* sold more newspapers the next day than on any day in its history.

2004 American League Championship Series, Game 4, New York Yankees at Boston Red Sox, Fenway Park, Boston, Massachusetts, October 17, 2004

You know what I remember most? Not Dave Roberts's memorable steal. Not even the Red Sox's 10–3 rout in Game 7. No, the thing that stayed with me was the reaction in Boston to David Ortiz's walkoff homer in the twelfth inning—the Red Sox's first victory of the series. The fans poured out of

Fenway, chanting and screaming in an incredible catharsis. I mean, few thought the Red Sox actually had a chance of coming back from a three-games-to-none deficit, but the fans were just so happy to get one win off the Yankees. And of course, history followed.

Jim Ross
Broadcaster, World Wrestling Entertainment

Oklahoma at Texas, Cotton Bowl, Dallas, Texas, October 10, 1970

Three of us traveled to the game with no tickets. We bought two tickets from a guy driving down I-35 holding two tickets up as he was driving. We pulled him over and my two friends, who were both bigger and older than me, threatened the guy with his life if the tickets were a fraud. We even got the guy's tag number to his vehicle. And don't ask how three larger-than-average men got into the Cotton Bowl with only two tickets.

This was the game where Oklahoma ran the Wishbone Offense for the very first time. The Sooners lost the game, 41–9, but it was more about how this game would affect the future of Oklahoma football that makes it so significant. They put the Wishbone in during an off-week, and it started the Oklahoma dynasty of the early seventies, including a big win in the Red River Rivalry the next year that was the first of five straight over the Longhorns. It was a new offense and, if run correctly, was almost indefensible. It was such a bold move by Chuck Fairbanks and his staff, including a young coach named Barry Switzer. The Wishbone started the "Switzer era," which included a National Championship in 1974 and '75. I wear the 1974 National

Championship ring every day for good luck. It was a surprise gift from my wife, who found one on a sports auction.

San Francisco 49ers at Atlanta Falcons, Georgia Dome, Atlanta, Georgia, November 9, 1992

I was on the Atlanta Falcons broadcast team in 1992, and this was a really moving experience. The team featured Deion Sanders, Andre Rison, Bill Fralic, and others, and that year the Falcons had one of the highest season-ticket sales numbers in the entire NFL. There were two Monday Night games scheduled that season, but the first one, against the San Francisco 49ers, was just an awesome night. I've always looked at myself as a fan that happens to just do broadcasting for a living, so experiences like this are always pretty cool for me. To broadcast the first-ever Monday Night Football game in Georgia Dome history was special. The Niners kicked our butts that night, 41–3, but it was still a great experience. It felt like a Super Bowl, since it had been years since the Falcons actually hosted a Monday Night game.

The highlight of the evening was interviewing radio analyst Hank Stram on my Falcon pregame show. He had so much fun talking about our mutual friends "The Big Cat" Ernie Ladd and Buck Buchanan that he blew off the rehearsal for his radio broadcast and did an extra segment with me. Afterwards, I told Hank that his partner, Jack Buck, was one of my boyhood heroes from his KMOX radio days with the St. Louis Cardinals. The next thing I knew, there was Jack Buck standing in our broadcast booth ready to come on my show because he said Hank had had so much fun. I was in sports heaven.

2001 Orange Bowl, Oklahoma vs. Florida State, Orange Bowl, Miami, Florida, January 3, 2001

I watched this game from the Oklahoma sideline as Oklahoma topped Bobby Bowden's Florida State Seminoles, 13–2, to win the national title. The Sooners entered the game 12–0, but Florida State was still heavily favored. It was the Sooners' first title under Bob Stoops. The atmosphere at the game was neat because OU led for a large part of the game, and Lee Roy Selmon and Brian Bosworth and Billy Sims were all on the sidelines. For a huge OU fan like myself, to be in that kind of company on the sideline was unforgettable—kind of like going to Yankee Stadium and sitting in a box with Mickey Mantle and Joe DiMaggio and Lou Gehrig. All these former Sooner greats and yours truly were standing together as one, cheering on our team, with no issues of age, race, or lifestyle. We were all crimson and cream with one common bond, our Sooner football team. I learned late in life it was okay for men to cry in public and to hug occasionally. I guess I had watched one too many John Wayne movies as a kid, as both those demonstrations of emotion and affection were taboo in our house as I grew up.

Wrestlemania X-Seven, Houston Astrodome, Houston, Texas, April 4, 2001

My first Wrestlemania was Nine and was outdoors at Caesars Palace—it was my first live broadcast for WWE, my first Wrestlemania, my first show at Caesars Palace, and the first time I ever wore a toga. But Wrestlemania X-Seven in the Astrodome was unique, because we broke the attendance record in the Astrodome, with even more people there than there were for games during the Houston Oilers' heydays. When I was growing up in Oklahoma, the local station always carried the Oilers' games, so the Astrodome was looked at as a spectacular, extraordinary venue. That made this a huge thrill for me. We had the advantage of having seats where the football field was, of course. The card was headlined by Stone Cold Steve Austin against The Rock, though, which certainly helped.

Bum Phillips was one of my heroes, because finally a guy that sounded like me made it to the NFL and got some TV time! I loved Bum's cowboy hat, and my late dad used to say, "I'll bet that hat cost old Bum over a hundred dollars." I always wear a 200X Resistol hat when I work on a WWE broadcast, and these specific hats run about a grand each. On that day, I actually thought about honoring Bum and not wearing my traditional black hat, but our producer quickly vetoed that idea. Walking around the 'Dome earlier in the day, I could almost hear Curt Gowdy doing play-by-play and talking about the Oilers' squatty fullback, "The Human Bowling Ball" Charlie Tolar from back in the old AFL days.

2004 Sugar Bowl, LSU vs. Oklahoma, Louisiana Superdome, New Orleans, Louisiana, January 4, 2004

Because the game was in the Superdome, this was like a home game for LSU. Between the game being played indoors and the presence of so many drunken LSU fans, this was one of the loudest, wildest atmospheres I've ever experienced at a sporting event. Oklahoma lost the game, 21–14, giving LSU a share of the national championship. It was an extraordinary day, though. We walked from the hotel to the Superdome and then walked back after the game was over, and there were as many LSU fans on the outside of the stadium as there were inside. And the outside fans were drinking just as much and got the celebration started for those inside to join when the game was over. I firmly believe that my black hat and my visibility with the WWE helped my wife and our friends make the trip back to the hotel from the Superdome after the LSU victory. There were not enough police to handle all the aggressive and drunk LSU fans who wanted to celebrate the 21–14 win and taunt the despondent Sooner fans. Drunk Cajuns and rednecks is a combustible combination, but so many of the LSU brethren recognized me from wrestling that our group was given a "free pass" from the harassment, and some of the LSU faithful even walked us back to the hotel to make sure "Good Ol' J.R. and his wife and friends didn't think bad of us." As far as raw, guttural, passionate emotion, that night was spectacular.

Chris Russo
Cohost, Mike and the Mad Dog,
WFAN Radio New York

Super Bowl XXV, Buffalo Bills vs. New York Giants, Tampa Stadium, Tampa, Florida, January 27, 1991

This game was during the Gulf War in the old Tampa Stadium. We got there really early because security was going to be very tight. I'll never forget how competitive this game was and that the Bills didn't win. I was shocked at how well the Giants' defense played against a powerful Bills' offense. They came back after giving up a safety to go down 12–3, then Scott Norwood missed the game-winning field goal. While everyone was leaving, they were playing "New York, New York" in the stadium. I know there have been a lot of really good Super Bowls since, but games really don't get as good as this one was. It was just a tremendous game.

Evander Holyfield vs. Riddick Bowe, Thomas & Mack Center, Las Vegas, Nevada, November 13, 1992

The atmosphere of a heavyweight title fight in Las Vegas is as good as it gets. The enthusiasm builds through the preliminary fights, and the energy and electricity are just amazing. The tenth round of this fight was incredible. Holyfield took an absolute beating in the round. He lost the fight, but he was a warrior and just hung in there against a much bigger guy. The performance he gave was admirable.

1995 NBA Eastern Conference Semifinals, Game 7, Indiana Pacers at New York Knicks, Madison Square Garden, New York, New York, May 21, 1995

The Pacers winning Game 7 from the Knicks in Madison Square Garden is one of the biggest surprises I think I'm ever going to see. The year before, the

Knicks were down three games to two but came back to take the series in seven games. In 1995 the Knicks were down three games to one but came back to force a seventh game, and everyone in the building expected the Knicks to repeat their feat from the season before and take the deciding game. Mark Jackson and Reggie Miller both played superb games, though, and Rik Smits was great in the fourth quarter. When Patrick Ewing missed the finger roll at the end of the game that would have tied it, the arena's feel was amazing as the ball just fell off the rim. A lot of people called in and said the miss reminded them of Bill Bradley's miss against the Bullets in Game 7 in 1971. This was a series everyone expected the Knicks to win after they made it to the finals in 1994. To see Ewing miss an easy shot was just a shock, and it surprised just about everyone. This ended up being the last game Pat Riley coached for the Knicks.

2000 National League Division Series, Game 3, San Francisco Giants at New York Mets, Shea Stadium, Queens, New York, October 7, 2000

I really thought the Giants would win this series. I knew how dangerous the Mets were but thought, after J. T. Snow hit the homer in the ninth to tie Game 2, that the Giants would win the series. The Mets came back to win that game, but I still had hope the Giants would win the series. Game 3 was at Shea Stadium, and I sat second row behind the Giants' dugout for the thirteen-inning, five-and-a-half-hour marathon that ended when Benny Agbayani homered off Aaron Fultz. The ups and downs and intensity in this game were awesome. In hindsight, the Mets won this Series in Game 2, but I didn't know that at the time. I remember standing up after Agbayani homered and listening to the crowd, which drove me nuts. I went into the Mets' locker room after the game to make sure they saw me because they all knew I am such a big Giants fan. That was just a brutal loss, but I was very proud of the Giants that night.

2004 American League Championship Series, Game 7, Boston Red Sox at New York Yankees, Yankee Stadium, Bronx, New York, October 20, 2004

I was in the building in Game 3 when the Yankees were killing the Sox and remember leaving after the seventh inning with them up big, saying to myself, "Well, if you are ever going to break a curse, it is going to take a cataclysmic event to do so." What could be more cataclysmic than coming back from three games to none to win a series? Did I feel that way in Game 4, when the Yankees were winning and Mariano Rivera was on the mound? No. But once the Red Sox came back to win that game, I started to get the feeling that something was aligned right. By the time Game 7 rolled around, I was very confident the Sox would win. After Johnny Damon hit that grand slam, it was an amazing scene as the Red Sox fans in Yankee Stadium had seven innings to celebrate. Watching the Sox fans celebrate was just tremendous. I sat with [WFAN's] Ed Coleman for the game, and Ed brought one of his father's old Red Sox sweaters with him, because his father had seen the Red Sox win their last World Series in 1918 as an eight-year-old. To come back after both the three games to none deficit and the way the Yankees won in 2003 made this one of the greatest games you will ever see.

Peter Schmuck

Columnist, Baltimore Sun

Houston Astros at Los Angeles Dodgers, Dodger Stadium, Los Angeles, California, April 9, 1981

My first regular-season game as a youthful Los Angeles Dodgers beat writer featured a relatively unknown substitute starting pitcher named Fernando Valenzuela, who filled in for injured veteran Jerry Reuss and pitched the Dodgers to a 2–0 victory on April 9, 1981. He would get off to an amazing 8–0 start that included four shutouts and even a game-winning hit, then went on to win the Cy Young Award and Rookie of the Year honors.

1986 American League Championship Series, Game 5, Boston Red Sox at California Angels, Anaheim Stadium, Anaheim, California, October 12, 1986

One of the most startling comebacks in playoff history. The California Angels entered the ninth inning with a three-run lead and seemed certain to close out the series against the Boston Red Sox in five games. Instead, they collapsed, setting up the Mets/Red Sox World Series that featured Bill Buckner's infamous gaffe. The fallout didn't end there, however. Angels relief pitcher Donnie Moore, who gave up a dramatic home run to Dave Henderson in the Angels ninth-inning collapse, never recovered from that fateful pitch and committed suicide three years later.

1989 World Series, Game 3, Oakland Athletics at San Francisco Giants, Candlestick Park, San Francisco, California, October 17, 1989

It's not one of my favorite sports memories, but few others are still as vivid as the afternoon when the earth shook under Candlestick Park in San Francisco, forcing the interruption of the 1989 World Series for nearly two weeks. The quake sparked a heated debate over whether it was appropriate to resume the Fall Classic, which was eventually won by the Oakland A's in four games.

California Angels at Baltimore Orioles, Camden Yards, Baltimore, Maryland, September 6, 1995

That September night might not have meant as much to me if Cal Ripken Jr. had not spent the previous five months bringing back strike-disaffected fans one autograph at a time. The record that was never supposed to be broken went down, and Ripken took an impromptu victory lap during which he shook hands with fans in every corner of Camden Yards. There wasn't a dry eye in the house.

Baltimore Orioles at Cuba, Latin American Stadium, Havana, Cuba, March 16, 1999

I was part of the delegation that traveled to Cuba in January of 1999 to work out the details for the Orioles' historic goodwill trip. Latin American Stadium was packed with Fidel Castro's invited guests for the March exhibition, but the event still captured the imagination of regular citizens in both countries and afforded me two amazing opportunities to tour the communist island.

Steve Serby
Columnist, New York Post

1968 AFL Championship, Oakland Raiders at New York Jets, Shea Stadium, Queens, New York, December 29, 1968

This was as cold as I have ever been in my life, seated high atop Shea Stadium watching Joe Willie try to beat the Raiders and get to Super Bowl III. Namath was one of my heroes, so much so that I grew a Fu Manchu, wore tie-dyed jeans and white shoes, and visited Bachelors III, the Lexington Avenue club the NFL eventually forced him to give up. My best friend's uncle, Bob Olen, a photographer I later would work with at the *New York Post*, got us the tickets. My friend Mike Welsch, who now works for the *Daily Racing Form*, and I were home on winter break from Ohio U. It was a nerve-wracking, ebb-and-flow game, with a happy ending. We thawed out at his uncle Bob's house on Long Island.

1985 NCAA Men's Basketball Tournament Finals, Villanova vs. Georgetown, Rupp Arena, Lexington, Kentucky, April 1, 1985

No one gave Rollie Massimino and the Wildcats a chance against Patrick Ewing and the Hoyas. It was electric inside Rupp Arena as Villanova provided evidence early that it would not be intimidated. Ed Pinckney, a kid from the Bronx, neutralized Ewing even though he spotted him 3 inches. Gary McLain, the brash point guard, was the brilliant floor general. When smooth Dwayne McClain wasn't operating inside, Harold Jensen was sharpshooting outside down the stretch. Villanova would shoot 22 of 29 and play what is remembered as The Perfect Game in one of the biggest upsets in college basketball history.

Super Bowl XXV, Buffalo Bills vs. New York Giants, Tampa Stadium, Tampa, Florida, January 27, 1991

Giants 20, Bills 19, Scott Norwood wide right with a 47-yard field-goal attempt in the final seconds. This was during Desert Storm, when media members waited two hours outside Tampa Stadium on a security line. The game, which was built to a crescendo by Whitney Houston's stirring rendition of the national anthem, was worth the inconvenience. The underdog Giants, led by Phil Simms's backup, Jeff Hostetler, played keepaway from the prolific Bills, and Bill Belichick's unorthodox defense kept quarterback Jim Kelly off balance, and when it was over, Lawrence Taylor and Carl Banks carried an exultant Bill Parcells off the field.

Kansas City Chiefs at New York Jets, Giants Stadium, East Rutherford, New Jersey, November 29, 1992

This was the most memorable, and easily the saddest, moment I've ever seen. The Jets' Dennis Byrd was a talented, personable defensive end from Oklahoma with a bright future—until it was taken away when he crashed into teammate Scott Mersereau while rushing the passer. I watched in horror from the press box at Giants Stadium. All of a hushed Giants Stadium prayed for Byrd after he crumbled motionless to the ground with a devastating spinal-cord injury. He never played football again but wrote an inspirational story about the human spirit when he did, indeed, *Rise and Walk*.

1996 World Series, Game 4, New York Yankees at Atlanta Braves, Fulton County Stadium, Atlanta, Georgia, October 23, 1996

I was seated in the auxiliary press box high down the rightfield line at Fulton County Stadium as pinch-hitter Jim Leyritz stepped in against Mark Wohlers. The Yankees, down two games to one, trailed 6–3. Leyritz was the tying run. Wohlers, a 100-mph fireman, hung a slider, and Leyritz crushed it into the left-field seats. I could tell from the trajectory of the ball that it was gone. I remember the Yankees jumping excitedly from their dugout to greet Leyritz and the hush in the stadium, not a single tomahawk chop in sight. The Yanks went on to win it 8–6 in ten innings to tie the Series on their way to beating the Braves in six to stand atop the baseball world for the first time in eighteen years.

Brad Sham
Broadcaster, Dallas Cowboys

Washington Redskins at Dallas Cowboys, Texas Stadium, Irving, Texas, December 16, 1979

This was the best football game I've ever seen. It was one of those games where everything was on the line. Both teams were really good, and the winner would win the division, while the loser might miss the playoffs. It turned out to be Roger Staubach's last regular-season game, and of course, it was Dallas versus Washington, one of the great rivalries in all of sports.

Early in the game, John Riggins ran 66 yards for a touchdown to help the Redskins build a double-digit lead, but the Cowboys came back to go ahead. The Redskins went ahead by double digits again, and the Cowboys came back, scoring two touchdowns in the last 2:20. Late in the game, the Redskins had a six-point lead and the ball, and Dallas was out of timeouts. All they had to do was make a first down and the game was over. They gave the ball to John Riggins, and Larry Cole came charging from his defensive-tackle position to tackle Riggins behind the line of scrimmage for a loss, forcing a punt. Staubach then led the Cowboys down the field and threw a touchdown pass to Tony Hill, and the extra point won the game, 35–34.

It was the greatest game I had ever seen, but what made it even more memorable for me was that, in those days, I was the color man for Verne Lundquist. But Verne had been assigned by ABC to do a boxing tournament in Japan, so I did that game with Charlie Waters, who had been injured in training camp. The whole time, as the Cowboys were coming back in the second half, every time they did something good, Charlie said to me, "You've gotta believe, Brad. You've gotta believe." Everyone left when the Redskins went ahead, but with five minutes left and the Cowboys coming back, I reminded everyone who had left that it wasn't over yet. Charlie turned on me at that point and said, "Shame on you, you lowly broadcaster who didn't believe. You have to love the Dallas Cowboys. You never give up." It was just classic radio, and the kicker to it all is that now Charlie is my regular radio partner. Whenever someone asks me what my favorite Cowboys game was, I always tell them this one.

1982 NCAA Men's Basketball Tournament Finals, North Carolina vs. Georgetown, Louisiana Superdome, New Orleans, Louisiana, March 29, 1982

This was the first Final Four that I ever got a chance to see in person. I had done college basketball for a long time and had the chance to cover these games as a reporter. I was sitting in the auxiliary press box, which was actually in the first row of the stands, next to my friend Jim Brock, who was the chairman of the Cotton Bowl Selection Committee and who knew everybody. I've gotten the chance to go to and work at a lot more Final Fours since then and have really developed an appreciation for the NCAA Tournament, which I think is the best sporting event in America, from the first game through the championship.

But this one is still the best. Georgetown's Patrick Ewing was blocking shots all over the place; Michael Jordan, James Worthy, and Sam Perkins were running up and down the floor for North Carolina. And for the game to end the way it did, with Jordan's shot, this game is just one I'll never forget.

Super Bowl XXVII, Dallas Cowboys vs. Buffalo Bills, Rose Bowl, Pasadena, California, January 31, 1993

I was lucky enough to be around some great Cowboy teams in the late seventies and early eighties and was also there to watch the team decline afterwards. So I think I was incredibly fortunate enough to still be there when they rose back to prominence in the early nineties. I watched the team suffer through a 1–15 season in 1989, then struggle again in the first half of the 1990 season. They made the playoffs in 1991 and won a playoff game, setting up 1992. No one predicted the Super Bowl that year, but I remember in training camp, when they got Charles Haley, thinking that things might have just changed.

The year went on, and they won some games they weren't expected to win, and the coaches couldn't believe what was happening. I remember leaving the LA Coliseum after they beat the Raiders; I was walking with offensive line coach Tony Wise, and he was shaking his head, saying he didn't know what was going on. I had to remind him that there might come a time during the season where they would have to admit that this team was pretty good. They had a magical game in the NFC Championship Game in San Francisco, and now it was on to the Super Bowl.

They beat Buffalo big, but the game was almost secondary. What made it memorable was walking out onto the field at the Rose Bowl around three hours before kickoff. It was one of those uniquely perfect South California days. There wasn't any smog, the mountains were almost tangible, there was dew glistening on the grass. I walked out to the middle of the field and saw the big Super Bowl logo, and I just thought to myself, "We are in the Rose Bowl, and this team, that was 1–15 in 1989, is going to play in the Super Bowl, just three years later, on this day, in this weather, and in this setting?" This is enough to sway an agnostic. The Cowboys won the game, but it wasn't really about that. It was the fact that they were there.

1993 Charity Shield, Manchester United vs. Arsenal, Wembley Stadium, London, England, August 7, 1993

I am a big soccer fan, and the Cowboys were playing in the preseason American Bowl against the Detroit Lions in London on the same weekend as the Charity Shield, which is the annual preseason game right before the English Premier League begins. In 1976, I was the PR director for the Chicago Sting of the North American Soccer League, and our coach was a man named Bill Foulke, who had been a star defender for Manchester United and was on the team when they were involved in a plane crash that killed several members of the team. I got to know him and became a big Man U fan, which I still am to this day. So it might have been an exhibition game, but I got to see Manchester United and Arsenal play in Wembley Stadium.

Boston Red Sox at Chicago Cubs, Wrigley Field, Chicago, Illinois, June 11, 2005

I am, to my detriment, a devoted, lifelong Chicago Cubs fan. I was in Chicago to broadcast a soccer game the weekend they hosted the Boston Red Sox. We had a Sunday game and were off Saturday, and I was able to make a phone call and get a credential for the game. So I went to watch the game. Because I am a baseball fan, I appreciate the history and tradition of the game, and this was the first time the teams were meeting in eighty-seven years and the first time ever that the Red Sox had played at Wrigley Field.

I had the day all to myself. I took the train and got there very early, just so I could soak up the atmosphere. I'm a native Chicagoan, but I failed to comprehend what a Cubs game had become. With this being the Cubs and Red Sox, though, this was even more special and magical. I walked around Wrigleyville, and it was like a college football atmosphere. People were partying, the restaurants were jammed, the streets were teeming, and it was a beautiful, warm June day. Before the game started, I got so infused with the atmosphere, I called my cousin, who lives in Natick, Massachusetts, and is a die-hard Red Sox fan, just to tell him where I was. And then it turned out to be one of the best baseball games I've ever seen. This was just one of the coolest things I've ever done. It was just a perfect day.

Dan Shaughnessy
Columnist, Boston Globe

1984 NBA Finals, Boston Celtics vs. Los Angeles Lakers, Boston Garden, Boston, Massachusetts, and The Forum, Inglewood, California, May 27–June 12, 1984

This series featured multiple Hall of Fame players. It was the last year of the 2–2–1–1–1 format. I remember going back and forth on planes with Jack Nicholson, since the Celtics flew commercial in those days. The heat in the Garden was tremendous, in Game 5 in particular. The Celtics really could have been swept in that series. They were blown out in Game 1, stole the second game after Gerald Henderson stole the ball following a Magic mistake, got blown out again in Game 3, got a clutch win in Game 4, and then just took over the series. The Kevin McHale takedown of Kurt Rambis was instrumental in Game 4 and changed the entire series. The Celtics won three titles in the Larry Bird era, two against the Houston Rockets. But those teams didn't match up anywhere close to beating the Lakers in the Finals.

1991 World Series, Atlanta Braves vs. Minnesota Twins, Fulton County Stadium, Atlanta, Georgia, and Hubert H. Humphrey Metrodome, Minneapolis, Minnesota, October 19–27, 1991

The way Kirby Puckett took over Game 6, followed by Jack Morris in Game 7, was astounding. There was tremendous drama and a lot of one-run games all Series. There is that great picture of Dan Gladden sliding into home and being upside down. There might not have been a Boston connection in this Series, but I was just enthralled the entire time.

1996 Summer Olympics, Women's Gymnastics, Georgia Dome, Atlanta, Georgia, July 23, 1996

Gymnastics was really starting to take off, and it was amazing being there to watch the whole thing unfold. I've seen a lot of Olympic moments, and this one, with Kerri Strug's remarkable vault, just stays with me.

Super Bowl XXXVI, New England Patriots vs. St. Louis Rams, Louisiana Superdome, New Orleans, Louisiana, February 3, 2002

The Pats had been to the Super Bowl twice before but lost and were huge underdogs in this game. The Tom Brady thing had picked up a lot of steam, as everyone was enamored with this magical wonderboy. The winning kick by Adam Vinatieri was incredible. Of course, the game that led up to this, the Tuck Rule Game, might have been even more dramatic. They were absolutely beaten in that one but stole that game and won it on a Vinatieri field goal, possibly the greatest clutch kick in the history of the NFL. That just started them on a roll that went on for three more seasons.

2004 Boston Red Sox Postseason, October 5–27, 2004

This was a culmination of eighty-six years. I think the Sox coming back from down three games to none against the Yankees in the ALCS is the greatest story in the history of American sports. Given all the layers that led into this Series, with the longtime rivalry and the whole Babe Ruth thing, plus the idea that no baseball team had ever come back from that deficit, this was astounding. I remember one of my shuttle flights from New York to Boston was Flight #1918, which I thought was very strange.

Watching that unfold and then watching the Sox subsequently annihilate the Cardinals without even a burp, to see the joy that it brought back to our region . . . we always wondered what it would be like. Would it take some of the mystique away? They are forever changed; it definitely made them different, but people were so happy. A lot of people went to graveyards and decorated them. The global response was overwhelming. It was a great privilege for me, having grown up in the Boston area, to write the page-one story for the *Boston Globe* that became a T-shirt and a poster.

Bob Sheppard
Public Address Announcer, Yankee Stadium

1956 World Series, Game 5, Brooklyn Dodgers at New York Yankees, Yankee Stadium, Bronx, New York, October 8, 1956
Don Larsen wasn't the ace starter you would expect to pitch a perfect game. The stadium was packed for the game against the Dodgers, with the masterful Sal Maglie opposing Larsen. It was a perfect day—clear, pleasant, sunny. Bit by bit, as the game went on, the crowd was aware that the situation was abnormal and that Larsen was unhittable. I think we held our breath until the

ninth inning, when the moment of real passion and panic hit me, when I had to introduce, with two out in the ninth inning, a fellow named Dale Mitchell as a pinch hitter. Mitchell was a very dangerous hitter, but luckily, Larsen got two strikes on him and Babe Pinelli called the next pitch for strike three, and the game was over. It was the most memorable thing I've ever seen in my fifty-six years at Yankee Stadium.

Cleveland Browns at New York Giants, Yankee Stadium, Bronx, New York, December 14, 1958

Pat Summerall's foot helped the Giants top Cleveland in the snow to give the Giants a share of first place with the Browns. The lines on the field were obliterated, so we weren't really sure how long the kick was, but Summerall was able to make what is now believed to be a 49-yard field goal and move the Giants into a one-game playoff the next week against the Browns at Yankee Stadium again.

Boston Red Sox at New York Yankees, Yankee Stadium, Bronx, New York, October 1, 1961

Roger Maris's chase of Babe Ruth's home-run record was a struggle all through the season, but on the last day of the season, he hit number 61. I was so moved, I immediately wrote a poem to celebrate it. I called it "Roger Maris Says His Prayers," and I've envisioned Roger Maris on his knees that night, looking up to heaven and saying:

> *They've been pitching me low*
> *They've been pitching me tight*
> *I've grown so nervous, tense and pallid*
> *But my prayer is full of joy tonight*
> *Thank you Lord, for Tracy Stallard*

It came almost immediately for me, since I dabbled a little bit in poetry. I handed it to Mel Allen, the longtime Yankee announcer, who was sitting next to me, and he read it on the air and told everyone to mail me at Yankee Stadium if they wanted a copy of it. I had to get the Yankee staff to handle the requests!

1976 American League Championship Series, Game 5, Kansas City Royals at New York Yankees, Yankee Stadium, Bronx, New York, October 14, 1976
When Chris Chambliss homered into the bleachers to defeat the Kansas City Royals, it was the only time in all my years at Yankee Stadium where I've seen a mob of Yankees fans run out onto the field. He didn't get around the bases easily and had to fight through everyone after crossing second base before scoring the winning run.

1977 World Series, Game 6, Los Angeles Dodgers at New York Yankees, Yankee Stadium, Bronx, New York, October 18, 1977
Reggie Jackson hits three homers on three successive pitches against three different pitchers, including Charlie Hough and his knuckleball. Incredible! This one speaks for itself.

Dan Shulman
Broadcaster, ESPN

1993 World Series, Game 6, Philadelphia Phillies at Toronto Blue Jays, Skydome, Toronto, Canada, October 23, 1993
I was hosting the pre- and postgame shows on the Blue Jays' radio network at the time, so I could actually sit in the seats during the game. I was sitting with my wife, enjoying Game 6, which the Phillies led, 6–5, going into the bottom of the ninth. At that point I left my seat to go to our broadcast location in the hotel at the ballpark, figuring it would take me a few minutes to get out there. There was a freight elevator I used to use that would help me bypass some of

the crowd, but for whatever reason, it stopped for a while while I was in it. When the building started shaking, I knew something big had happened, but I didn't know what. I never saw Joe Carter's home run.

1994 Winter Olympics, Ice Hockey Finals, Sweden vs. Canada, Haakons Hall, Lillehammer, Norway, February 27, 1994

I was working for CTV, a Canadian television network, doing the hosting, interviews, etc., for this game. This was before NHLers were playing in the Olympics, but two future NHL superstars played a pivotal role. There were thousands of Canadians in the stands who had made the trip across the Atlantic, and thousands of Swedes, who had made the short drive to Lille-hammer. The two teams played a tremendously exciting sixty minutes, were tied at 2, and then could settle nothing in overtime.

In the shootout, the two teams each scored twice in five shots, sending it to sudden death. Finally, on the seventh shot, Peter Forsberg made what is still the most amazing move on a breakaway I've ever seen, sliding a backhander under the glove of Corey Hirsch, and then Paul Kariya was stopped by Tommy Salo, giving Sweden their first-ever gold medal in hockey at the Olympics. Even though I'm Canadian, being at a moment of that magnitude, seeing the flag-waving, and watching gold medals being handed out was an experience I'll never forget.

1998 Great Alaska Shootout Finals, Cincinnati vs. Duke, Sullivan Arena, Anchorage, Alaska, November 28, 1998

I've been lucky enough to call a lot of great college basketball games, but this one stands out in my mind more than any other. Duke, led by Alaska native Trajan Langdon, was the heavy favorite going into the final against Cincinnati. The game was close throughout, and in the last few minutes, the teams traded baskets and the lead every time down the floor. Finally, Cincinnati inbounded with just three seconds left. They ran a hook-and-ladder-type play, to borrow a football term, and Kenyon Martin, who had caught the long inbounds pass, shoveled it to a streaking Melvin Levett, who dunked for the winning bucket. Langdon, ironically, was the guy Levett beat on the play.

The crowd was mostly pro-Duke most of the night, but the deeper into the game it went, the more the local fans started rooting for the underdog. Duke actually got the ball back and made a basket—but just after the final horn, and the Bearcats celebrated like they had won the NCAA championship.

2003 National League Championship Series, Game 6, Florida Marlins at Chicago Cubs, Wrigley Field, Chicago, Illinois, October 14, 2003

I was doing play-by-play for ESPN Radio, and will never forget the confidence Cub fans had coming home for Games 6 and possibly 7. They had Mark Prior going in Game 6, and Kerry Wood, if necessary, in 7, and they all thought it was *over*. And with a three-run lead in the eighth inning of Game 6, it looked like they were right. When Luis Castillo hit the ball, all I did was follow Moises Alou over to the wall, watched him jump, and then saw, plain as day, Steve Bartman reach up and touch the ball. It was clear to me he hadn't reached into the field of play, but I also felt right away, and still feel, that Alou probably would have caught the ball had it not been touched.

Immediately, there was a huge groan throughout the stadium, and then a lot of yelling and chattering. I think some fans were angry right away, but I think most just realized that the curse still lived, evidently, and that it was not meant to be. Even though the Cubs still led Game 6 at that moment, and of course still could have won the series by winning Game 7, I believe most Cub fans felt right then that they weren't going to win.

2005 National League Championship Series, Game 5, St. Louis Cardinals at Houston Astros, Minute Maid Park, Houston, Texas, October 17, 2005

I was doing play-by-play for ESPN Radio, and Minute Maid Park was as loud as any ballpark I'd ever been in. The Astros were one out away from getting to the World Series for the first time ever, and even when Brad Lidge gave up a walk and a hit, and even with Albert Pujols coming up, you still sensed history was about to be made. I just don't think anyone expected Pujols, as great as he is, to be the one making the history. He hit it so far, and it got quiet so fast at the stadium, an eerie feeling came over me as if what I thought I was seeing (and saying) wasn't really happening. The stadium was dead silent by the time the ball hit the glass above leftfield, and believe me, it didn't take long to get there.

Steve Somers

Host, The Steve Somers Show,
WFAN Radio New York

Los Angeles Dodgers at San Francisco Giants, Seals Stadium, San Francisco, California, April 15, 1958

My father, Sam, took me to my first major league baseball game, which just happened to be the first major league game played in San Francisco. The game was played in Seals Stadium, where the Giants played for two seasons on their arrival from New York and which is the same stadium where the old San Francisco Seals played, featuring players like Joe DiMaggio, Tony Lazzeri, and Frank Crosetti.

1962 World Series, Game 7, New York Yankees at San Francisco Giants, Candlestick Park, San Francisco, California, October 16, 1962

What an incredible finish to the World Series, with the Yankees taking this game 1–0. Willie McCovey lined out to Bobby Richardson with Giants on second and third and two outs in the bottom of the ninth. If the ball is hit to the left or right of Richardson, it is a base hit and the Giants win; if McCovey had gotten under the pitch a little, it would have been a home run. Willie Mays was on second, Matty Alou was on third after Mays had doubled down the rightfield line, and Roger Maris, in a foreign stadium and on a wet field (it had rained throughout the Series in both San Francisco and New York), made a great play on the ball and made a perfect cutoff throw to Bobby Richardson, who then made a perfect throw home to Elston Howard to keep Alou on third.

Should he have been sent home? I think if he was, he would have been out and the game would have ended that way. The pitcher was Ralph Terry, who two years earlier had given up the home run to Bill Mazeroski to win the 1960 Series for Pittsburgh, and with first base open, manager Ralph Houk went to the mound and allowed Terry to pitch to McCovey. Of course, Hall-of-Famer Orlando Cepeda was on deck, but they pitched to McCovey, who lined out to end the Series.

Fighting Muhammad Ali, Atlanta, Georgia, 1970

I was working in Atlanta for a TV station. Atlanta had always supported and defended Ali politically and personally and after he came back to boxing following his exile, and his first fight back was in Atlanta against Jerry Quarry. For charity purposes, he wanted to get in the ring with a few Atlanta area personalities, and I just happened to be one of them. So I put on the trunks and the gloves and got in the ring with him for three rounds. It was a great experience, and I put a huge beating on him . . . actually, he didn't hit me once but instead spent the three rounds dodging everything I threw (which wasn't exactly intimidating to begin with). Ali was arguably the most influential athlete of our lifetime, and it was a thrill doing something like this.

1994 Eastern Conference Finals, Game 7, New Jersey Devils at New York Rangers, Madison Square Garden, New York, New York, May 27, 1994

In my mind, this game is actually ahead of the Rangers winning the Stanley Cup. I was just blown away and overwhelmed by this game. It almost made winning the Stanley Cup anticlimactic. The whole stretch of games was just so personal and emotional, though. Grown men were calling my show in tears to talk about it. But in person, this game, with the ebb and flow, the Devils scoring with 7.7 seconds remaining to tie it, then Stephane Matteau's goal in double overtime—it was the best of all of them.

Pittsburgh Pirates at New York Mets, Shea Stadium, Queens, New York, September 25, 2003

It was a very memorable night in Shea Stadium, being a part of that program, honoring a true voice of summer baseball and the voice of the Mets, Bob Murphy. Unfortunately, it wasn't all that long before he passed away. I was with baseball royalty, sitting next to Mrs. Gil Hodges, even getting a kiss on the cheek, and a crowd of maybe twenty-five thousand or so, upon my intro, gave me a very warm hand, if you can believe that!

Jayson Stark

Broadcaster, ESPN

1980 World Series, Game 6, Kansas City Royals at Philadelphia Phillies, Veterans Stadium, Philadelphia, Pennsylvania, October 21, 1980

Some games just belong in a time capsule. This is one of them. If you're someone like me, who grew up in Philadelphia, and never thought you'd live to see the Phillies win a World Series, how do you leave this game off the list? Full disclosure: I was just a young guy learning to cover baseball—*really* cover it—back then. And I had a rocky relationship with a lot of the guys who played for this team.

But I was also a Philadelphian. So I knew what this night meant. I knew why that decibel level was mounting as sixty-five thousand people counted down the outs. I knew what every Philadelphian was thinking when Tug McGraw decided he *had* to pitch out of bases-loaded nightmares in the eighth *and* ninth innings. I even knew why all those police horses and attack dogs were on the field. This was, after all, Philadelphia. And I knew exactly what I'd just witnessed when McGraw pumped that twenty-seventh-out third strike past Willie Wilson, and people everywhere were crying and hugging each other. Nearly a century of baseball disaster, collapses, and suffering led everybody to that pitch, to that moment. So it wasn't just joy that erupted. It was relief. A lot of ghosts got zapped that night.

Houston Astros at Philadelphia Phillies, Veterans Stadium, Philadelphia, Pennsylvania, June 10, 1981

Talk about plotlines. How about all of these: Pete Rose was one hit from tying Stan Musial's all-time National League career-hits record, so Musial was in Philadelphia, at the game. But the 1981 baseball strike was about to begin, so this was Rose's last chance to get there before the strike freeze-dried this chase in time. You also had the most riveting pitching matchup it was possible for these two teams to conjure up: Nolan Ryan vs. Steve Carlton, at a time when they were dueling for the all-time career-strikeout lead.

So Rose got a hit off Ryan the first time up (a single through the middle) to tie the record. But you could almost see the flames flying out of Ryan's eyes as Rose soaked in the cheers. And 7⅔ innings later, Ryan hadn't given up *any* other hits, to Rose or anyone else. He punched out Rose for the *third* time—the first three-whiff game for Rose in four years—for the second out in the eighth. And it was clearly his night, not Pete's. Rose actually went back to the dugout, made eye contact with Ryan and gave him a little nod of salute. What a scene.

Then it happened. George Vukovich bounced a pinch-hit single up the middle, and Ryan twisted his back trying to pivot and catch it. So he had to leave. In came Frank LaCorte to protect a 4–0 lead. The next four hitters went double, walk, single, homer. And amazingly, the Phillies had a 5–4 lead. When the ninth inning began, Phillies fans were actually rooting for the Astros to tie the game so Rose could bat again. But they didn't. And Rose didn't break the record for two *months*. I'll never forget that one.

1988 World Series, Game 1, Oakland Athletics at Los Angeles Dodgers, Dodger Stadium, Los Angeles, California, October 15, 1988

This is my most memorable evening watching any World Series game I've ever witnessed. I guess this is the best way to sum up why that is: When something happens in a sporting event that your brain tells you can't possibly happen, there's this moment when it dawns on you what you're watching. So I'll never forget seeing Kirk Gibson hit that ball off Dennis Eckersley and then having this feeling come over me, as the ball was floating out there toward the fence, that I can replay in my brain to this day. It was almost as if time froze for a second. There was that baseball, flying through the night, and suddenly, I realized what this was.

This was a home run that couldn't possibly have been hit. Dennis Eckersley was the most untouchable relief pitcher alive. Kirk Gibson could barely walk. And then there was that baseball, heading toward history, and everything about that World Series was about to change. *Lives* were changed by that swing of the bat, that baseball: that Oakland team's place in history. Gibson's place. Eckersley's place. Tommy Lasorda's place. Even Orel Hershiser's place. What a moment. And I can't get that sight, of that baseball frozen in the sky, out of my brain.

San Francisco Giants at Philadelphia Phillies, Veterans Stadium, Philadelphia, Pennsylvania, August 15, 1990

I often wonder how many baseball games I've been paid to watch. It's in the thousands. I know that. But incredibly, some of my most indelible memories ever at a ballpark were games I just happened to go to as a spectator. The only four-homer game I've ever seen (Mike Schmidt, at Wrigley Field, 1976), I stumbled into holding a ticket, during a summer trip, years before I got a job covering the Phillies. I saw a cycle (by Gregg Jefferies, in 1995) while attending a game with the family. And I've seen two no-hitters in my life—*both* of them by accident. The first was in St. Louis (Bob Forsch, 1983), when I was basically stuck there, killing a day, in the middle of a work trip. So I wound up seeing a no-hitter and a three-hundredth win (Steve Carlton's) in the same week, only one of which was on purpose.

But one of the most fun nights I've ever spent at a ballpark came on August 15, 1990, when a buddy and I decided to take our six-year-olds to a game—and a no-hitter broke out. And not just any no-hitter. The first no-hitter pitched by a Phillie in Philadelphia in the twentieth century. So after the sixth inning, I actually had to abandon my little son in the stands. I headed for the press box, called my office, told them I was there and told them I'd find a way to write about this, somehow, if Terry Mulholland pitched his no-hitter. I had no computer. I had no notebook. I didn't even know how I was going to get home. But I scribbled notes on the back of some press-box scrap paper, wrote out a story longhand, dictated it, and then rented a car to get home. No runs. No hits. No way I'll ever forget that night.

1991 World Series, Game 7, Atlanta Braves at Minnesota Twins, Hubert H. Humphrey Metrodome, Minneapolis, Minnesota, October 27, 1991

There's nothing in baseball that gets the metabolism flowing more than Game 7 of a World Series. So I go back and forth all the time on which Game 7 still gives me more chills—the Jack Morris Game or the 2001 classic in Arizona when Mariano Rivera couldn't hold a one-run lead in the ninth after an awesome Roger Clemens–Curt Schilling mano a mano. But I'm going with 1991 because I'll always argue that, start to finish, it was the best postseason I've ever seen—and because Jack Morris pitched the greatest Big Game I've ever seen pitched. Possibly because it's the best Big Game *anybody* has ever seen pitched.

When you're at an event of that magnitude, and the zeroes keep accumulating on the scoreboard, and Morris keeps walking to that mound inning after inning, and your ears are literally throbbing because it's so freaking loud inside the Metrodome, there's a feeling that hits you that's hard to describe. You want all Game 7s to be great. And when you begin to comprehend that this one is going to be something beyond great, the adrenaline rush is overpowering. All these years later, I can still feel it. And I can still see Jack Morris out there, refusing to let his team get beat. Tremendous.

Joe Starkey
*Broadcaster, San Francisco 49ers/California
Golden Bears*

San Francisco 49ers at Chicago Bears, Wrigley Field, Chicago, Illinois, December 12, 1965

I've seen the Chicago Bears' three greatest individual record-setting games. Two came against teams for whom I was broadcasting. In 2005 it was Nathan Vasher going 108 yards with a missed field goal against the San Francisco 49ers. In 1977 Walter Payton ran for 275 yards against the Minnesota Vikings. But growing up in Chicago, my family had Bears season tickets, and we were in the stands at Wrigley Field on December 12, 1965, the day Gale Sayers scored six touchdowns. That was just an extraordinary and special game.

It was a very cold, wet, miserable day. The field was in terrible shape and was wet and sloppy. Former Chicago Bears running back and All-American at Northwestern Bill deCorrevont made the comment before the opening kickoff, "There is no way Sayers can do anything special today." That didn't stop Sayers that day, though. What I loved about watching him play was that, when he knew he was going to score, he had this habit of looking back, not to showboat, but to see if anyone was getting close to him. I still think he was the best running back I've ever seen. He had the ability to go one direction but then turn faster than anyone else I've ever watched. Defenses would think they had him, and then he would all of a sudden cut and make them miss.

It was an amazing day, and his reputation was already growing. But what made that day even more amazing was how he scored the touchdowns. There was an 80-yard screen-pass touchdown, four rushing touchdowns, and an 85-yard punt return for a touchdown. It was clearly one of the most incredible individual performances ever, as he accounted for 336 yards of total offense—113 rushing, 89 receiving, 134 on punt returns.

Boston Bruins at Toronto Maple Leafs, Maple Leaf Gardens, Toronto, Canada, February 7, 1976

I was broadcasting for the NHL's California Golden Seals at the time. We were in Toronto but had the night off, while the Bruins were also there for a game, so I decided to go see the game that night. Bob Wilson, who was the radio broadcaster for Boston, asked me before the game to help him on the broadcast because he had laryngitis and could barely talk, so I was happy to fill in and help, and here I am, all of a sudden, on a Boston Bruins broadcast when Darryl Sittler has the greatest individual game in the history of the NHL with six goals and four assists. You just couldn't believe it as the points kept coming. For starters, how often does a team score ten goals in a game? Sittler had ten points by himself. He had two assists in the first period, then three more goals and a pair of assists in the second, and another hat trick in the third period. This is one of those records that I find hard to believe will ever be broken.

1980 Winter Olympics, Ice Hockey Semifinals, United States vs. Soviet Union, Olympic Ice Center, Lake Placid, New York, February 22, 1980

I had been broadcasting NHL games since 1972 and had just left the Colorado Rockies, who were getting ready to leave Denver and become the New Jersey

Devils. I was in Lake Placid covering the Games as a broadcaster for the ABC Radio Network and for KGO Radio in San Francisco. I had the freedom to cover whatever I wanted. With my background in hockey and with some of the players, as well as with assistant coach Craig Patrick, I really zeroed in on the team during the tournament, even though, like everyone else, I never expected much to happen. Of course, the team played very well and advanced to the medal round to play the Soviet Union. With the game being tape delayed around the country, no one was watching live.

But as things developed, I saw what was going on, and, when the third period got underway, with the U.S. possibly in position to win, I called KGO, where the afternoon news was on. I told them what the story was, even though it sounded crazy, and asked them to hook me up so I could do the rest of the game on a telephone hookup as a live broadcast. I told them that I was willing to stake my job on it, that it had the potential to be an enormous story. They gambled with me and did it, even though it was prime time for radio news, and also called every affiliate up and down the West Coast and hooked them in, as well. While there was a live radio broadcast on ABC Radio, it was not being carried anywhere on the West Coast.

So I called the rest of the game. After the game ended, I'll never forget the looks on the Soviet players' faces. They were just totally stunned at what had happened and couldn't believe they lost this game. Outside the arena, the celebration was just unforgettable—it was New Year's Eve, Mardi Gras, and anything else you can think of all rolled into one. People are always surprised to hear that this game, not the Lateral Game, was the biggest moment I remember. There was nothing like the atmosphere in Lake Placid the night the U.S. beat the Russians. A bunch of college kids and minor leaguers beating the best professional team in the world during the "Cold War" era from the USSR was an international stunner and front-page news all over the world.

Stanford at Cal, Memorial Stadium, Berkeley, California, November 20, 1982

I didn't realize it at the time, but this turned out to be one of those moments that is going to last forever. The interesting part about this game was its importance—it was John Elway's last regular-season game, and if Stanford won as they were expected to do, they would be going to a bowl game for the first time in Elway's career. Cal was a middle-of-the-pack team, but there were indications that if they won, they also might receive a bowl invitation. So both teams had a lot riding on the outcome. What people also forget about this game is that many of us in attendance that day believe that this was one of the top five college football games of all time *before* the final play. It was just an extraordinary game.

Elway had one play that basically defined his college career—completing a fourth-and-17 pass from his own 13 in the fourth quarter on the drive that led to the field goal that we all thought ended the game. Apparently, though, there was an enormous disagreement on the Stanford sidelines regarding how much time to leave on the clock to set up the field goal. Also, Stanford celebrated so much after the field goal that the officials gave them a 15-yard penalty on the kickoff, so that also played a large role in the final play.

When the ball was kicked off and the Bears were throwing the ball all around the field, it just didn't seem possible that they could actually get it all the way to the end zone. I wasn't even thinking about it, actually. One thing that really surprised me about my call when I listened back later was that I didn't use the term "lateral" until the game was over. The reason for that was that, like every other broadcaster, I tend to just summarize the last play of the game—although I wish I had used the word, since it certainly would have played better on the air. There were a couple times I almost said it, but by the time I could, the ball was in someone else's hands already, so I was just going with the action.

The play just kept going, and all of a sudden, I see the Stanford band on the field. There were so many visual things going on at that point—there were no lights on, and since it was a late afternoon in November, we could barely see what was going on down on the field. It wasn't nearly as bright as it looked on television, so we were just trying to figure out who had the ball, because there were just so many people on the field. Plus, there was so much luck involved in the play. On the last lateral, Mariet Ford, when he threw it to Kevin Moen—there is no way on this planet that he knew there was a Bear standing behind him. He just couldn't know that, between racing down the field and all of the band members around him. He simply flipped the ball over his shoulder, and Moen was there to catch it and take it into the end zone, where he crashed into the band member, Gary Tyrell, in one of the most famous visuals in sports history.

Like everyone else, I didn't know if it was going to count or not. But I am proud of the fact that I did not make the mistake that was made on other broadcasts of the game. I didn't worry about the flags or whether the play was going to stand. I just called the action and worried about all that other stuff after the play was done, to make sure that I at least had the entire call of the play. When the referee put his arms in the air signaling the touchdown, the place went nuts. I have never seen anything like it. It was so loud, even if it was only from the Cal side of the stands. It was amazing just how many people were on the field at this point—Cal players, fans, band members. It was a visual scene like I've never seen at a sporting event before or since.

1998 NFC Wild Card Game, Green Bay Packers at San Francisco 49ers, Candlestick Park, San Francisco, California, January 3, 1999

One of the most entertaining, emotional, dramatic wins the 49ers have ever had was this game in the Wild Card round of the playoffs. The Packers owned the Niners at that point; Brett Favre was at his peak as a player and had beaten San Francisco five times in a row. Steve Young and the Niners just could not beat the Packers. On this day, though, Young completed a pass while falling down to a young receiver by the name of Terrell Owens with four seconds to go and three defenders around him for the winning touchdown.

Owens had dropped at least five passes during the course of the game. He looked like he could be a great receiver; he had tons of potential, but there was a real concern that he was one of those guys who just couldn't hang on to the ball. When Favre put the Packers ahead late in the fourth quarter, the feeling in the stands was, "Here we go again." But Young, with his reputation on the line about whether he could ever beat Brett Favre and the Packers, responded brilliantly. With five seconds to play, he dropped back, almost fell down (and to this day, I'm still not sure how he didn't actually go down, since he was almost parallel to the ground at one point), stepped up, and somehow Owens, with three Packers surrounding him, catches this rocket of a pass and falls in to the end zone for the score. Owens could not stop crying after the game, after he had struggled all day with drops.

The reaction to that game was as exciting as any I had ever seen. If they didn't lose Garrison Hearst to a broken ankle the next week against Atlanta, I truly believe that team would have gone back to another Super Bowl. That play was the last great moment for the future Hall of Fame quarterback. When the 1999 season opened the following September, on a Monday night in Tempe, Arizona, Aeneas Williams of the Arizona Cardinals would deliver a career-ending hit against Young. The resulting concussion forced him into retirement.

Dave Strader

Broadcaster, Florida Panthers

Maine Mariners at Adirondack Red Wings, Glens Falls Civic Center, Glens Falls, New York, November 17, 1982

Mel Hewitt was a journeyman tough-guy minor leaguer who was playing for the Maine Mariners when he scored three goals in a game, all against different goalies. At the time, no one could verify it, but to this day, I can't imagine it has happened before or since in professional hockey. It was the 1982–83 season, and I was in my fourth season as the radio voice of Detroit's American Hockey League affiliate, the Adirondack Red Wings. The Red Wings were hosting their archrivals from Maine at the Glens Falls Civic Center, and goaltender Gilles Gilbert was with Adirondack on a conditioning assignment from the parent club in Detroit. Claude Legris was dressed as his backup and Jim Rutherford, another goaltender who was with Adirondack at the time, wasn't dressed for the game. Jim was set to watch the game from the press box (I can still remember him eating a hot dog before the game).

The game began with Maine winning the opening faceoff and dumping the puck behind the net. Gilbert went to play the puck, and, as he turned to skate to the front of the net, wrenched his back and fell down. Maine got the loose puck, and Hewitt scored to make it 1–0. Gilbert was done for the night, and Legris went in to play goal. Rutherford had to leave the press box and get in uniform to back up Legris. In the second period, Hewitt scored against Legris, and shortly after the goal, there was a bench-clearing brawl. The only Adirondack player on the ice not paired up with anyone was Legris, so he skated the length of the ice and grabbed a kid by the name of Steve Tsujiura (who reportedly had a black belt in martial arts). Claude got the worst of the exchange, and he was tossed out of the game. Rutherford then went in to play goal, and Hewitt scored again! I've told the story a couple times on the air since then, and every time I see Jim Rutherford, who is now general manager of the Carolina Hurricanes, he asks me how many times I am going to tell that story. But it is such a classic, so I won't be retiring it anytime soon.

Detroit Red Wings at Calgary Flames, Olympic Saddledome, Calgary, Canada, October 27, 1995

There was an interesting scenario leading up to the trade in which the Detroit Red Wings acquired Igor Larionov from the San Jose Sharks. In 1995, following the first NHL lockout, the Red Wings rolled through the shortened regular season and then the playoffs, until they faced New Jersey in the Stanley Cup Final. The Devils swept the Wings in four straight. Early the next season, Wings' coach Scotty Bowman wanted to do something to shake things up.

At the time, the Red Wings had four very talented Russian players, and Bowman was always fascinated with the Russian style of play that focused on puck possession. I was now the TV voice of the Detroit Red Wings, and I was on the Wings' team plane (Red Bird One) for a road trip in October of 1995 when Scotty called Sergei Fedorov to the front of the plane. After their meeting was over, Sergei had a big smile on his face as he went back to his seat, so I knew something had happened. It was the deal for Larionov. Igor became the fifth Russian on the team, along with Fedorov and Viacheslav Kozlov up front and Slava Fetisov and Vladimir Konstantinov on defense.

The first game after the trade was in Calgary, and it would be the first time in NHL history that five teammates from Russia would take the ice together. The Red Wings not only won the game 3–0, the Flames had just eight shots on goal. The Russian Five (as they were called) had the puck all night, and their style of play quickly rubbed off on the rest of the team. I remember my Detroit broadcast partner Mickey Redmond saying that opposing players went to the bench after a shift against the Russian Five looking for the Dramamine to cure their motion sickness!

We stayed over in Calgary for a day after that historic game before heading to Winnipeg. The team wasn't able to practice at the Saddledome, so they skated at the nearby Corral. I had two copies of the official score sheet, and as the five Russians were walking toward me after practice, I asked all five to sign them for me. I gave one of the signed sheets to the Red Wings for their archives, and I saved one as a cherished memento of that game. That Detroit team ended up winning the Presidents' Trophy for the NHL's best record with

131 points, but they lost in the Western Conference Final to the eventual Stanley Cup champion, the Colorado Avalanche.

1997 Stanley Cup Finals, Game 4, Philadelphia Flyers at Detroit Red Wings, Joe Louis Arena, Detroit, Michigan, June 7, 1997

I was hired as the play-by-play announcer for the NHL's international TV broadcast of the Stanley Cup Finals in 1997. This was the first time the league had produced a separate telecast to send out to approximately two hundred countries around the world. I had just finished my first season covering the NHL on ESPN after spending eleven years as the voice of the Red Wings. Ironically, the NHL hired my longtime Detroit TV partner Mickey Redmond as the analyst for the series. The NHL hired us before the playoffs began, so we were thrilled that the Finals matchup ended up being the Red Wings against Philadelphia. Detroit hadn't won a Cup since 1955 and had been swept in the Finals two years earlier by New Jersey.

Detroit jumped out to a 3–0 series lead. The atmosphere for Game 4 at the Joe Louis Arena was electric. Darren McCarty's series-clinching goal after walking around Philadelphia defenseman Janne Niinimaa was a highlight-reel special. Detroit Captain Steve Yzerman had put a lot of thought into whom he would hand the Cup to first after accepting it from Commissioner Bettman. Steve called over Igor Larionov and Slava Fetisov together and handed them the Cup. It was a magic moment. Yzerman recognized not only their contributions to the team but the historical significance of how these two players paved the way for so many others. Larionov and Fetisov defied all odds in breaking free from the grip of communism to pursue their dream of playing in the NHL. If it weren't for Larionov and Fetisov, the transformation of the NHL into a true melting pot of international talent would have taken decades.

Years later I heard another story from that night from assistant coach Dave Lewis. With all the excitement about Detroit's being up three games to none and having a chance to win the Cup that night at home, right after the opening faceoff, with the puck in the Detroit zone and Philadelphia frantically trying to score the first goal, the bench was alive, and the crowd was going nuts. Lewis turned to Scotty Bowman, who was staring across the ice, not even looking at the play. Scotty faced Lewis and said, "Is that Gordie Howe?" Lewis asked what he was talking about, and Bowman repeated the question, "Is that Gordie Howe?" There was a whistle and a faceoff near the goal, and Bowman still hadn't looked at the action. Finally, Lewis looked over and said, "Yeah, that's Gordie Howe." Scotty asked, "Why isn't he in the owner's box?" Then Scotty turned his attention back into the game. There weren't many details that escaped Scotty's attention, no matter what was going on around him.

After the game, having been with the Wings for so many years, my family and I had the opportunity to have some pictures taken with the Stanley Cup. I have one picture with Mickey Redmond as I am pointing to his name on the Cup (Mickey won two Cups with Montreal in the sixties). I also remember seeing actor Jeff Daniels, a Michigan native and lifelong Wings fan, still hanging out on the ice with his kids at around 2:00 A.M., wearing his Red Wings jersey and taking in everything that had happened that night.

1998 Stanley Cup Finals, Game 4, Detroit Red Wings at Washington Capitals, MCI Center, Washington, D.C., June 16, 1998

I also worked this series for NHL International TV with Mickey Redmond, and it was an incredibly emotional experience. The Red Wings beat the Washington Capitals in four games, with the clinching win in Washington. Steve Yzerman again thought about whom he would hand the Stanley Cup to, although it was a fairly easy decision. Defenseman Vladimir Konstantinov had been involved in a limo accident just six days after the Wings won the Cup in 1997. He was critically injured and never able to play hockey again. The scene with Vladimir on the ice in his wheelchair after the clinching game in Washington one year later is something I'll never forget.

The best game in the series was actually Game 2 at Joe Louis Arena. Doug Brown scored one of the best goals I've seen in any of the Stanley Cups I have covered. Not only was it a great goal, but he also made a great defensive play to set it up, and that goal really turned the game around, leading to a Red Wings' overtime victory. The rest of the series was anticlimactic until the Cup presentation after Game 4. When they brought Konstantinov out in the wheelchair and Yzerman handed him the Cup, and all of his teammates, especially the Russians, gathered around him, it was quite a scene. It was emotional for both Mickey and me, because we had known Vlade since he came to the NHL.

Of all the Russian players on the Red Wings, Konstantinov was the most curious. He didn't have great command of the English language, but he always wanted to try to speak it, and on some road trips he would sit with us on the plane and just grin and nod and try to get involved in a conversation. Vlade would have won at least one Norris Trophy if his career had not been cut short. He was so respected as a person and an athlete, which made the accident a tragedy on so many levels.

1999 Stanley Cup Finals, Game 6, Dallas Stars at Buffalo Sabres, Buffalo Memorial Auditorium, Buffalo, New York, June 19, 1999

I was on the NHL International telecast again in 1999 for one of the most controversial moments in Stanley Cup history. My broadcast partner for this series between Buffalo and Dallas was former player Ed Olczyk. That season there was all kinds of controversy about the NHL's rule regarding players in the crease when goals were scored—if any part of the skate of an attacking player was in the crease when the puck entered the net, it was ruled no goal. But with rules like that, there always seems to be different circumstances that leave a little room for interpretation.

An example given to me earlier that season by one NHL referee was that if a player had control of the puck and was in the crease while he scored a goal, it would be allowed. The key word is control. The night of Game 6 in Buffalo, Eddie and I were not right at center ice in the main press box. Our broadcast position was near the end where Brett Hull scored the Cup-clinching goal. When the goal was scored, the place went nuts, and Hull skated away and got mobbed by his teammates. I don't remember if we had seen a replay yet, but Olczyk looked at me and signaled that Hull was in the crease when he scored. We showed a couple of replays, including the famous overhead shot, and my first reaction was that Hull had kicked the puck with his skate to his stick and his skate stayed in the crease as he shot the puck into the net. Did Hull have control of the puck as he scored? It depends on whom you ask. There was so much confusion afterwards and still a lot of bitter feelings in Buffalo today.

Pat Summerall

Broadcaster

Recipient of Football Hall of Fame's Pete Rozelle Award, 1994

Chicago White Sox at New York Yankees, Yankee Stadium, Bronx, New York, June 8, 1969

Frank Messer and Phil Rizzuto, the regular Yankee announcers, along with Mel Allen were all part of Mickey Mantle's retirement ceremony that day, so the Yankees needed someone in the booth during the broadcast. I had been doing the Yankees' pregame and postgame show, so they asked me to take that spot. Mickey and I were very good friends, and I got a chance to be part of this very special day. During the ceremony, Mickey took a ride around the field on the warning track, and it was a tribute I'll never forget.

Muhammad Ali vs. Jean-Pierre Coopman, Clemente Coliseum, Hato Rey, Puerto Rico, February 20, 1976

The fight was in Puerto Rico, and we went over a few days ahead of time and became friendly with Muhammad, who confided a lot of things in us. Coopman was a Belgian who called himself "The Lion of Flanders," but he couldn't fight a lick (which we sort of knew going in, even though it was a championship fight). Coopman was around 5 foot 11, 200 pounds, while Ali was this big physical specimen, and it looked like a mismatch from the very beginning.

It was a big crowd, and I was doing the fight with Tom Brookshier, and for the first few rounds, Ali just toyed with him. No one was hitting anyone, and the crowd was singing songs like "Let Me Call You Sweetheart." After the fourth round, Ali came over to where I was sitting at ringside instead of going to his corner, put his arms over the ropes, and said, "Let me ask you something, Pat. Did you get all your commercials in?" I told him I didn't know, and he said, "Well, I hope so, because this ain't good for you, it ain't good for me, and it ain't good for boxing. I've got to take this cat out."

In the fifth round, he starting hitting Coopman, and it went from sounding like someone hitting a grapefruit to sounding like rifle shots. He knocked him out two minutes into that round.

1984 U.S. Open Super Saturday, National Tennis Center, Flushing, New York, September 8, 1984

The second Saturday at the U.S. Open is referred to as "Super Saturday" and consists of the two men's semifinal matches plus the women's final. This day, all three matches went the limit. I got there fairly early in the morning, and our producer, Frank Chirkinian, suggested I head up to the tower to tape the Men's Senior Doubles match that was going on, since we were going to be on the air from noon to 5:00 and we needed to make sure we had enough tennis to air. We taped that for an hour and then started the regular broadcast of the first Men's Semifinal between Pat Cash and Ivan Lendl at noon with Tony Trabert and John Newcombe. That match went to a fifth-set tiebreaker, which was won by Lendl.

Tony and John then left, while I stayed up there for the Women's Final with Virginia Wade and Billie Jean King, which went three sets and saw Martina Navratilova beat Chris Evert Lloyd. We were supposed to be off the air at 5:00, but the women were still playing at that point, and there was still a second Men's Semifinal to come. When the women finished, Jimmy Connors and John McEnroe took the court for their match, which ended up starting at 7:30.

Around 10:00, Tony looked at me and reminded me about how long I had been in the tower without a break, unlike him and John, and asked if I needed to go to the bathroom. The tennis was so good, though, that I hadn't even thought about that . . . until he reminded me. At 11:18, I was finally able to leave the tower after McEnroe topped Connors in five sets, over twelve hours after first entering it but also after seeing an amazing day of tennis.

The 1986 Masters, Augusta National Golf Club, Augusta, Georgia, April 10–13, 1986

Going into the weekend, the feeling among most people was that Jack Nicklaus was too old to do anything in the tournament and too old to win another major championship. No one thought he would be a factor. After he made the cut, people started to take notice on a limited basis, and when he was near the leaderboard following the third round, it certainly turned some heads. His son was caddying for him, which was a little different, and that made it a little more emotional for me, since I knew them both so well.

He was close to the top of the leaderboard as he made the turn on Sunday, and as he played the back nine, there were roars that were distinctly for him. If you go to Augusta enough times, you know there was a particular roar when Arnold Palmer did something, or when Greg Norman did something, or when Jack did something. You could tell who the player was without even being there. The roars for Nicklaus started coming at 10, then 11, and so on. I was sitting in the tower at 18, and as the roars got louder and louder, they kept changing the leaderboard, with Jack eventually taking the lead. Nobody could believe it.

He birdied 16 and 17, and when he got to 18, it looked like all he needed was to par the hole to win the tournament. When he stepped to the tee, before he even hit his tee shot, the crowd just began to stand and applaud. After he hit a nice shot and started walking up the hill, the crowd rose like a wave and got louder and louder until it reached such a crescendo that if I had said anything, no one would have been able to hear it. It was one of those moments where the picture really told the whole story, and I didn't need to say anything. I looked at Ken Venturi, who was sitting next to me, and there were tears running down his cheeks. I know tears were running down my cheeks, as well.

Jack parred at 18 for a 30 on the back nine, and it looked like he was going to win, unless someone did something incredible behind him, which didn't happen. He dropped his putter and grabbed his son, hugging him. Again, there was nothing that needed to be said, so I stayed quiet until they were off the green and on their way to the scorer's tent. It was certainly the most memorable moment I experienced in my career.

AFL-NFL World Championship Game, Green Bay Packers vs. Kansas City Chiefs, Los Angeles Coliseum, Los Angeles, California, January 15, 1967, and Super Bowl XXXVI, New England Patriots vs. St. Louis Rams, Louisiana Superdome, New Orleans, Louisiana, February 3, 2002

No one realized that the game soon to be known as the Super Bowl was going to become such a big event. The first time it was played, it was actually a simulcast, with CBS and NBC both broadcasting the game with their own announcers but using the same pictures. I was on the CBS crew representing the NFL with Ray Scott, Frank Gifford, and Jack Whitaker, while Curt Gowdy and Paul Christman had the AFL side on NBC.

We thought there would be a lot of animosity between the networks, but we had a production meeting, and everything was very congenial. They flipped a coin to determine which crew would be in charge at the meeting, which NBC won. Everyone got along well except the technicians, who were in different unions; they actually had to erect a chain-link fence between the remote units to keep them from going after each other. The pregame and half-time shows were separate, but the postgame shows were the same, since we had to do that from the winner's locker room. I was the host of the show, and one of the stipulations we had to grant to NBC was that one of their announcers would be in the locker room with me, and I had to let him ask one question. Their announcer was George Ratterman, who was one of their analysts, and I handed him the microphone so he could ask a question. Of course, my producer immediately started yelling at me for giving him the microphone and to get it back. There were forty thousand empty seats in the stadium that day, and the most expensive ticket was twelve dollars—quite a difference from the way it is today.

And quite different from another special moment for me, the last Super Bowl I worked, my final broadcast with John Madden. That game, between the Patriots and Rams, was a great game that ended on a game-winning field goal by Adam Vinatieri and obviously was a very emotional and special event for me.

DB Sweeney
Actor, Eight Men Out, The Cutting Edge

1986 Benson and Hedges Cup Final, Middlesex vs. Kent, Lord's Cricket Ground, London, England, July 12, 1986

I'd never seen cricket before, but I read in the London sports pages that this was the final match of one of the titans: Clive "Big Cat" Lloyd. The opposition featured the reigning star of the day, Imran Khan.

I'm in.

Impossible ticket, the hotel concierge tells me. There's always a single to be found, in my experience. I find a guy at the pub next to the venue. After a few pints he agrees to pass me out his stub through the fence once he's gone in. Works like a charm.

The English are as fired up as they get for this one. Good times.

1986 World Series, Game 6, Boston Red Sox at New York Mets, Shea Stadium, Queens, New York, October 25, 1986

I had a roommate who was the son of a famous sportswriter. Thankfully, the son wasn't a baseball fan, so he offered me a press pass to the game if I would scalp his two seats and give him the money. I jumped at this, since I'd already spent a lot of dough going to Games 1 through 5. An undercover cop arrested me mid-sale in the Shea Stadium parking lot, but the press pass was safe in my sock. After getting released, I went into Shea and immediately down onto the field to watch BP. What's the point of having a press pass if you can't have some stinking access?

I remember being most impressed by a reserve named Mike Greenwell. As they began to roll down the cage, I noticed a bat was about to be crushed. What if it was Dwight Evans's favorite and its loss would be the difference between victory and defeat?! I reached down to remove and save it from damage, only to be rebuked by an unfamiliar-looking Red Sox player. "Where you going with that?" I said I was moving it so it didn't get wrecked. "Sure," he grunts, "you were trying to swipe it." As he turns away, I see it's Marc Sullivan, the backup catcher. Stung, I spend the early innings thinking you shouldn't be such a jerk to people when you're only on the team because your uncle's the general manager.

Super Bowl XXV, Buffalo Bills vs. New York Giants, Tampa Stadium, Tampa, Florida, January 27, 1991

I was about thirty rows up on the 10-yard line and couldn't tell Scott Norwood had missed "wide right" until the Giants fans in the end zone exploded. I was with my dad, a lifelong Giants fan. Perfect. . . .

1994 Stanley Cup Finals, Game 7, Vancouver Canucks at New York Rangers, Madison Square Garden, New York, New York, June 14, 1994

As a lifelong Blueshirt and friend to some of the Rangers players, I followed their run to the Cup very closely. I went to most of the Devils games and then traveled to Vancouver to see the games out there. But there was nothing like this game. I was in my usual aisle seat next to Doug Moss in the third row behind the visitor's bench. Bedlam. The greatest crowd noise ever. Snuck downstairs afterwards to the locker room and drank from the chalice. Sublime.

1999 Major League Baseball All-Star Game, Fenway Park, Boston, Massachusetts, July 13, 1999

I was on *Harsh Realm*, a FOX show, at the time. Since they were broadcasting the game, I had an unbelievable seat behind home plate.

Ted Williams waves to the crowd, and there's not a dry eye in the house. Then Pedro Martinez fans five out of the six hitters he faces. Most dominant pitching I've ever seen in person.

Michele Tafoya

Broadcaster, ESPN

Stanford at Cal, Memorial Stadium, Berkeley, California, November 20, 1982

I was in high school and had been accepted to both Stanford and Cal and was trying to decide which to go to. My sister was a senior at Cal and took me to the rally Friday night and the Big Game on Saturday. It has to be the most amazing finish to a football game I've seen to this day. We were sitting in the Cal student section around midfield. When the final play unfolded, it felt like slow motion. You were trying to keep your eye on the ball and follow the action, and all you could think was, "This isn't over. This isn't over!"

I remember everyone yelling about the band being on the field in the end zone to our left. The excitement in the student section was crazy. In some ways, the memory is just a blur. Once Cal scored the winning touchdown, the entire student section rushed the field, which in those days was artificial turf. After the game, the entire Bay Area was just buzzing. You couldn't go anywhere—be it a bar, a party, anywhere—without seeing the highlights on TV. The city of Berkeley was just alive that night. It wasn't just a win. I don't think anyone who was there at the time knew "The Play" would become the historic sporting moment it has. But we did know it was something special. I still get the chills when I see the "The Play" or hear the original radio call of it. I have to admit that I enjoy being able to say that I was there. Oh, and I decided to attend Cal!

EuroBasket 1995, Athens, Greece, June 21–July 2, 1995

These games took place just as the war in between the Croats and Serbs in Croatia was simmering down, but there was still a lot of tension in the Balkans. Croatia had become independent from Yugoslavia, which meant that a very powerful Yugoslavian national basketball team had also been split up. Two famous stars from Yugoslavia, Vlade Divac and Toni Kukoc, were no longer teammates. Kukoc now played for the Croatian national team, while Divac remained with Yugoslavia. The former friends were now enemies, both politically and on the basketball court.

Further adding to the drama was the fact that Yugoslavia was just return-ing to the games after a ban on international competition. No one was quite sure if they were as good as they had once been.

But as the tournament unfolded, it became clear that the Croatian team was on a collision course with their hated Yugoslavian rivals. As the teams played their way through the brackets, they appeared destined to meet in the championship game. But if Croatia played against Yugoslavia in the final game and lost, the result would be tremendous shame over losing to the coun-try that had brutally killed or maimed so many Croats. That notion was so daunting that I am convinced the Croatian national team purposely lost in the semifinals—Croatia was outplaying Lithuania in every way, but the Croatian head coach pulled his best player from the game, allowing Lithuania to claim the momentum and the spot in the finals against Yugoslavia.

The final result was that Yugoslavia won the gold, Lithuania the silver and Croatia the bronze. When Yugoslavia came to the medal stand to claim gold, the Croatians left the stand in protest. It was a dramatic moment that illus-trated how sport and nationality are so tightly intertwined.

2000 Summer Olympics, Sydney, Australia, September 15–October 1, 2000

From the Opening Ceremony all the way to the Closing Ceremony, these were the most remarkable Olympic Games I've ever witnessed. Every facet of the Games was perfect, from the weather to the transportation, from the Aussie hospitality to the international camaraderie. Around Sydney you could find giant TV screens strategically placed so that no one would have to miss any event, even if the event was miles away. Aussies and tourists alike would sur-round these screens, Fosters in hand, and cheer, no matter who won at what. The swimming venue was so raucous you would have thought you were at a soccer game at Wembley. The track and field competition was one of the most exciting ever, as Australian sprinter Cathy Freeman—of Aboriginal descent—made strides for her people with every step she ran. Even the equestrian events, which were highlighted by the home team's winning the Three-Day Event, were spectacular.

The Games ended with the most incredible fireworks display imaginable. An eight-and-a-half-mile "fuse" carrying fireworks along barges from Olympic Park all the way to the Sydney Harbor Bridge was referred to as the "River of Lightning." It was the ideal way to end these perfect Olympic Games. Good on ya, Aussies.

Washington Redskins at Green Bay Packers, Lambeau Field, Green Bay, Wisconsin, September 24, 2001

The first Monday Night Football game after the attacks on September 11, 2001, was September 24. The Green Bay Packers hosted the Washington Redskins at Lambeau Field. The country was just beginning to come out of the haze of 9/11, and the NFL's returning to action was a small measure of "getting back to normal." I was the reporter on ESPN's *Monday Night Countdown* that night. The security around the perimeter of Lambeau Field was like nothing I'd seen before. There was a palpable sense of tension, as we all knew the world had changed, and security at sporting events would never be the same again. We had to allow ourselves at least an extra hour to get our car thoroughly inspected and into the parking lot, to get our equipment past the bomb-sniffing dogs, and to get ourselves properly credentialed and into the stadium.

As part of the pregame festivities, local firefighters and policemen held an American flag shaped like the United States in the middle of the field. Just before ABC went on the air, the song "Proud to Be an American" was played over the stadium loudspeakers. I had never really liked that song, but I fell in love with it that night. As it played, all 59,771 fans waved the small American flags they'd been given at the stadium. Every last one of those flags was being waved as the song played, and everyone in the stadium was singing. As our crew walked off the field, we just looked at each other and asked, "Is the hair on the back of your neck standing up, too?" It was a remarkable moment. The game was secondary. At the end of the game the score was 37–0, Packers. But it was what happened before the game that I'll always remember.

2005 NBA Eastern Conference Semifinals, Game 6, Detroit Pistons at Indiana Pacers, Conseco Fieldhouse, Indianapolis, Indiana, May 19, 2005

Conseco Fieldhouse in downtown Indianapolis was packed with lifelong Pacers fans who had watched Reggie Miller's entire eighteen-year NBA career unfold in this basketball Mecca. Moments before the game ended, Larry Brown, who was the opposing coach for Detroit and had once been Miller's coach in Indy, called a timeout so that Reggie could walk off the court and receive a proper ovation.

I was working as the game's sideline reporter for ESPN, and I had been told all day that Reggie was not going to give a postgame interview. But this was an instance where it was not *what* you knew but *who* you knew. I am privileged to call Reggie a friend, having broadcast WNBA games with him for Lifetime Television for several years. I didn't want to exploit that relationship to get him to do this interview, but I knew everyone wanted to hear from the future Hall-of-Famer as he said goodbye to the game he so beautifully represented.

The moment the game ended and the buzzer sounded, the building erupted in chants of "Reg-gie! Reg-gie!" He stood on the court just kind of soaking it in, being hugged and congratulated by teammates and coaches. Somehow, through the mass of people, I made my way to Reggie, caught his eye, showed him the microphone I was holding and said simply, "You tell me, yes or no?" He said, "Okay, let's do this right now." Miller, one of the great trash-talkers in the game, is truly a humble man and a great professional. He delivered a moving interview, live on national television as the crowd continued to chant his name. Number 31 was hanging it up, and I got to conduct his final postgame interview. It was a thrilling and emotional moment for me both as a reporter and as his friend.

Rod Thorn

President, New Jersey Nets

1974 ABA East Division Finals, Game 3, New York Nets at Kentucky Colonels, Freedom Hall, Louisville, Kentucky, April 17, 1974

I was the assistant coach for the Nets at the time, and this was one of those low-scoring games that Kentucky always tried to get us into. The score was tied, and we called time. Kevin Loughery called for a play where Julius Erving had the ball and would take the last shot. Julius had the ball around center court and was dribbling out there. The clock was running and now was below ten seconds. Kevin was yelling, "Go, go!" But Julius was just standing there, dribbling, looking at the clock. Finally, he took a couple more dribbles, rose up, and hit the shot just before the buzzer sounded, giving the Nets the 89–87 win. The Kentucky crowd was just shocked. The Colonels' coach, Babe McCarthy, was sitting in his seat with his head in hands and just couldn't believe Dr. J had just done it again.

1987 NBA Eastern Conference Finals, Game 5, Detroit Pistons at Boston Celtics, Boston Garden, Boston, Massachusetts, May 26, 1987

I was sitting in Boston Garden, thinking the game was over. Detroit had played great, and Isiah Thomas put on an incredible show that night, which he usually did against the Celtics. Boston came back, though, but it looked like they were going to fall short. The Pistons had the ball, and all they had to do was get it inbounds. I was getting ready to put my coat on, when Larry Bird stole the pass and passed it to Dennis Johnson for the winning basket. Everyone thought this game was over, so when it happened, the place went absolutely crazy.

1989 NBA Playoffs Opening Round, Game 5, Chicago Bulls at Cleveland Cavaliers, Richfield Coliseum, Richfield, Ohio, May 7, 1989

This was the moment where Michael Jordan and the Bulls really started to take off. When Michael made the shot over Craig Ehlo, we all got the first big lesson on what a great clutch player he was. The Bulls had just gone up one, when Ehlo took a backdoor pass from Brad Daugherty to give the Cavs the lead and, everyone thought, the game and series. But the Bulls inbounded after the time-out, and Michael made that famous shot from the top of the key to win it. The crowd was just stunned. I remember looking at Cleveland GM Wayne Embry, who was standing in the tunnel, and he had his face turned to the wall, with a blank expression. The arena was almost quiet, except for the Bulls celebrating on the court.

Chicago Bulls at New York Knicks, Madison Square Garden, New York, New York, January 15, 1990

The Knicks were just an okay team at the time, while the Bulls were really good. There was one-tenth of a second on the clock and the game was tied at 106 when the Knicks inbounded the ball to Trent Tucker, who just threw the ball up from behind the three-point line. It went in to win the game. I ran into the commissioner after the game, and I remember him asking me if I thought the shot was on time, which I did not. Sure enough, it wasn't when we looked at it on tape in the league office. We timed it, and it took around six-tenths of a second. But with all of the human elements involved in starting the clock, it was able to happen legally in the game. From this shot, we had to institute a rule that said you needed at least three-tenths of a second on the clock to be allowed to catch and shoot off an inbound for it to be allowed. It will always be known as the "Trent Tucker Rule."

1997 NBA Finals, Game 5, Chicago Bulls at Utah Jazz, Delta Center, Salt Lake City, Utah, June 11, 1997

This was a critical game, with the winner of this game most likely winning the series. There were rumors running all over the arena that Michael Jordan was sick and that he might not be able to play in the game. When he came out to warm up, he was all bundled up, and it looked like he was not going to be able to play. But he played. And not only did he play, he played almost the whole game. He made some huge plays down the stretch, as he usually did, and the Bulls won the game. Afterwards, he was so exhausted, he could barely walk off the floor; he had to sit on the bench for a while before leaving the court. The atmosphere around this game was electric, it was a great game, and it was just incredible that Michael was able to play as well as he did.

Gary Thorne

Broadcaster, ESPN

1986 National League Championship Series, Game 6, New York Mets at Houston Astros, Astrodome, Houston, Texas, October 15, 1986

A lot of people consider this the best baseball game ever played, and I might have to agree. There was so much on the line for the Mets, because they believed that if they didn't win this game, they were not going to win Game 7 against Mike Scott. They had no confidence in hitting against him. So for them, this was really Game 7, and that is how they approached it. Houston knew that if they could just get to Game 7, they probably were going to win it. It was one of those games that refused to go away, because it seesawed back and forth endlessly. Each team made comebacks, starting with the Mets scoring three in the top of the ninth to send it to extra innings.

When Billy Hatcher homered in the fourteenth inning to tie the game, the Astrodome went absolutely nuts. Most people thought the game was over before that, and that the Mets were going to win, so when Hatcher came through, it rejuvenated not only the building but the game itself. It sent everything right back to where it was at the beginning, and it was just wild. A lot of people did not sit down for the rest of the game. It really was an electrifying feeling. To the other extreme, when the game ended and the Mets won after scoring three times in the top of the sixteenth (before giving up two runs in the bottom of the inning and hanging on for the 7–6 win), it was one of those deadly silences. It seemingly came so quickly, which is one of the ironies of games like this that go on and on forever with so much happening. When it ends, it just seems to end, and everybody sits there thinking there is more and that it can't actually be over. The Mets were delirious in their celebration, and thought that they had snuck under the bullet on this one. Watching the celebration, you would have thought they had won the World Series.

1986 World Series, Game 6, Boston Red Sox at New York Mets, Shea Stadium, Queens, New York, October 25, 1986

The feeling all season long around the Mets, starting in spring training, was that this was a team of destiny. It started in Florida in February; it was never about what happened in the regular season—it was about winning it all. There was chemistry on that team and a feeling of superiority that ran with them throughout the year. The '86 Mets were genuinely disliked because of their attitude. They loved beating the stuffing out of every team they played, especially the Cardinals. Whenever they hit a city on the road, guys would say it was "rape, pillage, and plunder" and get the hell out of the way.

When it got to Game 6 against Boston, and the possibility arose that things were actually going to end without a championship, it wasn't enough, and not even close to being enough. They had to win the whole thing, or the season would be a failure. They had won Game 6 in Houston and now had come back against Boston after losing the first two games of the Series at home before going down three games to two.

I honestly think losing was just one of those things that they refused to allow to happen. It was felt by every member of that team, but for those of us covering the games, it felt more like it was too late and that it just wasn't going to happen for them. And then they rose up one more time and won a baseball game that they shouldn't have won, and that's what the games are all about.

40th NHL All-Star Game, Northlands Coliseum, Edmonton, Canada, February 7, 1989

I happened to be downstairs during the pregame introductions of the players going out onto the ice and was standing next to Wayne Gretzky, who was going to be the last one introduced. There was tremendous anticipation in Edmonton for this moment. There wasn't any question that he was going to be greeted as the conquering hero and the prodigal son returning home. But everyone knew it was going to be a magical moment. No matter what he did beforehand, between the press conferences and team skates, the "moment" was going to be when he was introduced before the game and skated onto the ice.

The guys were standing in a line from the locker room to the Zamboni door, and Gretzky was last in line. He kept shuffling forward and shuffling forward, and with about five guys left, he started to cry. He was very emotional. This was his hockey home and where all the great games had been played and the great friendships had been made. The fans were doing what any athlete (or human being) would hope and that is receiving you back with open arms and an open heart. It was very emotional.

I have a vivid mind picture of standing there with the smoke machine going at the doorway, Gretzky being the last one and standing there as the lights are down and the spotlights are coming through the smoke. It was one of those Hollywood moments, and Gretzky was crying. After the introduction, it was a tumultuous, sustained applause that took the roof off. It typified him, though, because he really does care about the fans and that franchise and the others he played with. I thought that moment displayed what Wayne Gretzky was off the ice as well as any moment I've ever seen.

1994 Stanley Cup Finals, Game 7, Vancouver Canucks at New York Rangers, Madison Square Garden, New York, New York, June 14, 1994

One of the advantages I had in covering the playoffs in 1994 was that I wasn't a fan of any particular team, so I got the chance to stand back a little bit and just watch what was going on. From the Rangers side, this had turned into a death march. It was all or nothing, and this was it. The fans had had it and knew that if the Rangers were ever going to win, this was the team. Most of the players had the same feeling—if that organization was ever going to get it done, this was the season to do it.

When the series came back to New York after they lost Game 6, it became one of those situations where athletes decide that under no circumstances are they going to lose. You still have to pull it off, but if you go into a game with that attitude, and it is coming from the deepest part of your gut, you've got a pretty good shot at winning. I think that was felt that night by the fans and by the Rangers. Once the series went back to New York for Game 7, the reality that this was going to be the year had set in, and it was a genuine celebration from the time the game started.

1999 Major League Baseball All-Star Game, Fenway Park, Boston, Massachusetts, July 13, 1999

Ted Williams was my hero, so everything with me starts there. I had a chance to meet him and worked with him and traveled with him when he was doing some work for Upper Deck. That was very late in his life, but it established a small relationship between us. This night was going to be a great moment. You had the All-Century Team that had already been introduced and was surrounding the field. The current All-Stars were all there as well, and Ted was going to be the last person introduced.

When he took the field on his golf cart, Fenway Park just went nuts. But even more impressive in the depth of his importance to the game came through the players. The meeting where all the players moved in from their respective positions to where he was on the mound was not staged. It was a spontaneous reaction by the players. Of course, he threw out the first pitch that night and insisted on doing it by standing up from the cart and throwing it from the mound. He could barely stand up, but did, and threw the pitch.

I think that is what he was all about, though, both as a person and a player. He had a "no-give" attitude as a hitter, a fisherman, and a hunter. That is what his life was all about, and it was a very touching moment. I talked to the players afterwards who were there on the field, such as Tom Seaver, Joe Morgan, and Willie Mays; they were struck by it and touched by it. You've got to go pretty deep to touch guys like that who have lived those moments. And it happened that night.

Al Trautwig
Broadcaster, NBC Sports/MSG Network

1994 Winter Olympics, Men's 4x10 Kilometers Cross-Country Skiing, Birkebeineren Skistadion, Lillehammer, Norway, February 22, 1994

I did cross-country skiing at the Olympics for the first time in 1992 in Albertville and kind of wondered, as most Americans do, "Why?" Two years later, the Olympics were in Norway, where cross-country skiing is the national sport. The men's 4x10 relay is to cross-country skiing what the Super Bowl is to football. And it was clear from very early on at the Olympics that this race was going to be Norway's crowning moment. There was a big screen installed in downtown Oslo, and the night before the race, there were literally, from what I was told, over a hundred thousand people sleeping in the woods before the race. Some people say there were a half a million people there that day.

When the race was coming down to the end, it was obvious it was going to be between Italy and Norway. The Norwegian skier, Bjorn Daehlie, was one of the classiest guys but also had a little hot dog in him, although he was not the type to show anyone up. He stopped with about 1 mile to go to allow the Italian to go past him, but the Italian did not. When they entered the stadium, the Norwegian was in the dangerous lead position, and sure enough, that proved to be his doom, as the Italian was able to pass him at the end. The noise on the mountain that day, and how quickly it changed when the Italian beat the Norwegian by about 2½ feet after a 25-mile race, was unbelievable. It was so cold, and it was cross-country skiing, and I just couldn't believe what I was seeing and how much I cared.

1994 Eastern Conference Finals, Game 7, New Jersey Devils at New York Rangers, Madison Square Garden, New York, New York, May 27, 1994

There's no question that the Rangers winning the Stanley Cup was ridiculously over the top in terms of what you can imagine, but the game that got the

Rangers into the Stanley Cup Finals, when they beat the Devils in Game 7, was what taught me how fans behave when they are so emotionally invested that they are scared. You would think that the atmosphere in the overtimes that night would be crazy, but it wasn't. It was very quiet and really weird. I had never experienced something like that before, where the fans wanted it so badly that they were truly afraid. The best part about that game was when Stephane Matteau scored—and I still to this day don't know how the puck went in—there was a woman going absolutely nuts behind me. I looked up, and we made eye contact, and she yells, "This is my first game ever!" I told her never to go to another one.

1996 World Series, Game 4, New York Yankees at Atlanta Braves, Fulton County Stadium, Atlanta, Georgia, October 23, 1996

Personally, I had a lot emotionally invested and was still learning how not to be a fan and how being down two games to none doesn't mean you are done. When the Yankees were down 0–2, I thought they were finished. Then David Cone wins Game 3 and gives them a chance to believe, but they fall behind 6–0 in Game 4, and you start thinking it is over again and it wasn't meant to be.

They chipped away at the lead, but when Jim Leyritz came up, I certainly didn't allow myself to think "home run" in that situation. The homer only tied the game, but it completely changed that World Series and began a dynasty. Leyritz had one of those moments that allows him to walk into any stadium in New York and be treated like royalty. This home run gave Yankees fans belief that would last a decade.

1999 NBA Eastern Conference Finals, Game 3, Indiana Pacers at New York Knicks, Madison Square Garden, New York, New York, June 5, 1999

I realized Larry Johnson's four-point play needed to be on my list after seeing a tape of the game. When the play happened, I was at the other end of the floor, and you can actually see the look on my face. I had gone up to my wife and son during the time-out before the play, with eleven seconds left, and my son actually said to me, "Dad, all they need is a four-point play." I laughed but then couldn't believe when it really happened.

My favorite part of the whole thing is when Johnson hits the three-pointer and Chris Childs runs over to him and reminds him to relax, because he still has to make the free throw. Years later, the Knicks acquired Antonio Davis, who committed the foul, and every single day he went to practice, he had to walk past a photo on the wall at the Knicks' practice facility of Larry Johnson hitting the shot. This moment changed the way television covered basketball. I don't know how NBC had that shot, but broadcasters try to recapture that all the time.

2003 Ironman World Championship, Kona, Hawaii, October 18, 2003

Dick Hoyt has a son, Ricky, who was born a paraplegic. The Hoyt family raised the child but had no real connection to his soul—he can't talk, and they don't know if he can hear. Eventually, technology was created for Ricky to be able to communicate by pecking out letters, and the first words that Ricky Hoyt spoke were "Go Bruins." So his parents learned Ricky has a love of sports. They were with Ricky in a park one day, and there was a race. Ricky had a visceral reaction to the race that intrigued his parents, and he expressed to them that he wanted to do that.

Knowing that he couldn't, Dick entered a short race with Ricky, and the reaction they got from him made them realize just how powerful this was to Ricky. Eventually, it got to the point where Dick and Ricky ran the Boston Marathon and became the inspiration of New England. They entered more and more races and then set their sights on the Ironman Triathlon, which is a 2.2-mile swim, 112 miles on a bike, then a full marathon. This was the ultimate gift a father could give to his son. He couldn't make him talk or walk or anything else. All he could give him was the feeling he had when he was in a race.

The Ironman has to end at midnight after starting at 7 in the morning. But there is Dick, pushing his son through the race, beating the clock before midnight to complete the dream, knowing full well the clock is ticking on just how long he has the opportunity to do this for his son. It was beyond inspirational. It was someone doing something that only a father would do for his son.

Matt Vasgersian
Broadcaster, FOX Sports/San Diego Padres

Kansas City Royals at California Angels, Anaheim Stadium, Anaheim, California, September 30, 1992

In 1992 I was the single-A radio voice of the California League's High Desert Mavericks, a team owned by baseball's Brett Brothers—George, Ken, Bobby, and John. Ken Brett was working with the California Angels as their television color announcer and would often visit us up in the desert to check in on the team and enjoy watching minor league games in a stadium he and his brothers had built to become, at the time, one of the nicest in the minors.

Ken and I struck up a fast friendship, and as our season wore down, he was gracious enough to invite me to Anaheim to sit with him in the booth during a telecast during a home stand in late September. The Royals were in town for a four-game series and, being that George was approaching 3,000 hits, we decided that the most convenient time to hang out in the booth would be before or after the night of number 3,000.

So on the evening of September 30, with George Brett needing four hits for the magical mark, and the circus of friends, family, and media safely at least a day or two away, I sat in the Angels TV booth with Ken Brett and his partner Ken Wilson.

Top of the first vs. Julio Valera: George doubles to left.

Top of the third: base hit to right.

Top of the fifth: single to center.

As each at bat yielded yet another knock, the stadium started to buzz with the anticipation that "tonight might be the night." In this slightly-before-the-Internet age in sports, you could see people lining up to use the pay phones and hear the clickety-clack of wires spitting scores and headlines onto thin sheets of recycled paper. The press box at the "Big A" was functioning on all levels, and I had the best seat in the house, right behind the leading man's brother.

In the top of the seventh, against right-handed reliever Tim Fortugno and needing an unlikely fourth hit in his fourth at bat for the milestone, Brett lined a 3–0 pitch into right to earn a place in baseball immortality. As the future Hall-of-Famer got to first base, his first look was into the stands to recognize his wife and mother. His next look was right up to the Angels broadcast booth, where brother Ken raised a fist to share in the moment, sending immediate chills down the spine of a class-A radio hack sitting in the background. George himself was a little caught up in it too, as moments later he was picked off at first.

Ken Brett would become not only a closer friend as the years went on but eventually a colleague, as we worked together for a couple of seasons on FX's *Baseball Saturday* and the Fox Sports Net *Game of the Week* in the late nineties. Players and broadcasters alike have "favorite guys" in baseball, and Ken Brett was certainly mine. A guy who not only helps you out as a mentor but a guy who everyone loved being around. Whether it was downplaying his own great playing career over a couple of beers or inviting you out with some of his Hall of Fame pals (even though you knew you had little business being there), Ken Brett was the best.

When round two with a brain tumor finally proved too much for him to recover from in 2004, I couldn't help but remember that fantastic night in 1992, one that, fortunately, I had a chance to thank him for before he passed.

Cincinnati Reds at Milwaukee Brewers, Milwaukee County Stadium, Milwaukee, Wisconsin, September 28, 2000

On the night of September 28, 2000, Milwaukee County Stadium closed its doors for the last time. It was a night that certainly didn't sneak up on anybody, as a stadium farewell planned for the previous season was put on hold when a tragic accident claimed the lives of four construction workers at the new Miller Park just beyond right-centerfield. Thus County Stadium was coaxed into one more year of service before arriving at its final night as a host.

And people were crying. Was this the same County Stadium that each April showered fans with ice-cold water when frozen plumbing burst over the grandstand? Was this the same County Stadium with one functioning elevator? Was this the same County Stadium used to blame the Brewers' financial woes on for the last twenty years? County Stadium was the crazy aunt whom you rarely visited that passed after a long, fulfilling life and made you somehow feel like you missed her.

But something very important was reconfirmed to me that night—a top rule in the sports fans' unofficial guide to entitlement: it may be a bucket of bolts, but it's *our* bucket of bolts. As home to the Green Bay Packers, the Milwaukee Brewers, and, of course, the World Champion Milwaukee Braves, County Stadium had served its people well. For many Wisconsinites it was the first (and in some cases only) venue they'd ever known. And even though fans to a person agreed it was time for a new stadium, the reality that the old girl was about to go made for some real emotion.

So it was on this night that many of the theater's brightest stars reconvened to give Wisconsin fans one final opportunity to say goodbye, as after the final out one by one the former Packers, Brewers, and Braves made their way out from the visiting bullpen to home plate. Matching the appreciation and delight of the crowd was that of the players themselves, many of whom hadn't seen one another in many years, only to be reunited on such a memorable evening. Seventy-three-year-old ex-Brave Bob Buhl, barely able to get along all the way from the bullpen, wanted so badly to throw a pitch from the mound that the old guy took ten wonderful minutes to get up there and let it fly one last time. He passed away just a few months later.

The Apollo may have had Aretha Franklin and the Grand Ole Opry Hank Williams, but County Stadium had Hall-of-Famers Henry Aaron and Warren Spahn . . . gridiron greats Jim Taylor and Willie Davis . . . hard-hitting, hard-living Gorman Thomas . . . Wisconsin native and longtime second-baseman Jim Gantner . . . and of course huge applause for the still face of the franchise, Robin Yount.

My broadcast partner, ex-Brewer catcher Bill Schroeder, and I were grateful for the opportunity to punctuate the night's pictures with brief biographical nuggets and tidbits for the folks watching at home. As a guy who is most certainly his own worst critic, there haven't been many nights in my career where I've felt like I "nailed it," but thanks in part to Schroeder and the Brewers' then director of broadcasting Tim Van Waggoner, this was one of those nights. Bill and I encouraged each other to take the "less-is-more" philosophy and let the pictures speak for themselves while Van Waggoner produced a truly grand farewell, replete with perfect choices in music, timing, and drama. Bob Fosse couldn't have done it any better.

I had only been doing Brewers games for a handful of years, but being involved in this event made me feel a kinship with Milwaukee that's never really gone away. A part of me feels like it's home. September 28 also happens to be my birthday (a day that makes you a little more introspective anyway), and I remember leaving the parking lot that night thinking of the line from *Wayne's World*, "Milwaukee, or Mily-Wakay. It's Algonquin for the good land."

The good land indeed.

New York/New Jersey Hitmen at Las Vegas Outlaws, Sam Boyd Stadium, Las Vegas, Nevada, February 3, 2001

When I first heard about the plan to launch a rival football league created by (then) WWF czar Vince McMahon, I, like the rest of the sports world, didn't pay much attention. I remember changing in my dressing room (mentioning you had a dressing room: 15 yards for arrogance) in between episodes of the Fox Sports Net game show *Sports Geniuses* when I saw the story on CNN. "How stupid," I thought. "Compete with the NFL—hope that works out real well for you."

What exactly transpired between that day and the night of February 3, 2001, could look to some like a surefire strategy in how to derail what was shaping up to be a good career. Mmm, mmm . . . that Kool-Aid was tasty!

"You'll be given the freedom to call it like you see it."

"You'll be paired with a big-name analyst."

"This will be one of the most important pieces of programming on the network."

Great, I'm on board. It was a chance to get a little national play and break up the tedium of local baseball. Who among my peers wouldn't jump at the opportunity, given the above disclaimers? The weeks of hype leading to the opening kickoff had built some serious expectations. Bigger, more exciting, fewer rules, hotter cheerleaders—you name it. The problem with hype is that it makes you fair game for every pundit and critic this side of the Southwest Airlines in-flight magazine. And they were all waiting for us to fail.

At 8:05 ET, an estimated 9.7 million viewers tuned into NBC, only to be treated to the seemingly bloodied vocal chords of the inimitable Vince McMahon as he bellowed a phrase that's stayed with me like a double chili-cheese. . . .

"This . . . is . . . the XFL!!!!"

It was the kind of thing that sent chills down a guy's spine. Chills not from edge-of-the-seat excitement or because you knew you were on the verge of something big, but chills because it wasn't at all supposed to be like this. In the weeks prior to that opening kick, those with creative input agreed that "Mr. McMahon," for the sake of not alienating the football people and at least attempting to establish a modicum of credibility, should stay in the background. Somewhere along the way that plan changed, and come opening night there he was, front and center. At the time of "the scream," I remember making eye contact with Mike Adamle, the former NFL running back/announcer who was serving as a sideline reporter on our coverage for NBC, who at the time was some distance from me on the field. I couldn't help but note the exact look on his face that I knew I was carrying on mine. So this is how it's gonna be.

As far as the football goes, it was forgettable at best. The moment that best personified the telecast technology being better than the play on the field came by mistake, when Las Vegas Outlaw Kurt Gouveia picked up a fumble and started to return it over 80 yards for a touchdown. The former NFL Pro Bowler was about halfway into his return when his legs got heavy, allowing viewers at home to notice a rapidly evolving shot coming from one of the cameras on the field. Enter John Bruno, the veteran, Barney Rubble–bodied cameraman, who despite being 15 yards *in front* of the line of scrimmage at the time of the fumble had now *passed* Gouveia to shoot him as he backpedaled, all the while encumbered by a forty-five-pound camera apparatus strapped to his shoulders.

Other highlights of the night included coming back from a first-quarter break with WWF Superstar Triple H calling NFL commissioner Paul Tagliabue a wimp. *Good call!!* Another memorable telecast rejoin came via the serene pictures of a navel-to-neck look at a Las Vegas Outlaw cheerleader. No head, no legs, just boobs—a page torn right out of the *Girls Gone Wild* handbook. McMahon himself (now *producing* the madness in the truck) jumped right in on my headset, urging, "Matt, that's the XFL. That's what we're all about. That's America." The conflicting voices in my head became a bit much, leading me to utter the phrase (Dana Carvey/"Church Lady" style) that I'm confident led to my demise, "Well . . . I feel a bit uncomfortable."

As the telecast ended and we all attempted to make some sense of the last few hours, McMahon dispatched one of his henchmen, summoning me into a meeting with Vince himself. Hell, I half expected to be driven off into the desert and whacked by a squad of WWF goons. "You just don't get it," were the exact words McMahon used in telling me I was being demoted to the backup game. Even though the critiquing came as a bit of a relief, no one wants to be demoted from anything, and I was a bit miffed over the suggestion that I wasn't good enough to this gig. "Vince, this is your deal, and you deserve to have it treated the way you want," was my impulsive response.

It took me a while to realize how vindicating "You just don't get it" actually was.

Milwaukee Brewers at Pittsburgh Pirates, PNC Park, Pittsburgh, Pennsylvania, June 26, 2001

I've always enjoyed a good managerial snap. Longtime minor league skipper Tim Ireland once told me he judged his umpire run-ins by noting how many saliva-soaked sunflower seeds left his mouth and landed in his victim's eyelashes.

Baseball affords the fan a chance to see a grown man lose his mind in particularly comedic fashion. The view of a contentious football coach is oftentimes obstructed by surrounding assistants and players. Head coaches in the NBA dress in such a way that an inadvertent coat of polish is put on even the most boorish behavior.

A baseball manager, however, is afforded a completely different situation. To start he has the stage almost entirely to himself. Even mid-inning, with the defensive team on the field, all cases of managerial rage find all other action completely quiet (you never saw Earl Weaver going jaw-to-jaw with Ron Luciano while a runner was rounding third). Second, an on-field argument combined with the baseball-specific tradition of a manager suiting up in uniform puts the absurdity of a fifty-, sixty-, or seventy-year-old man wearing the same getup as his twenty-two-year-old second baseman into an even brighter light. In their early days Mets manager Casey Stengel was at his most cartoonish while taking issue with an umpire.

So it is with all due respect to Bill Parcells and Don Nelson that my fondest memories of "Bosses Gone Wild" come from the diamond. However, with so many choices—from Billy Martin kicking dirt to Lou Piniella bursting veins in his neck—summoning up a favorite seemed difficult until June 26, 2001.

During this otherwise pedestrian matchup between the perennially underachieving Brewers and Pirates at PNC Park, Bucs manager Lloyd McClendon took issue with umpire Rick Reed when Pittsburgh's Jason Kendall was called out on a very close play at first. Erupting out of the home dugout as though he were fired from a cannon, McClendon made his displeasure known from the outset. The standard gestures and salty language landed McClendon a rather predictable ejection from the proceedings. That was the moment of his brilliant, ad-libbed final touch. Digging into the ground, the Pirate manager pulled the first base bag out of the dirt, tucked it under his arm, and proclaimed, "If you ain't gonna use this I'm taking it with me." In an instant, our hero stormed off in a furious George Jefferson–style walk that brought a roar of approval from the crowd, his first-base bag in tow, kept safe from any further misuse.

It was hardly the stuff of Game 7 dreams or record-breaking heroics, but it was a moment that never fails to make me chuckle. As a broadcaster/fan I find myself occasionally overwhelmed by numbers and headlines; sometimes, the personal touches stand out most.

San Diego Padres at Los Angeles Dodgers, Dodger Stadium, Los Angeles, California, September 18, 2006

The final days of the 2006 season for the National League West played out in similar fashion to the end of the schedule each of the previous few years. A close race had often been misrepresented by the national media as a war of attrition—a battle of underachievers. In fact, for just about the entire season the Los Angeles Dodgers and San Diego Padres had played some competitive, spirited baseball, each taking turns atop the division, each harboring thoughts of playing deep into the fall.

San Diego had dominated the season series between the two Southern California rivals perhaps more thoroughly than ever before and had taken two of the first three games already in this series. On this night as well it appeared the Padres were on the way to drowning in the Blue once again. With San Diego leading 9–5, manager Bruce Bochy inserted righthander Jon Adkins, who in his first year as a Friar had proven steady and rather reliable. The following is a transcript of what happened on the field—not of the play-by-play from the booth but of the internal monologue I kept with myself throughout.

First batter . . . Jeff Kent. Home run. *Not a big deal. Let's just get this thing done because I've got to drive back to San Diego tonight for a home stand that begins tomorrow.*

Second batter . . . J.D. Drew. Home run. *Damn, they've just gone back-to-back here, and Trevor's gonna get a save now.*

San Diego inserts future Hall of Fame closer Trevor Hoffman to face Russell Martin, with their lead cut to a still-comfortable 9–7. Home run. *Three straight bombs—are you f'ing kidding me?*

At this point the rarest of sights was caught on camera at Chavez Ravine, as fans that had exited early (a Southern California baseball birthright) were seen turning around in the parking lot and running back inside the stadium.

Next batter . . . Marlon Anderson. Home run. I'm not exactly sure what I said on the air (I seem to remember a loud, amateurish moan), but I know what I was thinking.

There is no chance this has just happened.

Indeed, the Dodgers had struck for four consecutive home runs on eleven pitches. On but three previous occasions had this ever happened in major league history, and on none of those occasions did it take place during a pennant race with the home team trailing by exactly four runs in the bottom of the ninth. San Diego would manufacture a go-ahead run in the top of the tenth, but LA was destined to not only win this one but win it with style as Nomar Garciaparra hit (you guessed it) a two-run HR in the bottom of the tenth. To a man, those of us who cover the Padres feared the worst—that San Diego may not recover from such a brutal, bizarre beating. Our fears were unfounded, as not only did the Padres win the West a few weeks later, but the Dodgers would claim the NL wild card in a race that wasn't decided until the final weekend of the regular season.

George Vecsey
Columnist, New York Times

1966 NCAA Men's Basketball Tournament Finals, Kentucky vs. Texas Western, Cole Field House, College Park, Maryland, March 19, 1966

They didn't call it the Final Four back then. I stopped off in Maryland while driving to Florida to cover spring training for *Newsday*, not because the final was such a big deal. To this day, I am embarrassed at reading my faded clipping, that I did not describe the victory by five black starting players as an epic moment in American sports history. We thought it was, well, interesting, but not historic. Adolph Rupp, the coach of Kentucky, was probably a racist who resisted recruiting black players, but I have a vivid memory of his being gracious to the Texas Western players that day. ("You boys deserved to win," I recall him saying, over and over again.) I recently checked out my memory with Pat Riley, a northerner who played for UK that day. Riley said he recalled Rupp reacting like a gentleman.

1982 World Cup Finals, Brazil vs. Italy, Estadio Santiago Bernabeu, Madrid, Spain, July 11, 1982

I had played soccer, and I had watched the North American league, but I had no idea the sport could be so wonderful. *O Jogo Bonito*, the Brazilians call it in Portuguese. The Beautiful Game. In a funky little stadium in Barcelona, my first World Cup, Brazil moved the ball like magicians—Socrates to Falcao to Zico, bing-bing-bing, crisp runs, sharp passes. Then Italy counterattacked and won the entire World Cup, and I was hooked for life. To this day—my dirty little secret—I consider Brazil the keepers of the true flame, but my heart roots for Italy.

1983 Stanley Cup Finals, New York Islanders vs. Edmonton Oilers, Nassau Coliseum, Uniondale, New York, and Northlands Coliseum, Edmonton, Canada, May 10–17, 1983

The New York Islanders were the finest team I have ever covered—a clubhouse full of great athletes and strong personalities. They somehow managed to beat the brash young Edmonton Oilers in four straight games in the 1983 Stanley Cup finals, but as we watched Mike Bossy and Denis Potvin shake hands with Wayne Gretzky and Mark Messier on hockey's glorious handshake line after the last game, there was no doubt at all that the Oilers would be back. The next year the Islanders were old men, and the Oilers would win five of the next seven Cups. But in 1983 I had seen the Islanders hold off the Oilers—in retrospect, an amazing display of will.

1986 World Series, Game 6, Boston Red Sox at New York Mets, Shea Stadium, Queens, New York, October 25, 1986

It was midnight on a Saturday, very late for deadlines in the newspaper business. All of us in the press box had just filed our articles and columns reporting the Red Sox' first World Championship since 1918. The Red Sox were poised on the top step of their dugout, ready to swarm onto the field. Then the Mets staged their improbable rally, ending with the wild pitch to Mookie Wilson and the ground ball through Bill Buckner's legs. (I usually type "gnarled wickets.") We all groaned at the extra work and recalled our stories from our laptops and started all over again, knowing the Mets would surely win the seventh game, too, which, of course, they did.

2002 Winter Olympics, Ladies' Figure Skating, Delta Center, Salt Lake City, Utah, February 21, 2002

The Hughes family lives on the next peninsula from me, on Long Island. I went to their house when Sarah had a good showing in a world junior competition. Big family, good people, no prima donnas there. At the final skate of the 2002 Olympics, Sarah started in fourth place, but she gave such a joyous, uninhibited performance that, through the intricacies of scoring, she earned a gold medal. Hughes and her family and her coach were as stunned as the fans and the reporters. I don't expect to ever see another athlete perform with such glee, such energy, the moment of a lifetime for her and for many of us who witnessed it.

Tom Verducci
Senior Writer, Sports Illustrated

Miami Dolphins at New England Patriots, Foxboro Stadium, Foxboro, Massachusetts, December 12, 1982

Near-blizzard conditions had made scoring nonexistent at Foxboro Stadium until Patriots placekicker John Smith was about to try a 33-yard field goal late in the fourth quarter. Just prior to the snap, however, a man driving a John Deere tractor with a rotating sweeper steered toward the area of Smith's kick and conveniently cleared the spot. Smith, given sure footing, promptly drilled what would be the winning kick in a 3–0 game. As a Dolphins beat writer (my first full-time sportswriting gig), I immediately interviewed the driver—Mark Henderson still was seated on his charge—in the back of the end zone as Miami and incensed coach Don Shula, without mechanized aid, could not mount a comeback. Patriots fans were cheering the guy as a hero. It turned out the driver was a convict on work-release duty. Trying to write in the snowstorm, my feet wet and freezing fast, I had to laugh, reassured about my career choice. Sports provide great fodder for storytelling. You can't make this stuff up.

1991 World Series, Game 7, Atlanta Braves at Minnesota Twins, Hubert H. Humphrey Metrodome, Minneapolis, Minnesota, October 27, 1991

The tension and noise were so constant all that night in the Metrodome that you left with your ears ringing and your head hurting. With only one run being scored. That is the beauty of baseball. John Smoltz and Jack Morris pitched like champions, weaving in and out of trouble all night long, knowing full well that one mistake might decide the world championship. Years later, as I sat with Morris and watched a tape of the game, he told me that he never felt like he was in trouble the entire night. He was that confident.

2001 World Series, Game 7, New York Yankees at Arizona Diamondbacks, Bank One Ballpark, Phoenix, Arizona, November 4, 2001

Life during war times. The night began with the spooky but very real visage of stealth bombers flying over the rectangular hole in Bank One Ballpark, a reminder that our lives would never be quite like September 10 again. Security personnel spent the pregame hours welding shut the manhole covers of the streets around the ballpark. This was serious stuff. And then the Diamondbacks and Yankees gave us three hours of sublime diversion. Four of the six pitchers that night have good arguments for the Hall of Fame: Roger Clemens, Mariano Rivera, Curt Schilling, and Randy Johnson. And what had been an emotionally draining series—I can still hear New Yorkers at Yankee Stadium, the rubble of the Twin Towers still smoldering, singing "God Bless America" with real meaning—came down to the daydream of every child in a backyard: bases loaded, one out, bottom of the ninth, Game 7, score tied. And Luis Gonzalez lived the dream. He won the game, though as the events of 9/11 taught us, it wasn't right to call him a hero. It was only a game.

2003 Cal Ripken Baseball Hopewell Tournament Final, Montgomery vs. Hopewell, Hopewell, New Jersey, July, 2003

As Cal Ripken Baseball goes, this is Yankees–Red Sox. And we were locked in an extra inning game in which neither side was giving in. Multiple chances for both teams to end the game instead inspired another clutch out and another inning to play. And then my son, Adam, stepped up for his chance, with the bases loaded and two outs. He ripped a shot that bounced clear over the shortstop's head, sending home the winning run. And just like that, all the tension alchemized into euphoria. And the kind of pride and happiness I felt was unforgettable.

Cal Ripken Baseball, 10-Year-Olds, Middle Atlantic Regional Semifinals, Montgomery, New Jersey, vs. Bear, Delaware, Albany, New York, July 25, 2006

As manager of my town's 10-year-old travel team, I was staring straight at the end of our season from the third base coaching box: down 3–0 in the bottom of the fifth. We were 37–2 at that point, but we were left with only six outs left to a fabulous summer. We had hit only one home run the entire summer, so we were not a quick-strike team.

And then, out of nowhere, the most amazing sequence happened, starting with the top of our lineup: home run, double off the wall (from my son, Ben), single, home run. We win, 4–3. We win the finals the next day, too, avenging one of our two losses, and earn a trip to the Ripken World Series in Lafayette, Louisiana. I'll always remember the looks of pure joy on the kids' faces.

Suzyn Waldman
Broadcaster, New York Yankees

Minnesota Twins at Boston Red Sox, Fenway Park, Boston, Massachusetts, October 1, 1967

They were the hundred-to-one shot, the Cardiac Kids. It was the year of Yaz and his Triple Crown and the season that changed baseball forever in Boston. I was in the bleachers for every home game (thank you to Simmons College for being across the street) and heard or saw every pitch of that season. It was Billy Rohr's near no-hitter at Yankee Stadium, Jose Tartabull throwing out Ken Berry at the plate in Chicago, Tony C's horrid beaning on a warm August night. Ken Harrelson coming to Boston and throwing candy into the bleachers as a "Hello!"

But most of all it was October 1, 1967. There was a four-team pennant race going into the last day of the season. I was there when Jim Lonborg laid down a perfect bunt to start a sixth-inning rally, which led the Sox to an improbable win over the Twins. The Tigers had to win a doubleheader against California to clinch the pennant for themselves. . . . You've seen the films of overjoyed fans mobbing the field when Rich Rollins's pop-up landed in Rico

Petrocelli's glove. What you didn't see or hear was the voice of the late Sherm Feller saying, "Ladies and gentlemen, boys and girls, if you will return to your seats, Mr. Yawkey will play the second game of the Detroit-California game over the loud speakers."

And everyone did. Every now and then, Yaz would lean out of Mr. Yawkey's suite and wave. Detroit lost, and the joy in the stands was incredible. The Sox were going to the World Series for the first time since 1946. An older man near me was wearing a straw hat with "Go Go Red Sox" on it. He took it off his head, put it on mine, and said, "This will look better on you than me!" I still have that old straw hat! It was a celebration that could never happen today. Thirty-five thousand people hugging and kissing and celebrating in the stands turned into many more celebrating in Kenmore Square. No one turned over cars, no one hit anyone. People went into liquor stores, bought champagne, and passed the bottles around to total strangers who had become friends. . . . As the night went on, I realized that I was part of the greatest "love-in" sports had ever seen. To this day, every great event is compared to that day and that season, so long ago, in 1967.

Yale at Harvard, Harvard Stadium, Cambridge, Massachusetts, November 23, 1968

When I was a little girl, Saturday afternoons in the fall were spent with my family in my grandfather's eight seats at Harvard Stadium. My grandfather was in the Class of '16; my uncle, Class of '36; and rain or shine, we never missed a game. In 1968, Harvard and Yale both came into "The Game" with 8–0 records. Yale was on a sixteen-game winning streak and boasted both Calvin Hill and Brian Dowling on its team.

As Yale built up a huge lead, Harvard coach John Yovicsin put in the third string quarterback, a kid named Frank Champi, who miraculously brought the team back into the game. In the last forty-two seconds of the fourth quarter, Harvard scored two touchdowns and converted both two-point plays, with the final touchdown being scored by a local product, Vic Gatto, with no time remaining on the clock. The next day the papers actually said, "Harvard beats Yale, 29–29." Perhaps it was being with my family, enjoying a tradition that had gone on for so long or perhaps it was seeing the joy on my grandfather's face . . . but it was easily the best football game I've ever seen.

1975 World Series, Game 6, Cincinnati Reds at Boston Red Sox, Fenway Park, Boston, Massachusetts, October 21, 1975

He was the ultimate New Englander . . . the stoic, chiseled face and the New England work ethic. How perfect it was that it was Carlton Fisk who became the symbol of the 1975 World Series. The Red Sox had swept the great Oakland A's (with Yaz batting .455) to win the right to play the Big Red Machine. They were the classic underdog. They were good, but they weren't the Reds. Everyone in Boston knew it . . . but they rooted and hoped anyway.

Game 6? I remember Bernie Carbo telling me that when he rounded the bases after hitting his game-tying pinch-hit home run (and, of course, there is *no* Fisk Moment without Carbo) he said to Pete Rose, "Don't you wish you could hit like me!!?" Carbo and Rose were buddies, Carbo being a product of the Reds, and Bernie told me Rose laughed with him . . . enjoying the greatness of the game they were playing. The joy, the unbridled emotion of Carbo was catchy, and the fans, cold, tired, and just waiting for the rains to start, began to believe they could send this to a Game 7. When Fisk belted that home run in the bottom of the twelfth, the stands erupted, and the stoic New Englander, who never showed emotion, gave every bit of body language he could into keeping that ball "fair."

That they lost the Series was almost anticlimactic. The film you still see from 1975 is Fisk and that home run. Did the Red Sox lose the Series? Sure they did. But it's Fisk that everyone remembers, the symbol of New England. And I was there!

Cleveland Indians at New York Yankees, Yankee Stadium, Bronx, New York, September 4, 1993

Jim Abbott told me once that when he was a little boy, he wanted to be Nolan Ryan, not Pete Gray. That he had one hand didn't matter to him. He was going to make it. When he was a visiting Angels player, I once asked him about the pressure of pitching in Yankee Stadium. He smiled and told me, "This is nothing. The Olympics is pressure. The whole world is watching." When he was traded to the Yankees, I watched him talking to child after child who'd come to visit him—they also had one hand, and Jim never turned anyone away. He laid down a perfect bunt in one spring-training game against the Expos at West Palm, as we in the press box marveled at this extraordinary man.

And then there was September 4, 1993. Against a Cleveland Indian lineup that included Kenny Lofton, Carlos Baerga, Albert Belle, Manny Ramirez, and Jim Thome, Jim Abbott threw a no-hitter. I remember crying through the last three innings, watching the face of this brave young man and thinking how many lives he was changing that day. Baseball is baseball, but changing lives through baseball and being a role model to countless boys and girls is what Jim Abbott was all about.

1996 World Series, Game 4, New York Yankees at Atlanta Braves, Fulton County Stadium, Atlanta, Georgia, October 23, 1996

The Yankees were down early 6–0. All the New York writers were jammed in a section of the old Fulton County Stadium press box. As the Yankees started coming back from the extraordinary hole they had gotten themselves into, a reporter friend from the *New York Daily News* kept running to the back of the press box where I was sitting and yelling, "They are going to do it!" and would then go back to his seat. This went on all over the New York section of the press box.

Jim Leyritz's home run off Mark Wohlers to tie the game at 6–6 is legendary. But for me Wade Boggs's bases-loaded walk off Steve Avery, which gave the Yankees the lead in the tenth, was the greatest moment of the game. No one else in the lineup (probably in either lineup) would have taken that pitch except Boggs. He had told me a million times over the years that the plate is 17 inches wide, and if the pitch is at 17½, he was not going to swing at it. That was who he was as a player. I look for symbolic moments . . . that was one. Only Boggs could've pulled it off.

Dick Weiss

Columnist, New York Daily News

Recipient of Basketball Hall of Fame's Curt Gowdy Award, 1998

UCLA vs. Notre Dame, Athletic and Convocation Center, Notre Dame, Indiana, January 14, 1974

Like most young writers, I thought UCLA was invincible under John Wooden and Bill Walton was the ultimate weapon in a big game, but Digger Phelps and the Irish found a way to end the top-ranked Bruins' eighty-eight-game winning streak when guard Dwight Clay hit a jumper in the final seconds for the 71–70 win. Phelps got his team prepared by having them cut down the nets every day that week after practice. I also remember sitting on press row with Kenny Denlinger of the *Washington Post*, wondering why Wooden refused to call a time-out in the final three minutes when the Irish began to cut into a twelve-point UCLA lead.

1985 NCAA Men's Basketball Tournament Finals, Villanova vs. George-town, Rupp Arena, Lexington, Kentucky, April 1, 1985

I was covering college basketball for the *Philadelphia Daily News* at the time, and to this day I still have trouble believing what I witnessed. Heavy underdog Villanova played a near-perfect game that April 1, shooting 78 percent and 9 for 10 in the second half to beat a powerful Hoyas team that had Patrick Ewing in the NCAA championship game at Rupp Arena in Lexington. I can still remember Villanova guard Harold Jensen patting the late Jake Nevin, the Cats' legendary trainer who had been confined to a wheelchair with ALS, on the head for good luck after a time-out before going out to make a couple of clutch free throws in the final seconds and center Eddie Pinckney and forward Dwayne McClain running over to press row and screaming "April Fools" during the postgame celebration.

Miami at Notre Dame, Notre Dame Stadium, Notre Dame, Indiana, October 15, 1988

Talk about bad blood. I spent most of the week in South Bend during the buildup to the biggest grudge match I ever covered in college football. Miami was the defending national champion and ranked No. 1 in the country. Notre Dame was No. 4, and it was obvious the teams didn't like each other, as evidenced by the amount of students wearing "Catholics vs. Convicts" T-shirts. The 'Canes had dominated the Irish in the previous four years, and ND fans still had bitter memories of Jimmy Johnson ordering long passes late in a 58–7 victory in 1985.

This one started with a fight at the end of pregame warm-ups that spread into the tunnel leading to the locker room. Notre Dame's motto that year was "Never flinch," and they had the toughness to become No. 1 for the first time since 1973 that day after Pat Terrell returned an interception 60 yards for a touchdown, then batted down Steve Walsh's two-point conversion pass with 45 seconds left to seal the 31–30 victory.

1992 NCAA Men's Basketball Tournament, East Regional Finals, Kentucky vs. Duke, The Spectrum, Philadelphia, Pennsylvania, March 28, 1992

The Blue Devils' victory in the NCAA East Regional finals at Philadelphia had the most dramatic finish of any game I ever covered. I spent that year in Lexington writing a book with Rick Pitino, and the inspired Wildcats, who were finally eligible for NCAA play after spending two years on postseason suspension after a huge recruiting scandal, looked like they were on the verge of the ultimate upset against the defending national champions after guard Sean Woods scored on a floater with 2.3 seconds to play. But then Grant Hill made a perfect length-of-the-court pass to Christian Laettner, who drained a jumper at the buzzer. So much for best sellers.

I can still remember Mike Krzyzewski asking the late Hall of Fame radio announcer Cawood Ledford if he could address the Kentucky fans afterwards, telling them how proud they should be of their team's performance and the four senior starters—Woods, John Pelphrey, Darren Feldhaus, and Richie Farmer—getting their numbers retired at Rupp three days later.

2006 Rose Bowl, Texas vs. USC, Rose Bowl, Pasadena, California, January 4, 2006

Texas All-American quarterback Vince Young put on the greatest individual performance I'd ever seen since I started covering the national championship game in 1982, the last thirteen for the *New York Daily News*. Young, who lost the Heisman to SC running back Reggie Bush, completed 30 of 40 passes for 267 yards and rushing for another 200 on 19 carries as the Longhorns defeated the two-time defending national champions under the lights at the Rose Bowl.

It seemed strange watching a night game there, but this was Hollywood at its best. With SC clinging to a 38–33 lead, Pete Carroll went for a first down on a fourth and two at the Texas 45 with 2:09 left, in an effort to run out the clock rather than give the Horns one more shot. With Texas-stuffed Lendale White a yard short, Young took over. He was unstoppable on the Longhorns' final possession, taking Texas on a dramatic 11-play, 56-yard game-winning drive in the final 2:09 out of a no-huddle offense, breaking out of the pocket to score on an 8-yard run and a 41–38 triumph.

Jon Wertheim

Senior Writer, Sports Illustrated

Purdue at Indiana, Alumni Hall, Bloomington, Indiana, February 23, 1985

After beating North Carolina—and, in his final college game, a pretty fair player named Michael Jordan—in the 1984 NCAA tournament, the Indiana Hoosiers entered the next season with lofty expectations. The team, inexplicably, sucked. So much so that my friends and their families were doing the unthinkable: giving away their tickets to games. Thus it was that I sat in row H for Indiana's February 23 home game against rival Purdue. What began as another desultory game suddenly got a jolt when Bob Knight protested a bad call and became so enraged that he picked up a folding chair and, yes, zinged it across the court.

Even in the days before *SportsCenter*, this was instantly a highlight-show classic. In his later years Knight cut a polarizing figure, but at the time—four years removed from a national title and, it would turn out, two years prior to winning another one—he was an Indiana demigod. Lost amid a smattering of boos, I remember, was overwhelming approval that afternoon. He was The General, and he was just standing up for his troops. To an eighth grader, it was great stuff, a cartoon come to life. But in retrospect, what was up with this weird ambivalence (at best) of the fans at Assembly Hall toward what was, of course, an indefensible act? It was precisely the kind of enabling that gave rise to Knight's hubris and, more than a decade later, ultimately led to his ugly endgame at IU.

2000 U.S. Olympic Box-Off, Foxwoods Casino, Mashantucket, Connecticut, February 26, 2000

The 2000 Olympic boxing trials were held, oddly enough, at Foxwoods Casino in Connecticut. In the course of covering the event for *Sports Illustrated*, I had stumbled across a back staircase leading from the ring to the makeshift locker rooms, and this secret passage spared me from dealing with a self-righteous security guard. Sneaking down the steps after a heavyweight elimination fight, I got a spike of adrenaline when I heard a shrieking cry. I looked over the rail to see the losing heavyweight fighter—his name eludes me, which is ultimately the point—crying inconsolably.

Check that. Not crying. Sobbing, his entire chiseled body heaving. Still leaking blood and sweat, he was curled in a ball, mourning a dream that had just been administered its last rites. The other guy would be going to Sydney. The scene—a brute of a man all by himself in a dingy back stairwell, reduced to a blubbering baby—was almost unendurably poignant. We write about the winners and put them on TV and lavish them with money and fame and even put their faces on our cereal boxes. But here was a haunting reminder that, much as we all love winners, competition necessarily creates losers, too.

The 2000 Wimbledon Championships, Ladies' Semifinals, The All England Lawn Tennis Club, London, England, July 6, 2000

While tennis isn't as monochromatic as the stereotype would have us believe, it's rare to see an African American in the semifinal of a major tournament. It's rarer still to see two. The allegory of the Williams sisters has been repeated so often that it has taken on a biblical ring. And still, to my mind, it's the most underrated story in sports. Imagine, for a moment, if Tiger Woods had an equally talented sibling. Or if, say, Alex Rodriguez had a brother who also challenged for the MVP.

On a dreary July afternoon in England in 2000, Venus and Serena did battle for the right to play for the Wimbledon title. In the years that would follow, they would win a dozen titles among them, and tennis would grow accustomed, if not expectant, to the two playing each other on the biggest stages. But that afternoon, watching two sisters who'd once shared a bunk bed in Compton, play on the manicured grass of tennis's cathedral, the dimensions of their unlikely story were thrown into sharp relief. Venus awkwardly won the match and, blood being what it is, was more interested in consoling her sister than celebrating her victory. As the sisters walked off the court, there was an unmistakable sense that the twelve thousand fans were cheering less for the match than for the unlikely circumstances that had led up to it.

2002 U.S. Open Finals, Pete Sampras vs. Andre Agassi, National Tennis Center, Flushing, New York, September 8, 2002

The thought that great athletes ought to "go out on top" has become the hoariest of sports cliches. But in 2002 Pete Sampras was showing how even the most dignified, unsurpassed career could end badly. A shard of his former self, Sampras hadn't won a title all year, and at Wimbledon—his personal grass playground for the past decade—he was humiliated by a no-name. The tennis salon made its collective feeling clear: cut bait.

But it's easy to forget that, as well as we think we know athletes, they're much more keenly attuned to their bodies, their psyches, their capabilities. (Which, of course, is one of the reasons they're playing and we're watching.) Facing doubt from everyone but himself, Sampras entered the U.S. Open and promptly fired up something for the memory banks. For two weeks he was the Sampras of old, zinging lasers from the baselines and serving aces. His opponent in the final, Andre Agassi, was Sampras's rival dating back to the boys juniors. By that point, the Fates had written the script, and, on a late Sunday afternoon, in front of a packed house of American tennis fans, Sampras won in four sets. It was the last pro match he would ever play. Has an athlete ever authored a more ideal final chapter?

San Diego Padres at New York Mets, Shea Stadium, Queens, New York, May 10, 2003

It was one of those forgettable afternoon games that get lost in the folds of the 162-game pocket schedule. It was early in the season of 2003, and the Mets were playing the Padres. Assuming that the prospect of watching two sub-.500 teams on a Saturday would militate against a large crowd, I chose this date to take my son, Benjamin, to his first baseball game. Anyone who says taking your kid to his first game is a seminal moment of parenthood didn't do it with a two-year-old. Benjamin cried when Bachman Turner Overdrive boomed over the PA system (not that he could blamed for this). He was hot. He was thirsty. His Mets cap itched. I bought a few innings by splurging for a scoop of ice cream served in a batting helmet. But then the mascot was scary. The chicken fingers didn't taste like the ones Ben was used to. As extra innings lurked, Mike Piazza (mercifully) ended things with a walk-off home run. At least I think it was Piazza. My head was under the seat at the time, as I was scrambling to retrieve a juice box.

Gene Wojciechowski
Senior Columnist, ESPN.com

1992 NCAA Men's Basketball Tournament, East Regional Finals, Kentucky vs. Duke, The Spectrum, Philadelphia, Pennsylvania, March 28, 1992

If there is a heaven filled with great games, this is the one you first see as you enter the pearly gates. My goose bumps get goose bumps thinking about this game. It had the holy trinity (I'm sort of on a religious kick here, aren't I?) of game-day components: It was an NCAA Tournament game; winner goes to the Final Four. It had hoops pedigree (mighty Kentucky, with Rick Pitino rebuilding the NCAA-scarred Wildcats against mighty Duke). It had the kind of drama, tension, and excellence you see once every epoch. It remains my absolute, drop-dead favorite.

I remember the game, of course. I remember the stunning array of pressure shots. I remember thinking the game was over about ten different times. I remember the utter concentration on the faces of Krzyzewski and Pitino. I remember the overtime and The Play—Hill's heave to Laettner, who turns, shoots . . . and, ohmigod, it went in. I remember the exultation and the tears of joy and anguish. I remember seeing one of the Duke managers, I think, grab the ball and stuff it under his shirt as he ran off the court. He didn't want anyone stealing this miracle keepsake.

Afterward, because I was working for the *LA Times* and had later deadlines than most everyone else, I was one of maybe a dozen reporters who were there when the Kentucky locker room opened. Pitino looked as if he had just attended a funeral. You could hear a heart drop. John Pelphrey, who was one of the players "guarding" Laettner when he hit the game-winner, came from the bathroom/shower area to meet with the reporters. He started to speak and then, overcome with emotion, returned to the bathroom and started pounding the cinderblock wall. "I can't . . . I can't," he kept repeating. What do you do in those circumstances? I just stared at my shoes, amazed by the sheer emotion of it all.

I kept in touch with Pelphrey for several years after that game, even talked to him in Spain when he played over there, and he still had difficulty discussing that loss. But he has a special place in my Interview Hall of Fame because of what he did that night at the Spectrum. He didn't duck the press. He came out, tried to explain the unexplainable, and then couldn't go on.

As it turned out, I almost wasn't able to file my story. The union knuckleheads had broken down the press tables at courtside and disconnected the phone lines by the time I had finished writing. As deadline ticked closer, I had to beg a security guard to open up the Flyers offices so I could use one of their phone lines. I made it with maybe a minute or two to spare.

Every so often I see the Hill-to-Laettner highlight and still can't believe it. I even asked someone from the Duke basketball office to send me a copy of the game, which I watch every year or so. I just love the purity of that game, the quality of play, the moments.

Larry Bird Night, Boston Garden, Boston, Massachusetts, February 4, 1993

You've seen these farewell nights: sappy, formula driven, boooooring. This, though, was the perfect mixture of heartfelt appreciation for a player who had come to define a city's hoops heart. Bird might have arrived in Boston with a French Lick, Indiana, twang, but to the people in the Garden that night, his accent was as thick as New England clam chowder. He was one of them—no small feat in that town.

I admit it; I stole a bolt and a lug nut from the Garden floor that night. I had to. This was a farewell that has never been matched (sorry, Magic). The highlights they showed still made you do double takes. The speeches (especially Magic's) were pure sincerity and respect. The raising of Bird's number to the Garden rafters caused Adam's apples to catch in everybody's throats. I arrived at the Garden that night expecting little. I left knowing I had seen history.

1998 NBA Finals, Game 6, Chicago Bulls at Utah Jazz, Delta Center, Salt Lake City, Utah, June 14, 1998

Here's how you know Michael Jordan was the greatest who ever played the game: he made the shot . . . and I wasn't even surprised. You knew he was going to take the shot. That's a given. But what was weird about it—you knew he was going to make it, too. Quick, name all the players who you feel the same way about? I'm waiting. . . .

You can't quantify will. It is an intangible. But with the Jordan, it became more than that. You could almost touch it. That's how real he made it seem. He willed the Bulls to that win, to that championship. How can you cover a better game than when the sport's greatest player, on his last-ever shot, hits the shot that earns him another ring? Easy, you can't.

2003 National League Championship Series, Game 6, Florida Marlins at Chicago Cubs, Wrigley Field, Chicago, Illinois, October 14, 2003

Anybody who tells you there isn't a Curse of the Billy Goat didn't watch this game. I was there, sitting a few rows behind Ryne Sandberg and his wife. It was like watching time-lapse photography of a car wreck.

The Cubs were five outs away from their first World Series since 1945. They haven't won one since 1908. If ever a franchise was due, this was the one. Instead, you see a slicing foul ball down the leftfield line. At Wrigley, that line is separated by a sliver of grass about the width of a baseball. Then there's a padded wall (which figures, if you're a Cubs follower) and the Wrigley stands. Moises Alou reached for the ball and. . . . Wait! He didn't catch it? And why is he throwing that hissy fit?

Enter the much-maligned (undeservedly so, by the way) Steve Bartman, who, along with a half dozen other fans, reached for the ball. Except that Bartman touched it, sparking the very public tirade by Alou, which sparked a small meltdown by Mark Prior, which sparked a series of more baseball strangeness. The Cubs lost the game, of course. Then they lost Game 7. Then Cubs fans lost their minds.

After the Alou-Bartman play, you could almost feel the energy sucked out of the place. There was a sense of impending doom. As for Bartman, you feared for his health. Bartman wasn't to blame for that loss, but he became its symbol. I'm not sure I've been at a game (I had just begun working on a book, *Cubs Nation*) where an entire stadium and team turned on one fan. It was a compelling but unfortunate piece of theater.

USC at Notre Dame, Notre Dame Stadium, South Bend, Indiana, October 15, 2005

One of the best college football games played in the last, what, twenty-five years? Geez, I don't know, maybe, fifty? Ever?

Think about it: USC, million-game winning streak, Heisman Trophy winner Matt Leinart, Heisman Trophy winner-to-be Reggie Bush, Notre Dame Stadium, green jerseys, packed house, first-year coach Charlie Weis, so much at stake, quality plays out the wazoo, a controversial ending. . . .

This was a game where the performances were better than the hype. I'll remember it for the nutty ending—The Bush Push—but also for the sight of Weis walking into the USC locker room about thirty minutes after the game. He congratulated the Trojans and did so with his son, Charlie Jr., at his side. Sitting in front of a locker was Leinart, who was physically and mentally exhausted. His face was a mixture of dirt, sweat, and tears. Bush was so spent that he could barely speak at first. USC officials handed him Gatorade before he did his postgame interviews. But all he really wanted was a chair.

Alexander Wolff
Senior Writer, Sports Illustrated

North Carolina at Maryland, Cole Fieldhouse, College Park, Maryland, January 12, 1984

It was a routine, late-season ACC game, with nothing particular at stake. But watching Michael Jordan lock down his defensive assignments, and get his shots off at will, and toy with a very good Terp team (Len Bias, Ben Coleman, Adrian Branch), I had the premonition (which seemed to have eluded the Portland Trail Blazers, who would choose the brittle Sam Bowie as their No. 1 pick) that this guy was a remorseless talent unlike any to come through the college ranks. Late in the game, on a breakaway, Jordan threw down an exclamatory dunk, and in the locker room afterward someone asked him if he had meant to "send a message." He replied like an efficient secretary: "No messages." The attitude and demeanor that came with that comment we'd see again and again over the next dozen years.

1992 NCAA Men's Basketball Tournament, East Regional Finals, Kentucky vs. Duke, The Spectrum, Philadelphia, Pennsylvania, March 28, 1992

Sitting courtside in Philadelphia that night, members of the press couldn't get the phone lines to work. It's a detail I remember because the entire game seemed to leave those of us who witnessed it feeling as if the Spectrum had become untethered from reality. The final stretch of the game was pure can-you-top-this: Sean Woods's circus shot in the lane seemed to have won it, and then came Grant Hill's pass, and Christian Laettner's leap, and . . . well, we all know the rest.

1992 Tour de France, Stage 14, L'Alpe d'Huez, France, July 19, 1992

The L'Alpe d'Huez stage of the Tour de France, twenty-two switchback turns to a mountaintop finish, takes the measure of all cyclists; on my first Tour, a British journalist took me aside and said that, after witnessing the L'Alpe d'Huez stage for the first time, he never again used the word "heroic" to described the exploits of any other kind of athlete. Americans who jumped on the Greg LeMond and Lance Armstrong bandwagons won't recognize the name of Andy Hampsten, the slight, utterly drug-free son of two University of North Dakota English professors who won the stage. But he was a pioneer pro cyclist and superb climber who, though he won the Tour of Italy and the Tour of Switzerland, probably regards this July day as the greatest of his career.

EuroBasket 1993, Germany, June 23–July 4, 1993

With Sarajevo under siege by Serbian nationalist troops and ethnic cleansing still taking place throughout Bosnia and Herzegovina, a ragtag but multiethnic team of Bosnian players somehow reached the final round of the EuroBasket in Munich. Several members of the team had actually fled Sarajevo under cover of darkness, sprinting across the sniper's shooting gallery that was the airport tarmac, then escaping through the woods and by bus to safety in western Europe. One of them played in the very sneakers he wore that night;

another told the press during the team's unforgettable week in Munich, "If we have a national team, then surely we have a nation."

1994 Winter Olympics, Men's 1000 Meter Speed-Skating Final, Vikingskipet Olympic Arena, Hamar, Norway, February 18, 1994

The feckless fate of America's great speed-skating hope had become a kind of quadrennial soap opera that to Dan Jansen must have seemed altogether too up close and personal. That's why in Lillehammer, in an event that was hardly his best, in front of a Norwegian crowd that truly appreciated the fine points of the sport, it was so thrilling to see Jansen finally bag a gold. I'd never written about speed skating before, and I felt slightly guilty getting to write this particular story right out of the blocks. But I'm grateful to have had the chance.

Bob Wolff
Broadcaster
Recipient of Baseball Hall of Fame's Ford C. Frick Award, 1995

1956 World Series, Game 5, Brooklyn Dodgers at New York Yankees, Yankee Stadium, Bronx, New York, October 8, 1956

I've been lucky enough to call play-by-play for the championship in each of the four sports—World Series, National Football League, Stanley Cup, and NBA Finals. But, invariably when I am interviewed, there's a question about one game I called—the Don Larsen perfect World Series classic.

I was the Washington Senators announcer at that time and was selected to work the Series by the Gillette Safety Razor Company after they first utilized me that 1956 season on the All-Star Game in Washington. Four announcers were selected in those days for the Series assignment, two on radio and two on TV. One play-by-play man came from the American League winner, one from the National League champion. Mel Allen of the Yankees and Vin Scully of the Dodgers had those spots. One announcer came from the TV or radio network carrying the game, and Bob Neal from Cleveland was that choice. The sole sponsor, the Gillette Safety Razor Company, selected me as their choice, and I was thrilled to be on my first World Series. Others would follow.

Each announcer would work one-half of each game. I was on the radio team and was fortunate to do the second half of the perfect game.

During the commercial break before beginning my call, with the Yankees leading 1–0 on a Mickey Mantle homer and the Dodgers hitless and down in order, I whispered to the Gillette producer, Joel Nixon, that I would prefer to use every synonym in the book to let our worldwide audience know that a no-hitter was in progress but would prefer to avoid the specific words "no-hitter" or "perfect game" with respect to baseball superstition. Joel concurred as long as I left no doubt. It worked—not a letter came in saying someone wasn't informed.

In the back of my mind, I remembered the calls and letters that had come in after the 1947 Series game in which the all-time great sportscaster Red Barber was calling a Floyd "Bill" Bevens no-hitter in progress, also featuring the Yankees and Dodgers. Red used the words "no-hitter" just before Cookie Lavagetto of Brooklyn sent a drive off the fence, driving in the tying run and the winning run for the Dodgers. No question about Red's honesty, but given the choice, I went with baseball tradition.

The Yankees added another run off Dodger pitcher Sal Maglie in the second half of the game. With Larsen's pitching mastery dominating the game, it seemed to me in that ninth inning as if the entire focus of all the fans was on one question—would he do it? Would Don Larsen make baseball history? Would they be witnessing such an amazing event?

In the ninth inning, the roar of the crowd accentuated the drama. The noise swelled to fever pitch, subsided to an eerie silence before each ball and strike call was registered, and then unleashed an all-consuming crescendo as each of the final three outs was made. When Dale Mitchell checked his swing and Babe Pinelli made his final call behind home plate as a big-league umpire, the noise just exploded from every area of Yankee Stadium.

In that inning, I felt my body tightening as the tension kept rising and rising, and I had to keep reminding myself to keep reporting, not to falter, because I was so gripped by the emotion. And I noticed that my arm began to ache, that subconsciously I was pitching that final frame with Larsen. I never got into the box score for that body contribution, but my arm ached for a week after the game—and I enjoyed every minute of it.

1956 World Series, Game 6, New York Yankees at Brooklyn Dodgers, Ebbets Field, Brooklyn, New York, October 9, 1956

At the time there was no way of knowing, but as it developed, I called a historic hit in the 1956 World Series between the Yankees and Dodgers. Jackie Robinson's last major league hit in the tenth inning of the contest was a game winner. Brooklyn won the game, 1–0, as Jim Gilliam scampered home with the game's only run. A line shot to leftfield over a leaping Enos Slaughter evened the Series at three wins apiece. Robinson was hitless in Game 7 as the Yankees took that game 9–0 to win the Series. Robinson's farewell hit in Game 6 was a dramatic way to close out his great baseball career.

I discovered this when film director Spike Lee called me some years later seeking some Robinson material for a film he was making called *Crooklyn*. I checked my scorecard to confirm it. Robinson was the most exciting baserunner I had ever seen. When he got on base, with his ability to take off, the show began. Robinson would fake a steal moving a shoulder and arm or sometimes a quick step and then return to the bag as the crowd would go wild. Infielders were always on edge, and the pitchers kept throwing to the base. And then, when Jackie did take off, it was like a tornado ripping through town. Today's base stealers, for the most part, prefer not to call attention to their starts. They have great speed, but Jackie made the art a show by itself.

1958 NFL Championship Game, Baltimore Colts at New York Giants, Yankee Stadium, Bronx, New York, December 28, 1958

It was called the "Greatest Football Game Ever Played." Excitement is difficult to measure, but this game had everything. It was the first overtime NFL championship, and it had two climactic moments: first, Baltimore's Steve Myhra, with seven seconds left in regulation, booted a field goal to tie the game, then Alan Ameche plunged over the goal line for the Colts, to win the game eight minutes into the extra session. It had something more, though: a galaxy of pro football stars on both sides that were a Who's Who of the greatest.

Two years after I did the play-by-play at Yankee Stadium for Don Larsen's perfect World Series game, I was at the stadium calling this one—the game that put pro football into high major league exposure. TV and radio had combined to air football at its finest around the country, and the advertisers took notice.

The pinpoint passing of the Colts' Johnny Unitas stamped him as an all-time great, but there were also lineups of the game's elite—legendary Colts like Ameche, Myhra, Donovan, Berry, Moore, Mutscheller, and Marchetti, just to name a few. The Giants had Conerly, Gifford, Huff, Robustelli, Summerall, and Webster. When the losers were quoted as saying it was the greatest game they had ever played in, everybody knew that pro football had now arrived as a major sports attraction.

In those days, I worked the entire game. There was no analyst. At halftime, though, for a brief respite, I put my teenage spotter on the air to give his opinion of the game. That was Maury Povich's broadcast debut.

When the Colts returned home to Baltimore, fifty thousand fans were at the airport to greet them. My play-by-play highlights were being played on all the radio and TV stations and even on jukeboxes.

John Steadman, the sports editor of the *Baltimore News-Post*, had assigned himself to write a pregame story on how the game would come out. Amazingly, John's account looks like it had been written after the game, not before it. Myhra and Ameche came through in his fictional account, just as they did in the game. John picked Baltimore as the winner by the score of 23–17. That was right on target. The newspaper saluted him on the front page the next day, but I still salute John for the greatest prognostication I have ever read in sports.

New York Knicks vs. Cincinnati Royals, Cleveland Arena, Cleveland, Ohio, November 28, 1969

The Knicks were on a winning streak, the crowds at Madison Square Garden were sensing the possibility of their first-ever NBA championship, and the noise at Knicks games was deafening. Their win streak had now extended to seventeen in a row, and if New York could top Cincinnati in a game being played in Cleveland, the eighteen-game winning streak would set an NBA record.

I was at the mike sending the play-by-play back to New York, and it appeared that the streak might be shattered. The Knicks were down 105–100 with sixteen seconds remaining, when New York came roaring back to pull off one of the two greatest comebacks in Knicks history. The other was Knicks-Bucks in November of 1972, which we will get to shortly.

Willis Reed made a pair of free throws under pressure. Cincinnati player-coach Bob Cousy looped in a pass that was intercepted by Dave DeBusschere, which led to a basket, to put the Knicks within one. New York continued to pressure with seconds left. Walt Frazier stole the ball, dribbled to within 10 feet of the basket and let fly. He missed but got the rebound, put the ball up again, and was fouled. There were two seconds to go when Frazier made the first free throw to tie it and then coolly made the second to win it, 106–105.

The Knicks became media darlings. Watching the Knicks was a major sports occupation. Advertisers clamored to come aboard, and the NBA gloried in its new attention. The sport had reached its highest peak. And the hysteria continued all the way to the NBA title.

Milwaukee Bucks at New York Knicks, Madison Square Garden, New York, New York, November 18, 1972

The Knicks were on their way to a second championship season, but in this game at Madison Square Garden, there appeared no way New York could pull out a victory. They were trailing by 18 points with 5:50 left in the fourth quarter when they began one of the most incredible comebacks in the sport's history.

I was at the play-by-play mike becoming more and more amazed as the Knicks began to whittle down the lead, basket by basket. Not only were the Knicks scoring, but their fantastic defense kept shutting down the Bucks. Kareem Abdul-Jabbar could not break free from tenacious Willis Reed for a good shot. New York started to pile up the points, and the crowd was going wild as the Knicks inched closer and closer.

The miraculous climb to the lead became a reality when Earl Monroe put New York in front, 87–86. That was the final, with the Knicks scoring the last 19 points in a row. I was limp with emotion at the buzzer. What a game!

Chris Wragge

Broadcaster, WCBS-TV New York

1986 NFC Divisional Playoff, San Francisco 49ers at New York Giants, Giants Stadium, East Rutherford, New Jersey, January 4, 1987, and 1986 NFC Championship Game, Washington Redskins at New York Giants, Giants Stadium, East Rutherford, New Jersey, January 11, 1987

These two games bring back memories of some of the best years of my life. I was sixteen, a junior in high school, and a die-hard, die-hard Giants fan. Big Blue could do no wrong, and I bled blue from an early age, thanks to my dad. We had season tickets my entire life, and it was something that I always looked forward to, going to Giants games with him on Sundays. There was nothing like it, and it helped shape my career and me. The environment, the weather, and the noise at these games were just unforgettable.

In the San Francisco game, I remember Jerry Rice being open and streaking toward the end zone, but miraculously the ball popped out . . . it was like an act of God. Phil Simms was my idol growing up, and after seeing him go through so many trials and tribulations, for this to happen really made it feel like the tides had finally turned. From LT making plays all over the field (the interception he returned for a score almost caused me to fall out of the upper deck!) to Jim Burt knocking Joe Montana out, nothing went wrong that day, which is usually what happens when the final score is 49–3.

The next week, at the NFC Championship Game, the one image I'll forever take away from that game was in the closing minutes of the fourth quarter. The wind was swirling at Giants Stadium like it had never before. All of this garbage was flying around the stadium; it was like a mini-tornado of trash. Normally, you would think, "That's a bit odd," but at this time and at this juncture, it was unforgettable. My dad was to my left, my best friend was to my right, and we were all jumping around in excitement, freezing our butts off, knowing the

Giants were going to the Super Bowl. Next game: Pasadena! It was the culmination of so many years of sitting through the hardships; we finally got to see it all turn around. Thanks, Dad, and special thanks to the Giants!

2002 Winter Olympics, Opening Ceremonies, Rice-Eccles Olympic Stadium, Salt Lake City, Utah, February 8, 2002

This was the single greatest night of my professional life. Dick Ebersol of NBC Sports is my mentor; he took me under his wing and gave me some plum assignments, including this one. To be a part of the Opening Ceremonies broadcast in the first Olympics on our soil after 9/11 and to work with Bob Costas and Katie Couric, among others, on the broadcast was very special. When I found out I would be a part of this, I was floored. It was the crowning achievement of my career, and I will be forever indebted to Dick for giving me this assignment.

The Olympics have always had a big place in my heart, with one of the most vivid memories of my childhood being the 1980 hockey team. I grew up watching Jim McKay host the Olympics, and he tutored me my first couple of years in the business, and to have the opportunity to spend some time with people that I've looked at as pillars in this business was awe inspiring. During the Opening Ceremonies, they paid tribute to a number of the standout American Olympians of the past, and my job was to interview stars such as Cammi Granato and Picabo Street.

There was so much going on in Salt Lake City, given it was post-9/11. There was a weird feel, with security being heightened as much as it was. But being there to see all of the different cultures from around the world coming together and literally being on the surface itself in the beautiful stadium in Salt Lake City was something else. It was different from any other sporting event I had ever done. It was the Olympics, on the world's biggest stage, and the broadcast was the highest-rated Opening Ceremonies in the history of U.S. television. It was easy to get caught up in the grandeur of it all. It brought me back to my childhood again, when I watched events like this on television and could only dream of being there.

The 2004 Masters, Augusta National Golf Club, Augusta, Georgia, April 8–11, 2004

While with USA I had the chance to work around thirty tournaments every year for the PGA and had a chance to establish a rapport with some of the players. Phil Mickelson has a great public following but doesn't have a great relationship with many of the other players, whether it is jealousy or resentment or whatever the reason. He is the "People's Champion," but he is not the "Player's Champion."

By 2004 he had taken on that mythical title of "Best Player to Never Win a Major Championship," and the pressure was mounting after numerous close calls. This was the first time, though, where he took a step back and played golf, instead of being a home-run-hitting hero who hit bombs off the tee. He took on the approach of hitting more cut shots off the tee and played the game more conservatively than he usually did. He opted to manage the golf course instead of acting like a rebel, and it paid off. It lacked that Tiger vs. Phil drama on the 18th, but to see someone who had always struggled or fallen just short on the big stage finally come through, since I personally like the guy, it was nice to be there to see him get the monkey off his back.

I was standing right between the 18th green and the 10th tee when Mickelson made the putt to win, while Ernie Els was on the practice green getting ready for a possible playoff, and I didn't even watch the putt go in. I just focused like a cameraman on Phil the whole time, and his reaction, the 2-inch vertical jump, gave me chills. Golf needed something like this; someone other than Tiger Woods needed to step up, and Phil did.

The 2005 Masters, Augusta National Golf Club, Augusta, Georgia, April 7–10, 2005

I make it a point every year at the Masters to follow Tiger on the back nine because I love to watch him go through Amen Corner. On Sunday Tiger had to come out early in the morning to finish his third round, after it was postponed by rain, and I had a couple of hours before going on my USA Network show. The sun was coming up, it was chilly for April at Augusta, there was dew on the ground, and there was one of those "Friday the Thirteenth" eerie mists hovering in the air. I joined Tiger on 10, which he birdied, then followed him through Amen Corner, and it was birdie, birdie, birdie. The visual of him walking and emerging through the fog from the 13th tee was just incredible. To me, those first few holes of the day were where he won the tournament. The chip in the afternoon on 16 was one thing, but this is where he won.

My show was over on Sunday by the time he hit Amen Corner again for his Sunday round, and I picked him up there and followed him the rest of the day. I was standing right by the CBS broadcast tower on 16 and saw how difficult his chip was going to be. I had no idea he was going to approach the shot by using the green as a backboard but was in a perfect position to watch it happen. The chip started working back toward the hole, and the crowd got more and more excited, until it stopped on the lip. At that point, it went from the elation of watching this awesome shot to the silence of its not going in . . . to the roar when it dropped.

When you follow Tiger Woods, there are so many times when you shake your head in amazement and look at the person next to you for confirmation of what you just saw. This was the seminal moment. If you ever thought that someone was playing at a higher level than anyone else, this was all you needed to see. It was an amazing shot when it stopped on the lip. For it to actually go in, I think Verne Lundquist summed it up perfectly on the broadcast when he said, "In your life, have you ever seen anything like this?"

2006 National League Championship Series, Game 7, St. Louis Cardinals at New York Mets, Shea Stadium, Queens, New York, October 19, 2006

It is very easy, as a member of the media, to find yourself a little removed from the events you are covering. A lot of time is spent in press rooms, while the preference might be to be sitting in the stands, throwing down a couple of adult beverages. Since I was on duty, I made a pact with myself this night and vowed, even though it was cold and raining, to get one of the seats in the auxiliary press box so that I could watch the game outside. I wanted to feel the emotions of the fans and take in the whole experience.

When the ball came off Scott Rolen's bat in a 1–1 game in the sixth inning, I knew it was trouble. I've got my eye on the ball; now, I'm not clairvoyant, but I could also see in my peripheral vision Endy Chavez on the dead run. I immediately thought back to the Jeff Suppan home run in Game 3, and how close Chavez came to catching it, and thought he might have a chance to make a plan on this one if he timed it right. And boy, did he ever. It was an "Are you kidding me?" moment. To actually see him make this play . . . it is one of those plays where television doesn't do it justice. To see it in person, it was the single greatest catch I have ever seen, not just in person, but on TV, as well. I'll compare it to any of the great catches in history and still say it was better than any of them. It was one of those plays that make you look at the player in a different way. Regardless of where he plays, I will always look at Endy Chavez in a much different light. He could retire tomorrow, and when you hear the name Endy Chavez, you will think of that catch. That is what makes it one of those plays that transcend the game. It made me very happy about my decision to watch the game outside instead of from inside the press room.

Vic Ziegel
Columnist, New York Daily News

CCNY at Fordham, Rose Hill Gymnasium, Bronx, New York, February 5, 1957

I was a student at CCNY, a sportswriter for the school paper, *The Campus*. The CCNY team that year was a good one and would go on to play in the small-college NCAA tournament (this was before the Division II and III Championships). In 1951 CCNY had won both the NCAA and NIT, but the college point-shaving scandal ended those glory times for CCNY. The school left the Garden and went back to playing all its games at the small, badly lit gym on campus. We still played some of the old local rivals—NYU, St. John's, Fordham—but they were well out of CCNY's class. The scores were invariably one-sided.

But not this night at Fordham. CCNY hung close, and in the closing seconds, Joel Bernardo sank a long field goal to give CCNY a 58–56 win. Bedlam. But not for me. I had to write the story.

Muhammad Ali vs. Joe Frazier, Madison Square Garden, New York, New York, March 8, 1971

The atmosphere in the Garden, as the hours ticked off before the first bell, was electric. I remember being warned to hold my ticket firmly as I entered the Garden because people who were flashing their tickets had them ripped right out of their hands and resold on the street. The fight itself was not a great one; Ali had been away too long, and he wasn't ready to face Frazier's fierce attack. But Ali made it close. Even when he was knocked down in the last round, he came to, in somebody's phrase, the minute his ass hit the canvas.

Muhammad Ali vs. George Foreman, Stade du 20 Mai, Kinshasa, Zaire, October 30, 1974

The fight was held in Zaire at 4:00 in the morning, so the fight could be shown at 10:00 P.M. in New York on closed-circuit television. We spent a week in Zaire, living in one-room houses, in a camp usually reserved, we were told, for visiting diplomats. It was an amazing adventure as much as a dramatic sports event. Ali promised to dance all night in the ring, but it was obvious he could no longer live up to that boast. He came up with the rope-a-dope, seemed to be absorbing terrific punishment, but it was Foreman who punched himself out. The end, Foreman on the canvas, was a shocker, but one we all enjoyed. After I wrote my story and sent it in, the heaviest rainfall I have ever seen began. Walls of pure white. Now I know what they mean when they say the rain came down like sheets.

Muhammad Ali vs. Joe Frazier, Araneta Coliseum, Quezon City, Philippines, October 1, 1975

It was intensely hot inside the arena, the temperature well above 100 degrees. "The closest thing to death," Ali said of the fight, and, for once, he might not have been exaggerating. Ali was supposed to win easily, but Frazier's pride wouldn't accept defeat. The fight swung back and forth, until Ali began pulling away in the late rounds. Frazier was absorbing terrific punishment, but he kept coming on, the only style he knew. Finally, his trainer, Eddie Futch, a great boxing man, wouldn't let Joe get off the stool before the fifteenth round. He did the right thing. Hours later, at a postfight party, Frazier was singing, in front of a rock group, "Knock, knock, knockin' on heaven's door."

110th Belmont Stakes, Belmont Park, Elmont, New York, June 10, 1978

Their Derby was close, but Affirmed was too good that day. Alydar came closer at the end of the Preakness, but Affirmed, with seventeen-year-old Steve Cauthen riding, won the second leg of the Triple Crown by a neck. The Belmont, hotly anticipated, let no one down. This time, Alydar's strategy was different. He stayed much closer to Affirmed's early pace and put his head in front as they entered the stretch. In races like that, the horse moving in front would usually continue in the lead or lengthen it. Not this time. Affirmed, it seemed, didn't turn on his best stuff until the other horse passed him. Suddenly, it was a dogfight right to the wire. Everybody screaming, beating their program against a chair. At the end, again, Affirmed. This time by a nose.

INDEX OF EVENTS

—**Sugar Ray Leonard vs. Roberto Duran, Louisiana Superdome, New Orleans, Louisiana, November 25, 1980:** Andres Cantor

—**1980 NFC Championship Game, Dallas Cowboys at Philadelphia Eagles, Veterans Stadium, Philadelphia, Pennsylvania, January 11, 1981:** Merrill Reese

—**Houston Astros at Los Angeles Dodgers, Dodger Stadium, Los Angeles, California, April 9, 1981:** Peter Schmuck

—**Houston Astros at Philadelphia Phillies, Veterans Stadium, Philadelphia, Pennsylvania, June 10, 1981:** Jayson Stark

—**Chicago Bears at Kansas City Chiefs, Arrowhead Stadium, Kansas City, Missouri, November 8, 1981:** Wayne Larrivee

—**1981 AFC Wild Card Game, Buffalo Bills at New York Jets, Shea Stadium, Queens, New York, December 27, 1981:** Steve Levy

—**1982 University Cup Finals, Moncton vs. Saskatchewan, Moncton Coliseum, Moncton, Canada, March 14, 1982:** Elliott Price

—**1982 NCAA Men's Basketball Tournament Finals, North Carolina vs. Georgetown, Louisiana Superdome, New Orleans, Louisiana, March 29, 1982:** Mike Francesa, Brad Sham

—**1982 World Cup Finals, Brazil vs. Italy, Estadio Santiago Bernabeu, Madrid, Spain, July 11, 1982:** George Vecsey

—**Northern Illinois at Northwestern, Dykes Stadium, Evanston, Illinois, September 25, 1982:** Gary Miller

—**Harvard at Penn, Franklin Field, Philadelphia, Pennsylvania, November 13, 1982:** Merrill Reese

—**Maine Mariners at Adirondack Red Wings, Glens Falls Civic Center, Glens Falls, New York, November 17, 1982:** Dave Strader

—**Stanford at Cal, Memorial Stadium, Berkeley, California, November 20, 1982:** Joe Starkey, Michele Tafoya

—**Miami Dolphins at New England Patriots, Foxboro Stadium, Foxboro, Massachusetts, December 12, 1982:** Tom Verducci

—**1983 NCAA Men's Basketball Tournament Finals, North Carolina State vs. Houston, University Arena, Albuquerque, New Mexico, April 4, 1983:** Mike Francesa

—**1983 Norris Division Semifinals, Game 1, St. Louis Blues at Chicago Blackhawks, Chicago Stadium, Chicago, Illinois, April 6, 1983:** Elliott Price

—**1983 Stanley Cup Finals, New York Islanders vs. Edmonton Oilers, Nassau Coliseum, Uniondale, New York, and Northlands Coliseum, Edmonton, Canada, May 10–17, 1983:** Helene Elliott, George Vecsey

—**Kentucky at Kansas, Allen Fieldhouse, Lawrence, Kansas, December 10, 1983:** Kevin Harlan

—**1984 Orange Bowl, Miami vs. Nebraska, Orange Bowl, Miami, Florida, January 1, 1984:** Roy Firestone

PHOTO CREDITS

Name	Photo Credit	Name	Photo Credit
Ernie Accorsi	New York Giants	Roy Firestone	Magic Turtle Productions
Rich Ackerman	Rich Ackerman		
Al Albert	Indiana Pacers	Stan Fischler	MSG
Kenny Albert	FOX Sports	Mike Francesa	WFAN Radio
Marv Albert	New Jersey Nets	Jay Glazer	FOX Sports
Steve Albert	Steve Albert	Jim Gray	ESPN
Kevin Allen	*USA Today*	Jay Greenberg	*New York Post*
Maury Allen	Jackson Pokress	Tom Hammond	NBC Sports
Dave Anderson	*New York Times*	Kevin Harlan	Turner Sports
Jim Armstrong	*Denver Post*	Merle Harmon	Merle Harmon
Marty Aronoff	Marty Aronoff	Ernie Harwell	National Baseball Hall of Fame Library
Brian Baldinger	FOX Sports		
Carl Beane	Tim Samway/ Bosox Club	Dan Hicks	NBC Sports
		Steve Hirdt	Steve Hirdt
Len Berman	NBC Sports	Keith Jackson	ABC Sports
Craig Bolerjack	Utah Jazz	Gus Johnson	MSG
Mike Breen	ESPN	Daryl Johnston	FOX Sports
Christine Brennan	Jennie and Leslie Backoff	Steve Jones	Portland Trail Blazers
		Harry Kalas	Philadelphia Phillies
Rob Burnett	Craig Sjodin/ American Broadcasting Companies, Inc.	Peter King	*Sports Illustrated*
		Tim Kurkjian	ESPN
		Wayne Larrivee	Green Bay Packers
Andres Cantor	Futbol de Primera	Dan LeBatard	ESPN
Linda Cohn	ESPN	Will Leitch	Deadspin
Stephen Collins	Randall Slavin	Steve Levy	ESPN
Bill Conlin	*Philadelphia Daily News*	Josh Lewin	Texas Rangers
		Jim Litke	Associated Press
Seth Davis	*Sports Illustrated*	Verne Lundquist	CBS/Craig Blankenhorn/Landov
Matt Devlin	Charlotte Bobcats		
Jim Durham	ESPN	Bill Macatee	CBS Sports
Ian Eagle	YES Network	Jack McCallum	*Sports Illustrated*
Helene Elliott	Gary Ambrose/*Los Angeles Times*	Curt Menefee	FOX Sports
		Gary Miller	ESPN
Mike Emrick	NBC Sports	Jay Mohr	JayMohr.com
Michael Farber	Lou Capozzola/*Sports Illustrated*	Chris Myers	FOX Sports

Name	Photo Credit	Name	Photo Credit
Bob Neal	Bob Neal	Joe Starkey	San Francisco 49ers
Dave O'Brien	ESPN	Dave Strader	Florida Panthers
Keith Olbermann	MSNBC	Pat Summerall	FOX Sports
Bob Papa	NBC Sports	DB Sweeney	db-sweeney.com
Edwin Pope	*Miami Herald*	Michele Tafoya	ESPN
Elliott Price	Team 990	Rod Thorn	New Jersey Nets
Mel Proctor	Mel Proctor	Gary Thorne	ESPN
Merrill Reese	WBCB Radio	Al Trautwig	NBC Sports
Jimmy Roberts	NBC Sports	Matt Vasgersian	FOX Sports
Ken Rosenthal	FOX Sports	George Vecsey	Marianne Vecsey
Jim Ross	WWE	Tom Verducci	*Sports Illustrated*
Chris Russo	WFAN Radio	Suzyn Waldman	Lou Rocco
Peter Schmuck	Gene Sweeney Jr./ *The Baltimore Sun*	Dick Weiss	Howard Simmons/*New York Daily News*
Steve Serby	*New York Post*	Jon Wertheim	*Sports Illustrated*
Brad Sham	Dallas Cowboys	Gene Wojciechowski	ESPN
Dan Shaughnessy	John Louis Ioven Jr./ *The Boston Globe*	Alexander Wolff	*Sports Illustrated*
Bob Sheppard	New York Yankees	Bob Wolff	National Baseball Hall of Fame Library
Dan Shulman	ESPN	Chris Wragge	WCBS-TV
Steve Somers	WFAN Radio	Vic Ziegel	Pat Carroll/*New York Daily News*
Jayson Stark	ESPN